What Your Colleagues Are Saying . . .

The Big Book of Tasks for English Language Development, Grades K-8 by Nancy Akhavan is a clear and useful text for teachers new to instructing English learners. Pre-service and early career teachers who are learning about how to structure lessons will find solid advice and guidance. The book is organized into sections that align with the WIDA proficiency levels: entering, emerging, developing, and bridging. In each section, Akhavan explains multiple strategies that are appropriate for each proficiency level. She also includes "Watch fors and work arounds" so teachers can anticipate how students might react or engage in the lesson. I have taught many pre-service teachers about these activities; this text would be a valuable addition to a syllabus on teaching primary and intermediate literacy. In a classroom setting, this text will provide research-based, effective strategies that can be implemented during intervention blocks or during embedded Tier 1 ESL.

—Sara Hamerla, EdD
Administrator, Multilingual Department
Waltham Public Schools and Visiting Lecturer
Education Department
Framingham State University

Teachers understand the *why* behind the importance of designated English language development but often struggle with *how* and *what* to do. This book identifies how to effectively utilize designated ELD time, create a safe learning environment, and build confidence in a new language. Teachers get the *what* in a bank of lessons designed with rigor and appropriate scaffolds they can count on to meet the needs of English language learners.

—Amy Williams, EdD
Program Manager
California Education Partners

The Big Book of Tasks for English Language Development, Grades K–8 is an amazing resource for educators. It brings a wide range of research on language development together in a user-friendly practical guide. Aligning effective practices and strategies with language performance levels will give educators a clear direction and pathway to support all language learners at an appropriate level.

—Cari Carlson
Assistant Superintendent of Learning Services

This book is an amazing resource for any teacher who supports English learners! It is a teacher-friendly guide full of practical tips and strategies that reinforce great pedagogy and solid teaching practices. I highly recommend principals to provide this great tool for their teachers as a planning support and a great professional reference. As an EL myself and bilingual teacher of several years, I wish I would have had this reference to guide my lesson planning—it would have saved me time and made my job so much easier. Thank you, Nancy Akhavan for providing teachers with such a great resource.

—Janie Sifuentes-De La Cerda
Elementary ELA Manager-Fresno Unified School District
Fresno, CA

The Big Book of Tasks for English Language Development, Grades K–8

Dedication

To my father and mother Bob and Charlotte Pritz, who passed in 2021 and 2022. I am raising a glass of champagne to you, just as you always did for me on special occasions. This book is for you. Thank you for teaching me to appreciate and love the diversity of life, and the discovery of ideas.

The Big Book of Tasks for English Language Development, Grades K–8

Lessons and Activities That Invite Learners to Read, Write, Speak, and Listen

Nancy Akhavan

FOR INFORMATION:

Corwin
A SAGE Company
2455 Teller Road
Thousand Oaks, California 91320
(800) 233-9936
www.corwin.com

SAGE Publications Ltd.
1 Oliver's Yard
55 City Road
London EC1Y 1SP
United Kingdom

SAGE Publications India Pvt. Ltd.
Unit No 323-333, Third Floor, F-Block
International Trade Tower Nehru Place
New Delhi 110 019
India

SAGE Publications Asia-Pacific Pte. Ltd.
18 Cross Street #10-10/11/12
China Square Central
Singapore 048423

Vice President and Editorial Director: Monica Eckman
Executive Editor: Tori Mello Bachman
Associate Content Development Editor: Sarah Ross
Product Associate: Zachary Vann
Project Editor: Amy Schroller
Copy Editor: Lynne Curry
Typesetter: C&M Digitals (P) Ltd.
Proofreader: Theresa Kay
Indexer: Integra
Cover Designer: Scott Van Atta
Marketing Manager: Margaret O'Connor

Printed and bound by CPI Group (UK) Ltd, Croydon, CR0 4YY

Library of Congress Cataloging-in-Publication Data

Names: Akhavan, Nancy L., author.

Title: The big book of tasks for English language development, grades K-8 : lessons and activities that invite learners to read, write, speak, and listen / Nancy Akhavan.

Description: Thousand Oaks, California : Corwin, [2024] | Series: Corwin literacy | Includes bibliographical references.

Identifiers: LCCN 2023052024 | ISBN 9781071904121 (paperback) | ISBN 9781071937419 (epub) | ISBN 9781071937426 (epub) | ISBN 9781071937440 (pdf)

Subjects: LCSH: English language—Study and teaching (Elementary)—Foreign speakers. | English language—Study and teaching (Elementary)—Activity programs. | English language—Study and teaching (Elementary)—Standards—United States. | Second language acquisition. | WIDA Consortium.

Classification: LCC PE1128.A2 A338 2024 |
DDC 372.6/044—dc23/eng/20240109
LC record available at https://lccn.loc.gov/2023052024

This book is printed on acid-free paper.

24 25 26 27 28 10 9 8 7 6 5 4 3 2 1

Contents

3

Section 3: Tasks for Students at the Developing Level of English Language Proficiency 64

4

Section 4: Tasks for Students at the Expanding Level of English Language Acquisition 94

For downloadable resources, please visit the companion website:
resources.corwin.com/bigbookELD

This Book at a Glance

In this book, I focus on engaging tasks that support students' developing language proficiency. Each one is designed to streamline your teaching—and provide opportunities for students to produce language and communicate, both orally and in writing. The overarching principle is that students need to communicate messages, ideas, and information as much as they are receiving messages, ideas, and information. That's the surest way for them to develop fluency with the English language. I've laid out each task with the following features to make it easy for you to use the book as you are actually teaching.

2

Picture Retelling

Listening

A light introduction to inform students, but notice how brief it is. We want to move right into the action of the task.

This feature helps you know when students are ready for it.

WHEN YOU MIGHT OFFER IT

When students are able to understand the gist of a story read aloud.

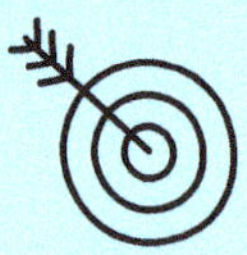

Tie the target goal to your standards and your success criteria.

TARGET

Students can put pictures in order after listening to a story read aloud.

Inviting students to retell a story you have read aloud to them is a powerful way to develop learners' listening comprehension. The routine also helps them understand story structure. Since students new to English are often not speaking in school, they need alternative ways to retell a story. They can point to pictures to put them in order, or they can manipulate the pictures them

I give you the basics for launching the task.

Your Instr

Materials: Simple p ure books – photocopy the picture pages and/or cut out images from the beginning, middle, and end of the book. You don't need to copy every page—just the big events that depict the beginning, middle, and resolution. A well-known story like "The Th introductory one or any narrative with a simpl

The explicitly stated purpose—so important for students to hear!

Name It: Today we are going to retell a story You are going to use pictures to retell the story students can connect to what you are saying).

What You Might Say Next: "When we retell st we understand. We think about the characters Often, they have a problem they have to so don't say everything about the story, but the think of what happened in the beginning of th and at the end of the story. I have pictures read story I am going to read today." (Point or hold up the pictures/book so students can make connections to what you are saying.)

A light appetizer to inform students, but notice how brief it is. We want to move right into the action of the task.

20 ▲ The Big Book of Tasks for English Language Development, Grades K-8

Ideas for how to demonstrate and also involve students—I purposely didn't script it in full because it's best if the words come from you!

2

Model/Do Together: Read the story aloud, stopping often to restate what is happening in the story, using simple language that summarizes the setting, characters, conflict, and action. Point to pictures as you go. After you are done reading and using the pictures you have cut out, ask students to help you retell. Support

of sequence by usi

Ideas for students doing the doing! Having students communicate ideas, information, and thoughts is the heart of the tasks.

Release: Once

work with a partne

Watch Fors and Work-Arounds

Students may us mix of their heritage language and English to retell or may spe udents are understand xpress their comprehen dent in, this is natural. I g skills in English, th ey their

Ideas for support and differentiating when students need your coaching in the midst of or after completing a task.

understanding. ... eir thoughts accurately, so it makes sense they would rely on their heritage language to ensure they are doing so. Encourage students to use the language they have to work on retelling the stories. Asking students to only speak English will not help them acquire English. It raises negative emotions and shuts down students' desire to participate.

The Research Support for the Tasks

There is substantive research serving as the foundation for the tasks in this book. Each task incorporates the best learning from research on language acquisition. In that fashion the tasks focus on the four modes—listening, speaking, reading, and writing—and spiral the expectations. (See Appendix A for a full listing of the research that backs each task in the book.)

You will notice that the tasks begin with lots of oral language development through listening, adding in speaking opportunities, and then including modeled writing and shared reading. As the oral language develops into academic contexts, the reading experiences are shared reading and read-alouds; the writing is shared writing and independent writing. As students move to the bridging stage of English language proficiency, the tasks focus more on independent work with the oral language involving lots of partner work and listening to academic information presented orally or visually in video. Of course, students at this point are reading independently, working with partners, and writing extensive pieces.

In the chart that follows, you will see the levels addressed in this book, and how the tasks involve listening, speaking, reading, and writing in ways that support students' developing proficiency.

Stage of language proficiency	Listening	Speaking	Reading	Writing
Entering and Emerging	With visuals, realia, and TPR for comprehensible input. Partnering with other heritage language speakers.	Not expected, but choral response is encouraged	"Shared" in the sense that students can scan the text and look at pictures	Modeled, drawing, labeling
Developing	With visuals, sentence frames, gestures, and lessons broken into smaller chunks of information for comprehensible input. Partnering with other heritage language speakers.	One or two words Short phrases	Shared reading Read aloud	Modeled, guided
Expanding	Academic content with comprehensible input.	Scaffolded and support	Shared, read aloud, independent	Guided, independent
Bridging	Academic content with less comprehensible input.	Independent, collaborative, and partner	Independent	Independent

Acknowledgments

There are many, many teachers I work with each year as I coach and consult in classrooms and schools. I have learned so much from each person I have collaborated with. Thank you to all of you who have shared their thinking with me and helped me continue to grow as an educator. To Tori Bachman, thank you for believing in me and my work with historically underserved students. As do you, I believe all students have the right to an outstanding literacy education. I appreciate you helping me be part of the lives of students, teachers, and education leaders across the United States and internationally. To Wendy Murray, thank you for always crafting my words and helping me say just what I want to say.

About the Author

Nancy Akhavan is an independent consultant and author. She previously was an associate professor in the Department of Educational Leadership at Fresno State University. She has held various positions as teacher, principal, and district office leader. She has led literacy programs for schools, grades K–12, for over thirty-five years. She currently consults with teachers, as well as district and school leaders, to implement effective reading and writing instruction to close equity gaps and provide support for all students to have all possible opportunities. Nancy is the author of thirteen professional books including *Small Group Reading With Multilingual Learners* (Corwin, 2023) and *The Big Book of Literacy Tasks: 75 Balanced Literacy Activities Students Do (Not You!), Grades K–8* (Corwin, 2018).

Introduction

This book you hold in your hand, *The Big Book of Tasks for English Language Development, Grades K–8* is a sequel to *The Big Book of Literacy Tasks* (Corwin), which was published in 2018. In the six years since then, as I traveled the United States and abroad working with schools, the question kept coming up: "Would you write a book like this one for multilingual learners?"

The answer is yes. And here it is.

I have an extensive background in English Language Development, and so this resource has long been on my mind and in my heart. As a California-based educator, it's in my professional DNA to design research-based teaching and learning for highly diverse student populations. Students acquiring English are not faring well in our classrooms. For example, 80 percent of Latinx students are not reading on grade level in fourth grade (NCES, 2022). According to the US Department of Education (2022), 75.9 percent of multilingual learners speak Spanish as their heritage language. While Latinx students make up most of the multilingual learner population in the US, it's more productive to acknowledge that English language learners across the board are struggling academically and linguistically. So, what do we do about it?

The short answer—and an uplifting one—is that multilingual learners need access to the same dynamic instruction that all students do. You teachers do an amazing job, and what I hope this book reminds you is: *You got this.*

Multilingual learners need access to the same dynamic instruction that all students do.

Supporting multilingual learners is a matter of changing our instruction so it focuses on practices that have high impact for students as they acquire language. It's not about doing more—it's about doing smarter. It's about supporting students to feel confident in their abilities to communicate and engage with peers and you!

In this book, I focus on teaching English language development. This is a book on teaching multilingual students so that they can acquire English. I stress this point at the outset because English Language Development (ELD) that is designated instruction is strikingly different than the teaching we provide multilingual students alongside students whose first language is English in integrated learning situations. Students acquiring English should receive both integrated and designated English language development. Edelman et al. (2022) found in their research that students receiving thirty minutes of designated ELD at each grade level scored similarly to students who speak English as their heritage language by third grade as measured by English language knowledge assessments. As I wrote about in my book on teaching multilingual students to read, *Small Group Reading With Multilingual Learners: Differentiating Instruction in 20 minutes a Day* (2023), ELD is specially designed instruction to help students increase their language acquisition in English (Wright, 2019).

An Important Note About Terms in This Book

I want to speak also about the terms I use. In my previous book I used the term *multilingual learner* to note the students in classrooms that are acquiring English as an additional language and that students communicate in multiple ways through multiple languages and literacies. In this book, I chose to use the older term *English learner*. I made this choice because I am sharing information about the teaching of English to students for whom English is not their heritage language. While some argue that the term is laden with non-asset-based connotations, I want to be clear about the reason for my choice. I often hear, "ELD is good for all students." But ELD is specific and substantially different than teaching academic language development to students whose heritage language is English (Wright, 2019; Bialik et al., 2018).

In ELD, we provide a safe space for students acquiring English to explore language and communication without judgment, without rebuke, without the pressure that they may experience to listen, speak, read, or write when in groups with students whose heritage language is English. ELD is designed just for students acquiring English. All students have rich assets that they bring to the classroom, and when we have English learners in our classrooms, we have an opportunity to learn from them about their lives, their experiences, and about their heritage language. Students acquiring English are assets—their knowledge and lived experiences can enrich the lives of all people in our schools and classrooms. So, why do I choose to use the term *English learner* in this book? It's because the term is embedded in the term *ELD: English language, English learner.*

There are four key principles to keep in mind as you try these tasks. The common thread? Clear expectations! The biggest barrier to multilingual learners' achievement is the education system's tendency to lower expectations for these students. "Lower" books, "lower groups," "lower tasks." The sixty tasks in this book expect the most from every child *and* provide the extra scaffolds students acquiring English need to succeed. We don't lower expectations, ever. We provide specifically designed instruction and activities during a lesson (thirty-minute minimum daily) so learners have access to learning about how to communicate, learn, and become knowledgeable in English and also learn how English works.

Principle 1: Multilingual Students Need Active Learning

iStock.com/FatCamera

All students need purposeful, active tasks where they are doing the cognitive lift during the lessons, not you. The teacher's role is to facilitate the work for students, not do it for them. Too often, we go home at the end of the day more tired than the students because we do so much, and we don't release often enough (with scaffolding) to ensure students are doing the doing. We do this because we want our students to be successful, but if we over-support and over-scaffold, we can undermine our best efforts to ensure student independence (Ellis & Shintani, 2013).

If we over-support, and over-scaffold, we can undermine our best efforts to ensure student independence.

In *The Big Book of Literacy Tasks,* I wrote that engaging tasks are at the center of the classroom dynamics and day-to-day routines. Additionally, I said that these tasks are the glue that connects teachers and students. I still believe this to be true. Active tasks engage readers cognitively and help them become independent, strong learners. The tasks in this book are no different, except that we are focused on helping students acquire an additional language.

When teachers invite me in to watch them teach, they ask me to help them know when the tasks they are doing aren't active. In giving them feedback, one thing I say is that active and passive tasks look different when we notice what the student is doing during the lesson. During active tasks, students are owning the cognitive lift—essentially doing the thinking and the work. That is why during great tasks students are stretched, just a bit, to try something new. Active tasks involve the students answering the questions (asking the questions also), discussing, and writing. Active tasks have a signature style, as shown in the chart that follows.

Active Task Signature Style	Passive Tasks
Students think about what they want to say and express themselves as best as they can.	Students sit and listen while the teacher does all or most of the talking and thinking (it's ok for students to listen, just not *all* of the time).
Students talk with a partner or with the group about their thinking.	Students sit quietly while the teacher calls on one student at a time to share their thinking (the problem is that only one student is active and the remainder of the class is *honestly*, not probably listening attentively).
Students read with a partner or on their own.	Students wait for the teacher to read everything aloud (read-alouds are a fabulous way to teach language; it's just that we cannot do them *all* of the time).
Students are invited to think about what is important in what they heard or read.	Students wait for the teacher to tell them what was important.
Students write their own thinking down, or write narratives, opinions, and informational essays or reports (even if they need to draw lots of pictures to support themselves).	Students copy what the teacher wrote.

Notice how in the active tasks students are doing the thinking, talking, reading, and writing. In the passive tasks, students are overly supported by the teacher. In the tasks in this book, students will be guided to do the work in any way they can as it is through supported practice that students acquire language and develop skills (Genesee et al., 2005).

Principle 2: Language Develops on a Continuum

iStock.com/andresr

Multilingual students progress along a predictable continuum of stages of English language proficiency. As the teacher, you are mindful of these stages. You use your awareness of each child's current stage to plan, implement, and adjust lessons. Students acquire language in a predictable flow. The flow is a continuum rather than movement through discrete stages. Although your local or state assessments might label students as being at a particular "stage" or "level" of language acquisition at a given time, students' language proficiency is continually evolving across the four domains (listening, speaking, reading, and writing). For example, a student may have more proficiency in speaking and listening than reading or writing, or vice versa (Cloud et al., 2009).

Six Levels of Language Proficiency

The stages along this continuum include entering, emerging, developing, expanding, bridging, and reaching.

Students move along this continuum from speaking their heritage language(s) to emerging as a multilingual student by adding one or more languages and then becoming more and more fluent in both languages (Gottlieb, 2016; Wright, 2019). A body of work by an organization called WIDA has developed a continuum of language proficiency descriptors, which help us to understand what students may be able to do during instruction. WIDA uses six levels to describe language proficiency: **entering**, **emerging**, **developing**, **expanding**, **bridging**, and **reaching** (Kohnert & Pham, 2010; Wright, 2019). While the labels for the stages may vary slightly in different states, countries, or districts, these are the labels used most in theory and in practice.

Keep in mind: The labels are not as important as understanding what a student "can do." Knowing what students can do affords you the opportunity to create experiences so students can successfully participate in lessons. In each section of this book the section opener will provide an overview of the level of English language proficiency.

The descriptors I use in the tables at the beginning of each section are the descriptors that cut across the terms used in different states across the US. They don't match exactly any one document. I do this purposefully in order for the terms to be as familiar as possible for those of us working in states who use similar, but not exact, terms as the WIDA framework uses. In my view, "levels," "stages," and "phases" are interchangeable labels. The labels don't matter. The students do.

Activate the Domains of Language

This continuum integrates the four domains of language: listening, speaking, reading, and writing. The four domains, also known as modes, do not develop at the same rate (Gibbons, 2015). Therefore, students are at different places on the continuum of development of each language mode at any given time.

Listening and reading are receptive modes and speaking and writing are productive modes; in other words, students are producing language when they are speaking and writing. For instance, students will understand more of what is said than what they can say, and students will be able to say more than they can read or write until they reach fluency in all four modes.

Students are in different places on the continuum of development of each language mode at any given time.

Now, let's look at the characteristics of each stage in the chart that follows.

I've organized this book into sections of tasks that are particularly apt for these levels, but always remember to let your students be your guide. They may have skills that overlap the levels, and you will be the best judge of what they are ready for. By the time students are in the reaching level, they are thriving with the English language and beyond the tasks in this book!

The Continuum of Language Development

Entering	
Level Characteristics	**What Students Can Do**
Students at the entering level have minimal comprehension of what is being said in English. Students will not be speaking much or often. Students' receptive modes are still developing.	• Communicate through pointing, gestures, and drawing. • Find or point to familiar objects, items, or people that are named orally for them. • Repeat simple phrases and words in unison with others. • Orally name objects they see. • State personal likes and dislikes using pictures to help them.

(Continued)

(Continued)

Emerging	
Level Characteristics	**What Students Can Do**
Students at the emerging stage are beginning to use language, in particular, their listening and speaking abilities. Students at this stage have limited comprehension of what is said, at first.	• Speak in one- to two-word phrases; respond with familiar phrases and use key words. • Form sentences using present tense verbs. Restate some language associated with texts and short stories. • Categorize and label. • Connect oral language to print. • State their preferences in one or two words. Participate in social interactions with peers, perhaps using both their heritage language and English, or by gesturing.

Developing	
Level Characteristics	**What Students Can Do**
Students at the developing stage of proficiency will speak in short sentences and begin to communicate more often socially. Students will be able to connect causal- or content-related relationships in texts together. Students' use of verb tenses is expanding and they are beginning to learn irregular conjugations. Students will know that different words are used to express similar ideas and they will expand in their vocabularies both socially and with academic language.	• Follow sequential directions one step at a time. Begin to write using sentence starters and drawings. • Respond orally to show agreement or disagreement and state personal opinions. • Communicate orally about content and give oral reports on content. • Write statements about books read and connect ideas together. • Make frequent grammatical and pronunciation errors. • Identify details and key ideas in texts and make simple comparisons about text and story elements.

Expanding	
Level Characteristics	**What Students Can Do**
At the expanding stage, students' language proficiency is expanding beyond social language use and beginning to use language for academic purposes. Students at this level need to be challenged to increase their English skills in more contexts and learn a greater variety of vocabulary and linguistic structures.	• Compare story elements. • Propose ideas to contribute to conversations. • Have good comprehension of social conversations, but they will not have complete comprehension of academic conversations. • Use technical and specific vocabulary.

(Continued)

<table>
<tr><th colspan="2">Expanding</th></tr>
<tr><th>Level Characteristics</th><th>What Students Can Do</th></tr>
<tr><td>Students apply their language skills in more sophisticated ways; students can produce statements about texts, convey their opinions, and explain information and ideas. Academic conversations will need to be scaffolded.</td><td>• Identify multiple sources for ideas and information.
• Will still make some errors in grammar and pronunciation.</td></tr>
<tr><th colspan="2">Bridging</th></tr>
<tr><th>Level Characteristics</th><th>What Students Can Do</th></tr>
<tr><td>Students at this level continue to learn and apply a range of higher-level English language skills in a variety of contexts, including comprehension of and production of academic texts.
Students will make fewer grammatical and pronunciation errors but will still need academic language and tasks to be scaffolded.
Students continue to need contextualized academic tasks.</td><td>• Evaluate texts and books, including story and text elements, and other literary elements and nonfiction text topics.
• Describe how factors relate in texts and lead to outcomes.
• Understand and use increasingly difficult academic vocabulary as they read texts that are comprehensible through the use of diagrams, pictures, and rich descriptions.
• Support claims with evidence from various sources and use claims and evidence to argue and persuade.</td></tr>
<tr><th colspan="2">Reaching
(Note: This level is not addressed in this book, as students are proficient enough they don't need dedicated language development instruction.)</th></tr>
<tr><th>Level Characteristics</th><th>What Students Can Do</th></tr>
<tr><td>Students at the level of reaching proficiency continue to learn and apply a range of high-level English language skills in a wide variety of contexts, including comprehension of and production of highly technical texts.
They need far less contextualization of texts and ideas.
They need minimal scaffolding of texts and information to be able to read, write, and discuss texts.</td><td>• Use technical language connected to specific content areas.
• Use a variety of sentence lengths and of varying complexity.
• Extend oral and written discourse in both fiction and nonfiction.
• Speak and write comparable to peers who are proficient in English.</td></tr>
</table>

Source: WIDA (2019); Krashen (1988); Scarcella (2003); Wright (2019)

Principle 3: See Students Through an Asset Lens

iStock.com/Weedezign

Understanding students' assets is an inherent responsibility of a teacher (Stembridge, 2020). Teachers know this, of course, but sometimes the error-focused nature of standardized testing causes a deficit lens to prevail. Seeing strengths is of particular importance for educators whose cultural background is different than their students. Reflecting on students and seeing students' strengths and gifts is one way to see and appreciate their assets. Then we can leverage students' assets and fold them into the design of the learning experiences throughout the school day (Stembridge, 2020).

Seeing strengths is of particular importance for educators whose cultural background is different than their students.

Equitable learning opportunities are based on students' assets. Writes Stembridge,

"Our goal as educators is to see our students as asset-filled beings and then to apply that awareness in classroom instruction."

What does it look and sound like when we apply this goal to our instruction in English language development? It's going to look like a lot of peer work, because collaborative practice has been shown to be highly effective in developing multilingual learners' social and emotional and academic strengths. And it's going to sound like a lot of beautiful, young voices as students talk together to deepen ideas, problem solve, and find commonalities (Honigsfeld & Dove, 2013).

For educators, an asset-based approach may involve doing a "flight check" on your current beliefs, possible implicit biases, and practices. There are so many excellent resources on culturally responsive practices. It's beyond the scope of this book to explore all the facets of equity, but the following reflection activity is a simple way of enhancing an asset-based mindset.

Think of a student or a group of students that you work with and reflect on the student's gifts and their cultural capital. What does the student bring to the classroom that can expand their learning and the learning of others?

____

____

____

How might you draw out the student's individual and family strengths? (send-home activities, surveys, cultural events)

____

____

____

How can you express students' assets in the classroom?

____

____

____

Show Students They Are Valued and Belong

When students feel seen, known, and valued, their cognition is actually enhanced (Steele, 1995). We do that by getting to know each student and using affirming language and being curious about their lives. Research shows that teacher language is a crucial aspect of a student's belief in themselves as a learner. So, in a book on English language development, you will find a "shadow" layer in every task of language that emboldens students. A few more research-based ways of playing to students' strengths include the following:

- Having a culturally and racially diverse classroom library *that reflects your current students* and using these texts during instruction as well as independent reading and read-alouds
- Designing conversations about texts that include all voices, from all students
- Scaffolding specifically so that students acquiring language and students of an array of backgrounds have voice in your classroom
- Differentiating with instruction, grouping, and use of tools to ensure students learn at high levels

- Not expecting students to respond in one way, such as when the teacher asks a question and calls on students one by one to answer—instead, students can answer in teams or groups
- Providing intensive academic intervention
- For your students who are of color, discuss excellence in people of color and provide information on achievements made by people of color (Howard, 2020).

(adapted from Busholtz et al., 2017; Hammond, 2015; Howard, 2020)

Develop Students' Familiarity With the Language of School

All students benefit when our lessons are clear, our collaborative practice aligns with what was demonstrated, and we plan a series of learning tasks that scaffold students' skill building—*and* their knowledge building. With multilingual learners, you want to use extra care to ensure to explain academic language like *compare, evaluate, responsibility,* and *freedom.* Students acquire language when they are at ease, supported, and are invited to use language for purposeful classroom work. Remember to do the following:

- Contextualize academic language by using pictures, diagrams, drawings, web-based videos, and so forth.
- Discuss academic terms and content before launching into a lesson to frontload information, vocabulary, and ideas.
- Provide students with ample time for reading authentic and engaging materials.

Principle 4: Design Instruction to Reflect How Students Acquire English

iStock.com/fstop123

Finally, supporting English learners requires that we remember that language is the currency of human connection. It's social. Thus, children acquire English in two ways. One way is by studying how English works, and another way is by being immersed in understandable English used for authentic purposes of communicating with others. What I mean by *English that is understandable* is that the language being used to teach the lesson is comprehensible to students at their current level of proficiency—the student can comprehend what is being said or read. When language is comprehensible, students can understand and begin to talk; they basically begin to "pick up" how to express themselves (Krashen, 1988). Students then use the momentum of talk to listen, read, and write.

Of course, using accessible English is not enough. Students acquiring English need carefully scaffolded lessons. The scaffolding is what makes this book different from *The Big Book of Literacy Tasks*. Each task has purposeful supports specifically for English learners, so it's important to do them with students. Making charts, pair shares, providing sentence stems, kinesthetic activities—these are not fun extras, but crucial components for multilingual students.

Use Language at the Edge of a Student's Range

Noted expert on language acquisition Krashen (1982) studied language acquisition in multilingual learners and found that students best learn language when the language they are working with is just a little bit harder than what they can do on their own, without support. This idea sounds as though it contradicts what I said above about using understandable English in lessons, but it doesn't! What these ideas have in common is that we need to teach into students' zone of proximal development (ZPD; Vygotsky, 1978). The "zone" is when a learner is close to mastering a skill set required to complete a task but still needs the guidance of an expert to do so. If we give a task that is too easy, the student is bored and isn't learning. If we give a task that is too hard, the learner may give up in frustration. When the task is a "just right" challenge, an expert uses various techniques to help the students perform a task independently.

With the ZDP in mind, the tasks in this book will stretch students by using language with them that is just a little beyond their current level of comprehension. This ensures that we are expanding students' vocabulary and background knowledge. If you believe an English language development (ELD) task is too easy, push for an academic conversation with your students. Make pictures and charts while you talk. Pull out new books or texts on the same topic and take the learning deeper. In short, I encourage you to adjust the difficulty level of the task based on your students. Mostly, I hope that you have fun teaching these tasks to your student acquiring English. Please know that they can do more than you likely think they can when it comes to content learning—don't water things down but rather scaffold up. Believe in the power of multilingualism!

Tips for Teaching Students New to English in Small Groups

The idea that students acquire language when they are comfortable and supported was developed by Krashen (1982). This theory is called the *affective filter.* The theory describes a condition of student comfort for learning. That is when a student is emotionally distraught or socio-emotionally not supported in the classroom and in their learning environments, the student may experience difficulty acquiring English. The fear of making mistakes in front of peers impedes their ability to learn. Low-anxiety learning settings improve student motivation, esteem, and self-confidence. These factors remain high, making it more likely that students will be able to focus on the lesson and the language being used in the lesson (Peregoy & Boyle, 2016).

You may wonder if you need to exclusively form groups for students based on English language acquisition level. The short answer is "no." However, you want to ensure you are providing activities in lessons that support all students' abilities so everyone can participate and learn. While whole group lessons can be intimidating and not be targeted enough to meet the needs of a student new to English, if they don't have emotionally safe opportunities to work with peers, they will not be exposed to the language proficiency of other students, either in their heritage language or English (Akhavan, 2019).

You may be teaching ELD whole group to a group of students who are all acquiring English, or you might be teaching ELD in small groups. To get started with groups, create a dedicated space for small group instruction. You may choose the library corner or clean off a rectangle or kidney-shaped table and move it to a convenient location in your classroom (Akhavan, 2019).

Knowing that the four domains of language (listening, speaking, reading, and writing) occur naturally together in the classroom when we focus ELD instruction on topics of interest to students, we can work on building background knowledge about interesting topics, facilitate listening and speaking opportunities about these topics, and also include reading and writing activities.

SECTION ONE

iStock.com/ChrisGorgio

TASKS for Students at the Entering Level of English Language Proficiency

	Section I • Everyday Tasks for Students at the Entering Level of English Language Proficiency	
1.	Total Physical Response	Listening
2.	Picture Retelling	Listening
3.	Building Vocabulary Using Realia	Listening
4.	Building Vocabulary With Word Banks	Listening
5.	Word Journals	Listening & Writing
6.	Choral Reading	Listening & Speaking
7.	Zoom the Room	Speaking & Listening
8.	Practicing Simple Phrases	Speaking & Listening
9.	Answering Yes or No	Speaking & Listening

Overview

As you work with students who are new to English, often called *newcomers*, refer to the stages of language acquisition on page 4 and see the WIDA description of the Entering level, below. Students new to English may experience a silent period, which is a period of time (days, weeks, months) when they may say nothing at all (Krashen, 2003; Himmele & Himmele, 2009). Not speaking, but rather taking in language, is completely normal and to be expected. Don't expect students to do what you have asked. They may prefer to watch and listen, enjoying participation by experiencing the lessons. Once they are ready, they will begin to talk and interact more.

As students progress from no understanding of English to some understanding of English they will move from being **new to English** to being at the **emerging level** of language proficiency. Additionally, students new to English may be new to living in the country where you are teaching and may be experiencing many changes in their personal lives. These students may have experienced trauma prior to arriving in your classroom if they are political refugees (Souers & Hall, 2018). They need support and understanding from the adults at school. Small group instruction can provide students with a learning setting that is more intimate and less overwhelming. For teachers, it provides the opportunity to differentiate lessons for the students, or differentiate objectives and activities (Akhavan, 2014). We can attend to targeted skills, and in this way, help close the gap.

When students are new to English, we will likely be doing the reading and writing, reading aloud and using interactive writing to help students compose ideas. We will also be creating experiences for students to listen to information about interesting topics and talk once students feel comfortable.

WIDA'S Descriptor for English Language Proficiency Levels for the Entering Level

Level 1 Entering	What Students Are Able to Do
Listening	Point to stated pictures, words, and phrases
	Understand repeated words, and phrases
	Point to objects and people
Speaking	Emerging use of words and phrases
	Use single words, phrases, or chunks of language
Reading	Match icons and symbols to words, phrases, or environmental print
	Listen to stories with limited language and strong visual support
Writing	Draw in response to a prompt
	Label pictures of familiar or repeated words and phrases

Source: WIDA (2012, 2020)

10 Tips for Success

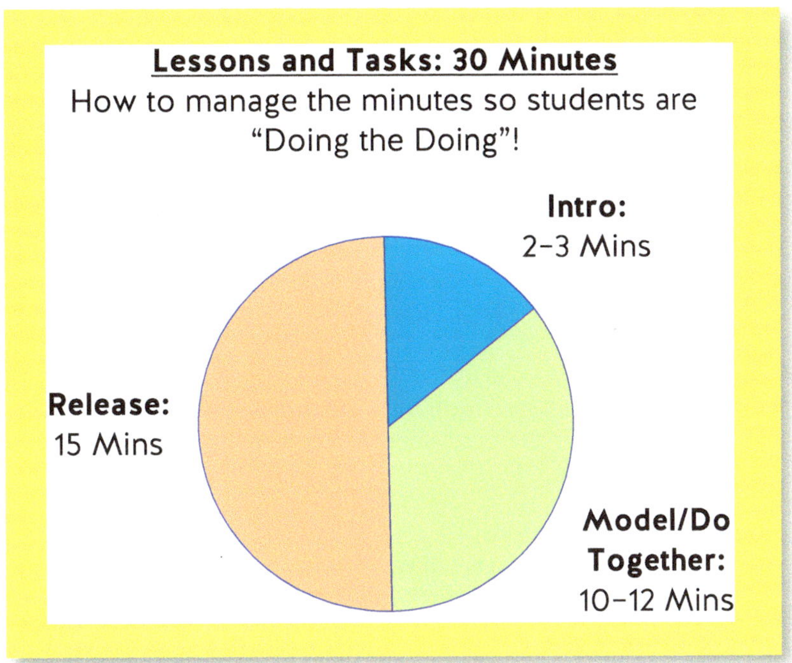

1. Take two to three minutes to introduce the lesson. At this stage of language acquisition, brevity is key. If you speak the heritage language of the students, it's helpful to preview (very quickly) for students what they will be doing in their heritage language.
2. State the purpose of the lesson. Students do better when the "Why" is clearly communicated at the outset.
3. Model for ten to twelve minutes. For students new to English, you will model the entire task.
4. Use visuals to help you communicate your messages, expectations, and content.
5. Look for ways to connect the visuals, real objects, and content to students' lives and interests. It puts students at ease when they see you are bringing in what you know of them to teaching and learning.
6. Release students to do the task. Reserve fifteen minutes. Look if students need more time, though, and continue it the next day. At this stage, generally students aren't ready for independent or partner work; it's more realistic that you conduct the task and students copy you.
7. Altogether, including release—plan on thirty minutes.
8. As students work, and when and if you bring them back together, look for those students who you can tell are still shaky with the task. Don't single them out but remind the group that you are always there with any question.
9. Plan to meet one-on-one with any students who need additional support.
10. Plan on reviewing students' strengths and needs once a week. Formative assessments of their participation, oral language, and understanding are the engine of your planning.

Total Physical Response

Listening

WHEN YOU MIGHT OFFER IT

Once students are feeling comfortable enough in class to play a game along with you.

TARGET

Students can follow along with the teacher.

Total Physical Response, known as TPR, is a kinesthetic activity in which students get moving! Students move to commands or signals that you give. Brain research has shown that physical movement during learning activates different processes, helping students make connections between the words said and the meaning of those words.

Your Instructional Playbook

Materials: No materials are needed at first. When students know the games or songs you might be using, you can write out the commands or lyrics on a slide or chart and students can read while moving. One popular song for this game is "Head, Shoulders, Knees and Toes."

Name It: Today we are going to play a game where we move our bodies to what I am saying. It will be fun!

What You Might Say Next: "Let's practice. Touch the part of your body or move your body the way that I tell you to. Do what I do and say. You can watch me if you are not sure what I am saying."

If you're happy and you know it, clap your hands.

(clap, clap)

If you're happy and you know it, touch your toes.

(touch toes, touch toes)

If you're happy and you know it, then your face will surely show it. If you're happy and you know it, touch your elbows (touch).

If you're happy and you know it, sit down.

(sit)

If you're happy and you know it, walk to the door.

(walk)

If you're happy and you know it, then your face will surely show it. If you're happy and you know it, stand by your desk.

(stand)

Model/Do Together: Start out by practicing a few commands. Tell students to touch their head, toes, or any other body part. Model it for them and make sure students are following along. Say the words slowly so students have time to hear the word, think about what it means, and watch you move. As you play the game over and over again, you can mix it up. You can have students move about the classroom to work on prepositions or verbs. For example: "Walk to the door," "Stand to the left of Mariam's desk," and so on.

Watch Fors and Work-Arounds

Students may be in the silent period where they don't talk or talk very little. They may not be comfortable repeating after you. This is perfectly fine. Students need to feel comfortable and safe when they begin speaking, so ensure your classroom atmosphere supports risk-taking. If students are saying words incorrectly, simply model the correct way; don't call out students for incorrect mispronunciations. You can encourage and celebrate any attempts students make to say the words.

Picture Retelling

Listening

WHEN YOU MIGHT OFFER IT

When students are able to understand the gist of a story read aloud.

TARGET

Students can put pictures in order after listening to a story read aloud.

Inviting students to retell a story you have read aloud to them is a powerful way to develop learners' listening comprehension. The routine also helps them understand story structure. Since students new to English are often not speaking in school, they need alternative ways to retell a story. They can point to pictures to put them in order, or they can manipulate the pictures themselves and order the pictures on their own.

Your Instructional Playbook

Materials: Simple picture books – photocopy the picture pages and/or cut out images from the beginning, middle, and end of the book. You don't need to copy every page—just the big events that depict the beginning, middle, and resolution. A well-known story like "The Three Little Pigs" is a good introductory one or any narrative with a simple story line.

Name It: Today we are going to retell a story after I have read it to you aloud. You are going to use pictures to retell the story (point or hold up pictures so students can connect to what you are saying).

What You Might Say Next: "When we retell stories, we can think about what we understand. We think about the characters and what happened to them. Often, they have a problem they have to solve, right? When we retell, we don't say everything about the story, but the main events. We tell what we think of what happened in the beginning of the story, during the middle, and at the end of the story. I have pictures ready for us to use to retell the story I am going to read today." (Point or hold up the pictures/book so students can make connections to what you are saying.)

Model/Do Together: Read the story aloud, stopping often to restate what is happening in the story, using simple language that summarizes the setting, characters, conflict, and action. Point to pictures as you go. After you are done reading and using the pictures you have cut out, ask students to help you retell. Support students in making their choices. Scaffold students' sense of sequence by using words like *first*, *then*, *next*, and *last*.

Release: Once students have practiced retelling stories with you, have them work with a partner, or in a small group to retell stories using pictures.

Watch Fors and Work-Arounds

Students may use a mix of their heritage language and English to retell or may speak only in their heritage language. That's okay! If students are understanding you when you read aloud in English but need to express their comprehension of the story in the language they feel more confident in, this is natural. It may reflect that although they have acquired listening skills in English, they still need to lean on their heritage language to convey their understanding. In my experience, they earnestly want to share their thoughts accurately, so it makes sense they would rely on their heritage language to ensure they are doing so. Encourage students to use the language they have to work on retelling the stories. Asking students to only speak English will not help them acquire English. It raises negative emotions and shuts down students' desire to participate.

Building Vocabulary Using Realia

Listening & Speaking

WHEN YOU MIGHT OFFER IT

Once students have been in school for a short time and have acclimated and are ready for a small group lesson to learn vocabulary.

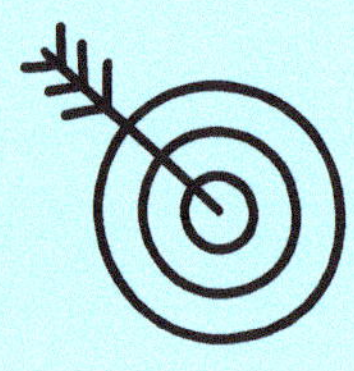

TARGET

Students can repeat the name of an object after the teacher and identify the correct object.

Realia is a real object that you use to help students acquire vocabulary. By touching moving objects, students are supported in making connections between words and the meaning of words. Visit places like the Dollar Store to gather a variety of inexpensive little objects for vocabulary-building like small toys and household items. Once students have acquired basic words, you can use picture cards, but in the beginning real items are more powerful.

Your Instructional Playbook

Name It: We are going to learn new words today. I've brought in some items that we use often, so this new vocabulary is going to be helpful for you to know.

What You Might Say Next: "When we work with real objects, we can connect the word to what it means so we can begin to use the words when we talk in English."

iStock.com/Stefan_Alfonso   iStock.com/davidnay   iStock.com/Olga Andreevna Shevchenko

Model/Do Together: Choose five objects. Introduce the objects and their name in a sequence. It might go something like this:

- Hold the item, say its name, and ask students to repeat it.
- Practice saying the name of the object with students a few times.
- Pass the object around or have students touch it, and say the name again.
- On a whiteboard or chart paper, write the object's name and draw a little picture, or add a photo next to the word. For objects in the room, you can use a sentence strip to label the object.
- Invite students to touch and say the name of the objects in the days after this lesson.

iStock.com/JakeOlimb iStock.com/CSA Images iStock.com/Polina Ekimova

You can also use picture cards to teach vocabulary. At the beginning of the year, though, use real objects that students can touch and pass around.

Watch Fors and Work-Arounds

Students may not know the names of objects and cannot participate. If students are quiet during the task, and don't try to say the names of the objects, it could be that they don't remember their names. Or it could be that they are not comfortable speaking in English. It is perfectly normal and acceptable for students to remain quiet when they are new to English. This stage, also known as the preproduction stage, means that you need to talk more and explain more so that students can feel comfortable during the task.

Building Vocabulary With Word Banks

Listening & Speaking

WHEN YOU MIGHT OFFER IT

When students are ready to say a few words out loud.

TARGET

Students will be able to repeat after the teacher and identify the correct word and picture.

Developing students' vocabulary is a daily, all-year affair. Research shows that it helps students to focus on words that are high utility and to cluster conceptually similar words. That's why using word banks is powerful. Word banks help children organize dozens of new vocabulary words into sensible categories. Sometimes your focus will be on "everyday" words students would benefit from knowing, such as *mom, table, book*. Other days, you stock your word banks with words about various emotions. And word banks can reflect books, concepts, and content you are teaching, of course, too.

Your Instructional Playbook

Materials: Pictures of items and things captured from the Internet and organized on slides, Word cards with pictures (optional), chart paper, pictures printed out (optional).

Name It: We are going to learn new words that will help us understand more of what we hear. We will also be able to say more things to express ourselves.

What You Might Say Next: "As we learn more words, we can understand more of what everyone is saying, plus we can say more ourselves. I bet there are things you would like to get better at asking for and have more ways to tell how you feel or what you think!"

iStock.com/Mieszko9

iStock.com/Far700

Model/Do Together: There are various ways you can use pictures to teach words that you will add to a class word bank. No matter what, remember that with students new to English, the idea is for them to learn the label in English of *things they already know about in the world*. Emergent bilinguals do not need to relearn concepts of typical things, items, ideas, and feelings. Following are two different ways you can approach this modeling:

Picture and say: Say the word describing a picture you display. Say it again slowly so students can hear the sounds. Invite students to repeat the word and say it with you. Chat about the word and use it in a simple sentence. Invite students to repeat the word on their own. They can also repeat the sentence you say or make up their own sentence. Repeat this process with a new word. Plan to introduce three to four new words at a time.

Picture, say, and write: Show students a picture by putting it on a table in a small group. Say the word the picture represents and then write the word on a whiteboard. Ask students to think of a sentence and then write it on the whiteboard for them to see and say aloud with you. (If using a pocket chart, vary steps accordingly.) Continue with additional words. Keep the number of new words introduced to a minimum.

Conclude activity with a word bank. Wrap up the activity by adding the words to a word bank (either one that is already on display or a new one). Use chart paper or cardstock; with a thick marker, write the word, and draw or paste a picture beside it. These visual references around the classroom are so beneficial to children acquiring English. Organize words in a word bank around topics or themes like feelings, or household items, or food, parts of the body, adjectives, prepositions, and so on.

Watch Fors and Work-Arounds

Students need additional practice. Avoid the one-and-done trap! Practice the words introduced often until students are comfortable with the word set, then dive into a new theme or topic of words to explore with students.

Word Journals

Listening & Writing

WHEN YOU MIGHT OFFER IT

Once students have acquired a few words in English and are ready to have words handy to look up.

TARGET

Students take ownership of learning words by keeping their own word journals.

Once you notice students have begun to use words and phrases from Task 4 on their own, help students with logging word meanings in their own word journals. Students need access to the journals any time of day to help them with writing or logging a word they are working to remember. While they will record words you present, they will also log words of their choice.

Your Instructional Playbook

Materials: Composition books, one per student

Name It: We are going to make personal word journals so you can have your own dictionary.

What You Might Say Next: "We learn new words throughout our lives. Many adults jot down new words and phrases that interest them in notebooks. So, throughout the year, you can copy words from our word cards we use in class together, or you can record words you want to add. I will help you spell the words, and you can draw a picture to remember what the word means."

iStock.com/ChrisBoswell

My family has an orange grove, and I have always loved walking in it. When I model learning new words, writing, and reflecting, I often draw on this favorite place for details.

Model/Do Together: I introduce this activity by holding up my Words That Wow Me dictionary and encourage students to name their own notebooks. I share a recent word discovery, saying something simple like, "The other day, a friend said she was going on an awe walk. An 'awe walk'? What's that? I knew the word *awe* means a sense of wonder, like awe of a beautiful mountain or the sight of an eagle soaring. I discovered that it means going outside for a stroll, where you pay attention to nature. I love this new noun, which has been added to official dictionaries recently. So, I am going to write it in my dictionary and do a sketch of me walking in my favorite spot, an orange grove."

Watch Fors and Work-Arounds

Students fluent in their heritage language can write the definitions of the words in English in their heritage language. Students can also use a mix of English and their heritage language, a process called *translanguaging*, to write definitions or make notes about the words. Use of students' heritage language will strengthen their knowledge of content and vocabulary in English.

Word banks that are visual provide a support for students to write words in their journal.

6 Choral Reading

Listening & Speaking

WHEN YOU MIGHT OFFER IT

When students are able to follow along with you while you read.

TARGET

Students can read print while the teacher reads a poem, text, or book. Students articulate the words after the teacher says them.

Choral reading is a type of shared reading where the students read along with the teacher. Your role is to give students opportunities to hear how you pronounce words and how the language flows. Students new to English are unlikely to be actually *decoding* the words along with you, but that is just fine for now; they can repeat along with you, and they may even begin to memorize the words through repeated readings. When they memorize words, they are memorizing how to say the word. They are not reading.

Your Instructional Playbook

Materials: Poems, song lyrics, rhymes printed on chart paper or typed on a slide; add clip art visuals that relate to the meaning of the text.

Name It: We are going to read together today so we can practice saying words.

What You Might Say Next: "First, I am going to read aloud the poem/song/rhyme, and the second time I am going to read it and you will repeat after me. After that, we will read it all together." (You can sing the lyrics to simple songs also.)

Model/Do Together: Ensure text is visible to all students. Read through the text moving your hand underneath the words so students see the sound-to-print match. Read the text in small chunks of about two lines so students new to English have an easier time processing it. Students may only be listening to how the sounds in English work or they may be able to read some words, but either way, going slower is better until they have worked with the text repeatedly. You can reread the poem, song, or lyrics multiple times, over days and weeks, as a fun and engaging activity for students.

Watch Fors and Work-Arounds

Some students may be in the silent period, where they are not yet speaking in class. Have the students clap to the beat along with you or move their arms. You can also play a song on YouTube and encourage students to move, dance, or act out the lyrics.

iStock.com/ChrisGorgio

7 Zoom the Room

Speaking & Listening

WHEN YOU MIGHT OFFER IT

When students are ready to practice reading a simple word to another student.

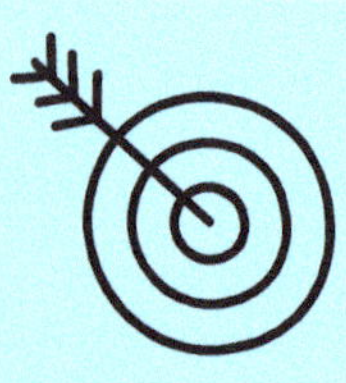

TARGET

Students can read words they have practiced multiple times.

When it comes to developing vocabulary, using oral language and collaborative practice with peers is critical. In this activity, students get a chance to move about the room and hear how classmates pronounce letters and words. It's guided, it's low risk, it's game-like, and thus builds all students' confidence.

Your Instructional Playbook

Materials: letter cards or word cards for every student; a bell or chime

Name It: Today you are going to have fun moving around the room to practice saying aloud letters and words with various partners.

What You Might Say Next: "When I see everyone standing with their chair pushed in, I am going to ring a bell to start the activity. Hold your card so it's facing out. We want your partner to be able to see it and read it aloud. Ready?"

iStock.com/Margolana

Word cards can be cut apart and given to students. Have an ample supply of them!

Model/Do Together: Follow this procedure: Each student stands and pushes in their chair. When given the signal, students walk around the room, not touching anything or anyone, not talking. When given the signal (bell or chime), students are to get back-to-back with the nearest student. Those without a partner raise a quiet hand and the teacher pairs them. Students turn to face their partner, read their letter or word, listen to their partner, trade cards, and wait for the teacher to tell them to start their "zoom" again. Repeat several times to give students several words/letters to practice.

Watch Fors and Work-Arounds

Students may take advantage of walking around the room and not properly interact. Be very clear in your expectations. You can teach your expectations for interaction before Zooming the Room the first time.

Students are ready for more. Students will read material posted around the room and write an exit ticket. Students repeat the same steps as in Zoom the Room but now they have to read words and labels you have posted around the room, including word banks and the sound wall. This activity is a powerful way to keep the visual references in your classroom relevant and in your students' awareness. Label your classroom, labeling everyday objects. The more labels the better.

Practicing Simple Phrases

Speaking & Listening

WHEN YOU MIGHT OFFER IT

When students are feeling comfortable saying a few words in English.

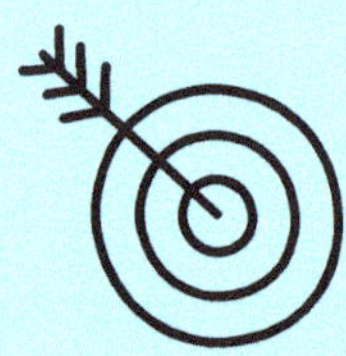

TARGET

Students can say common phrases to ask for help or get around school.

Students need the opportunity to practice saying simple phrases in an environment that is supportive. Begin with phrases students tend to need right away, related to basic needs like asking to go to the bathroom, or asking for help if sick or injured. Note that some students may be in the silent phase (see page 4 in the introduction) and may not say the phrases during the lesson, no matter how nurturing you make the classroom environment.

Your Instructional Playbook

Name It: We are going to practice how to say things that might help you get around the school. This might be a bit difficult at first, but it will become easier the more we practice.

What You Might Say Next: "I am going to make a list of things that we might want or need to say or ask. Would you help me think of topics? (As students offer ideas, write them on a chart paper. Your chart paper might look like the list below.) Now let's look at our list, and I am going to write a phrase we can use for each one. Sound good?"

iStock.com/Mohamed Rasik

I need to use the bathroom.

Example of dialogue cards to support students as they learn high-utility phrases.

Model/Do Together: As you craft each phrase, use simple words and be brief. Draw or paste a picture next to it. Practice saying the phrases with the students. Set students up in pairs to ask each other questions. They don't have to answer in words. They can point or gesture to answer questions as needed. It's important to not make the language practice artificial but keep it as real as possible. Choose phrases that will truly help your students flourish at school.

A list of ideas for the phrases include the following:

I need to use the bathroom.

I don't feel good (point to head or stomach).

I am hungry.

I need a Band-Aid (point to injury).

I need a pencil.

I need to sharpen my pencil.

I lost my . . . (book, pencil, crayon).

Where is the office?

Where is . . . (breakfast, lunch, cafeteria, bathroom, office, classroom)?

As you continue practicing different words and phrases, you can mix up the ways that students practice. You can invite students to:

- Model for each other
- Practice in a fishbowl setting with two to three students who feel confident in the center and the remaining students surrounding them in a circle watching and listening.
- Practice using sentence strips. Write phrases on sentence strips and randomly hand them out. Doing a hand up, pair up, share up, students can practice phrases with each other. You can also set up a pocket chart and have the phrases on sentence strips and matching pictures pasted on index cards available.

Release: Once students feel comfortable asking for help, encourage them to say the phrases any way they can. Don't overcorrect. Just communicate and encourage.

Watch Fors and Work-Arounds

Students may not hear the sounds in English well enough to repeat them correctly in sentences. Don't correct students individually. Instead, model the correct pronunciation by saying the words slowly so the students can hear each word and the sounds in the word. Students may answer each other in their heritage language after saying the sentence or phrase in English. This response is more than okay! It indicates that students are interacting and even understanding the word or phrase in English but are not yet ready to answer in English. Also, don't introduce too many phrases at any given time. Take it slow and make it fun! I suggest three to five times per week, and as the year progresses, be ready to retire the activity if students no longer need it or don't seem engaged by it.

Answering Yes or No

Speaking & Listening

WHEN YOU MIGHT OFFER IT

Once students are able to ask questions for help or say short phrases.

TARGET

Students can state how they feel or what they think in a short phrase.

As students become more comfortable speaking, they may feel ready to express their opinions. A motivating way to get started is by having them agree or disagree with a simple yes or no statement. I call them opinion games, and you can give them your own twist. For example, you can start by making a statement to students that a thing is the *best*, the *worst*, *good* or *bad*. Students can then think about what you said and answer on their own, agreeing or disagreeing with you.

Your Instructional Playbook

Materials: Yes/no cards. Using index cards, make two cards for each student. Write yes on one card and no on the other card.

Name It: We are going to play a game that I call the *opinion game*. You are going to practice sharing what you think about things I say. You may agree or disagree with me.

What You Might Say Next: "Your voice and your ideas are important to me. I want to know more about your opinion on things."

Model/Do Together: Show the yes/no cards and demonstrate how to hold up a card to express an opinion. Next, display a question on a whiteboard or doc cam. Then, answer your own question. For example, write *Chocolate is the best ice cream* on the board and hold up the yes or no card depending on what you think. Additionally, you can write a sentence stem on the board to help students ready to answer more fully in English.

Sentence stems might include the following:

> Yes, I agree.
>
> No, I don't agree.
>
> Yes, I agree. I like ________________.
>
> No, I disagree. I don't like ____________.
>
> Yes, I agree. I think ________________
>
> No, I don't agree. I think ____________.
>
> Yes, I agree because ______________
>
> No, I don't agree because ___________.

Watch Fors and Work-Arounds

Don't rush the process by making students talk before they are ready. Remember the phases of language acquisition (see introduction page 4) and know that students will speak as they are comfortable and confident. It is important to keep the students' affective filter low as they begin expressing their thinking orally. If students say something incorrectly, model it immediately afterwards correctly. For example you might say, "*You agree with me. You like chocolate ice cream.*" Also look for puzzled expressions and be prepared to provide context by drawing pictures, having pictures handy on cards or on a device, or showing a video snippet with a device. For example, in this instance, some children might not yet know what ice cream is.

SECTION TWO

iStock.com/ChrisGorgio

TASKS

for Students at the Emerging Level of English Language Proficiency

Section II ● Tasks for Students at the Emerging Level of English Language Proficiency		
1o.	Retelling Fiction	Listening & Reading
11.	Retelling Nonfiction	Listening & Speaking
12.	Read Aloud With Simple Group Discussion	Listening & Speaking
13.	Visual Vocabulary	Listening & Speaking
14.	Zoom the Room: Sound Walls	Listening, Speaking, & Reading
15.	Shared Reading Predictable Text	Listening, Speaking, & Reading
16.	Read Aloud and Partner Talk	Listening, Speaking, & Reading
17.	Daily Activity Sequencing	Listening, Speaking, & Reading
18.	Teaching Sounds and Reading Decodable Text	Reading
19.	Word Manipulation With Onset and Rhymes	Reading
20.	Writing Dialogue Journals With Sentence Frames	Writing

Overview

In the emerging level of English language proficiency students possess a range of skills and behaviors. (See page 4 of the introduction for more details on the stages.) Some students at the emerging level may experience a silent period, which is a period of time (days, weeks, months) when they say nothing at all (Krashen, 2003; Himmele & Himmele, 2009). This is completely normal. These children most likely understand what you are saying, but don't expect them to do what you have asked. Work with students with the language they have and in the ways they are comfortable responding to engage them with lessons (Wright, 2019).

As students progress from some understanding of English to a greater understanding, they move from the **emerging level** of language acquisition to the **developing level** of language acquisition (the **developing** level tasks are in the next section). You will want to ensure a good balance of listening, speaking, reading, and writing overall in the lessons.

The tasks are designed to help students acquire language and are most engaging when you use them to meet social studies or science objectives, or other content-area goals. For example, you may read to the class about different types of clouds that make up the weather and the task involves labeling a drawing and writing a short sentence about clouds.

To refresh your memory of what to expect of learners at this stage, the following is information from WIDA.

WIDA's Descriptors for English Language Proficiency Level for Emerging

Level 2 Emerging	What Students Are Able to Do
Listening	Point to stated pictures, words, and phrases
	Follow one-step directions
	Match oral statements to objects, figures, or illustrations
Speaking	Name objects, people, pictures
	Answer who, what, when, where, and which questions
	Say frequently used words and phrases with emerging precision
Reading	Match icons and symbols to words, phrases, or environmental print
	Identify concepts about print and text features
Writing	Label objects, pictures, diagrams
	Draw in response to a prompt
	Copy or draw icons, symbols, words, and phrases for meaning

Source: WIDA Consortium (2012); WIDA Consortium (2020)

10 Tips for Success

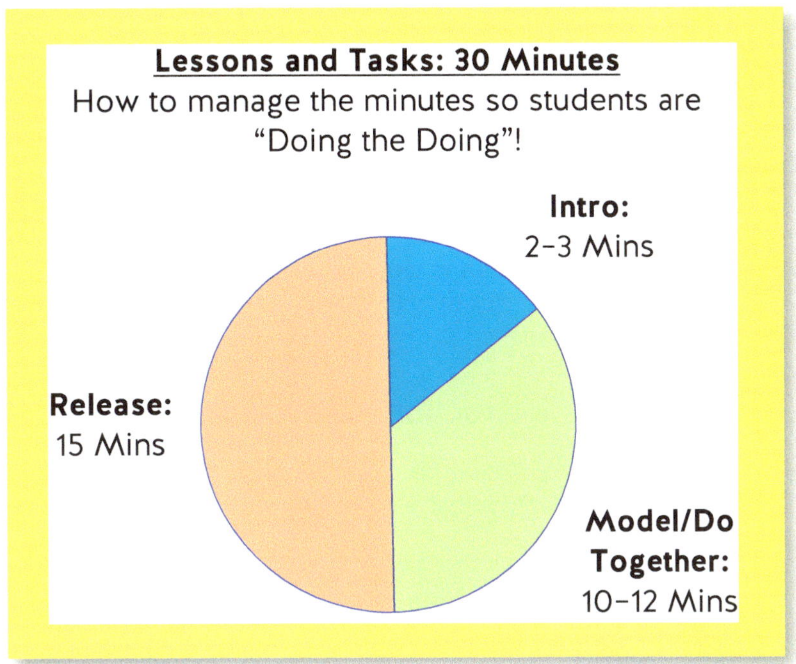

1. Some tasks emphasize one or two domains of language (like listening and speaking). Other tasks involve all the domains. To choose the tasks that students are ready for, consider data you have collected about students' readiness.
2. **Keep your introduction to two to three minutes.**
3. State the purpose of the lesson and use visuals to ensure that students understand. If you speak the students' heritage language, or a student in class does, explain what will be happening during the tasks.
4. Reassure students that you are going to show them how to do everything that is asked of them and you will do a lot of the work together.
5. **Model for ten to twelve minutes.**
6. Use visuals to help you communicate your messages, expectations, and content. Look for ways to connect the visuals, real objects, and content to students' interests.
7. Focus the lessons on topics that include social studies and science. ELD content needs to be based on *content*.
8. **Plan twelve to fifteen minutes of guided work and peer work**. You may find that students need to work with you through guided activities more than working with peers at first.
9. At this stage of English language development, students need lots of support from you, so some tasks in this section don't have a "release" component.
10. Altogether—plan for thirty minutes per task.

Retelling Fiction

Listening & Reading

WHEN YOU MIGHT OFFER IT

When students begin speaking in short phrases and can follow along with you when listening to a story read aloud.

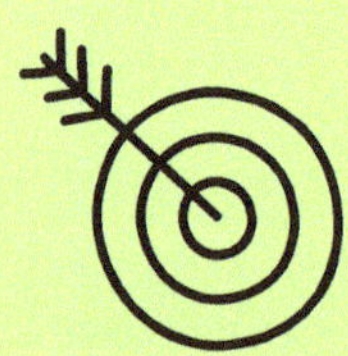

TARGET

Students will be able to read sentences on sentence strips to retell a simple story.

Retelling for many students is a spontaneous activity they embark on if asked what a story is about. But for the student acquiring English, retelling can be daunting. First, students may not have understood enough of the story to share the beginning, middle, and end. Second, they may not be able to say the words to retell. This is why it's good to make the retelling visual and tactile. In this task, students use pictures and sentence strips to retell a story they have heard you read aloud several times on previous days.

Your Instructional Playbook

Materials: Picture book or short story with picture; sentences written out on sentence strips that state the beginning, middle, and end of the story

Name It: Today we are going to retell a story after I read it out loud. Let's start with a story we know.

What You Might Say Next: "After I read the story out loud, you are going to retell the story by putting sentence strips together in the correct order."

Model/Do Together: Read the story aloud, stopping often to restate what was happening in the story. Run your finger under the print and point to pictures as you go so students can follow along. After you are done reading, ask students to help you retell the story, using the pictures and sentence strips that you have prepared. Start with three sentences, one for the beginning, one for the middle, and one for the end. As students progress in their listening ability and reading ability, add in additional details from the middle and use five sentence strips.

Revisiting the story of "Goldilocks and the Three Bears," sentences might include the following:

Beginning example:

Goldilocks ate the porridge, but it was too hot.

Goldilocks sat in the chair, but it was too big.

Goldilocks lay in the bed and it was just right.

You can also use sentences with temporal words:

First, ____________________.

Next, ____________________.

Last ____________________.

As students develop proficiency:

Goldilocks went into the house of the three bears.

Goldilocks ate father bear's porridge, but it was too hot.

Goldilocks sat in father bear's chair, but it was too big.

Goldilocks sat in baby bear's chair. The chair broke.

Goldilocks lay in baby bear's bed and it was just right.

Sentence frames with temporal words:

First, ______________________ happened.

Next, ______________ did (or other verb) ______________.

Also, _________________ happened.

Additionally, ______________ (name of character) ______________ (verb).

Release: Invite students to put the sentences in the correct order. After they practice, you can invite students to try putting the sentences in order without using the pictures to help them understand the sentences. Repeat with new stories and texts as appropriate.

Watch Fors and Work-Arounds

Continue to offer this lesson over time as you read stories out loud to students. Start with the simplest sentences with the least complicated language students can retell. Then, gradually increase the amount and sophistication of language. You can vary using and not using pictures as well. It's fine if students talk together to decide the correct order. Cooperative learning, during which students work in small groups to complete the task, is a powerful, natural extension of this activity. As you listen to student groups put sentences in order, remember it's fine if students speak in their heritage language to figure out the words in English. This is an asset and should be encouraged!

Retelling Nonfiction

Listening & Speaking

WHEN YOU MIGHT OFFER IT

Once students can get the gist of nonfiction text of medium complexity read during shared reading.

TARGET

Students can retell the main points in a nonfiction text.

Stories have a structure that can be easier for students to comprehend (characters, setting, problem, solution) than informational texts. But for students acquiring English, and all students, we need to be doing more nonfiction work, not less! We can build content knowledge and students' reading skills through nonfiction read-alouds. Listening and having you point out text features helps children learn the structure of nonfiction texts, including topic sentences, supporting details, and main ideas. Retelling solidifies these understandings and supports comprehension.

Your Instructional Playbook

Materials: Short text on a high-interest topic, with picture(s), sentences written out on sentence strips that state the main ideas from the text.

Name It: Today we are going to retell a nonfiction article (text) after I read it out loud. Let's start with a topic we are interested in. After I read the text out loud, you are going to retell the main ideas in the text by putting sentences in the correct order.

What You Might Say Next: "What do you know about this topic already?" Create a word bank (see Task 4) writing down vocabulary words and phrases they share, or that you pull from text.

Model/Do Together: Read the text aloud, stopping often to restate what the main ideas are in the text. Point to pictures as you go so students can see how the pictures help them. Once you are done reading, invite students to retell the text. Have them rely on the sentence strips that you have prepared and the pictures. (The sentence strip statements should capture either three of the main ideas or the big idea and three supporting facts.) Introduce this activity with just three sentences, one fact per sentence. As students progress in their listening and reading abilities, add in more details.

Looking at the text *Todos a Comer! A Mexican Food Alphabet Book* by Dr. Ma. Alma González Peréz, you might write the following sentences:

[G is para guacamole. The *aguacate* is mashed and then diced tomatoes, onions, and peppers are added. P es para pan dulce. Pan dulce is a rich variety of treats.]

Four example sentences from this book might be:

Two of our favorite letters are G and P.

The G stands for guacamole. Guacamole is made of *aguacates* (avocados).

The P stands for pan. Pan is good for breakfast.

You can also use sentences with order words:

The first fact______________________________________.

The second fact ____________________________________.

The third fact______________________________________.

As students develop proficiency, add in additional details.

Sentence frames with order words:

The text is about ____________________________________.

The first main idea is ________________________________.

Second ____.

Lastly ____.

Release: Invite students to put the sentences in the correct order. After they have done that practice, you can invite students to try putting the sentences in order without using the pictures to help them understand the sentences. Repeat with new texts as appropriate. For extra challenge, invite students to generate three sentence strips for a nonfiction text they have read independently.

Watch Fors and Work-Arounds

Students are overwhelmed after you read aloud. Read an appropriate amount of the text, so as not to confuse students with too much language. It would be fine to choose only some of the sentences to read aloud from complicated or complex text.

Scaffold this lesson over time as you read informational text out loud to students. Start with the simplest sentence set with the least complicated language. Then, gradually increase the amount of words in the sentences. You can vary using or not using pictures as well. Students may talk together to figure out the correct order. Again, cooperative learning is a strong follow-up to this activity and it's more than okay for students to use their heritage language to figure out the words in English.

Read Aloud With Simple Group Discussion

Listening & Speaking

WHEN YOU MIGHT OFFER IT

As soon as students are able to comprehend most of what is read aloud, get them to talk about the reading.

TARGET

Students can carry on a conversation after listening to text read aloud.

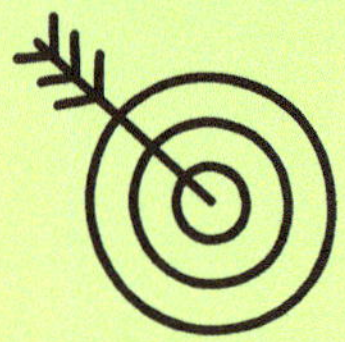

Once you have read stories aloud to students and they are comfortable discussing stories (simple one- or two-word discussions; see Task 10), students are ready to answer questions you pose that require more thinking. This read-aloud-based task provides an opportune time to bring in culturally relevant stories. Find books that reflect the backgrounds of students in your class, and look for ways to connect their interests, families, and knowledge to the ongoing discussion.

Your Instructional Playbook

Materials: Books that have less complex text but have enough meaning in them for students to discuss. Students new to English are not yet ready for complex texts in English. Of course, as soon as they develop skills in listening comprehension, you can increase the complexity of the books you use.

Name It: Today I am going to read a story aloud and we are going to talk about the text and share what we think. I want to hear your thinking, and remember, you can share your thoughts in any way you can. You can always just answer yes or no to the questions I ask if you don't know the best answer.

What You Might Say Next: "Introduce the idea of answering questions you ask by saying yes or no. (You can use yes/no cards, or have students write yes/no on whiteboards. Ensure students know that they can say anything they are thinking about the book, but the minimum they need to think about is saying *yes* or *no* to the questions you pose.)

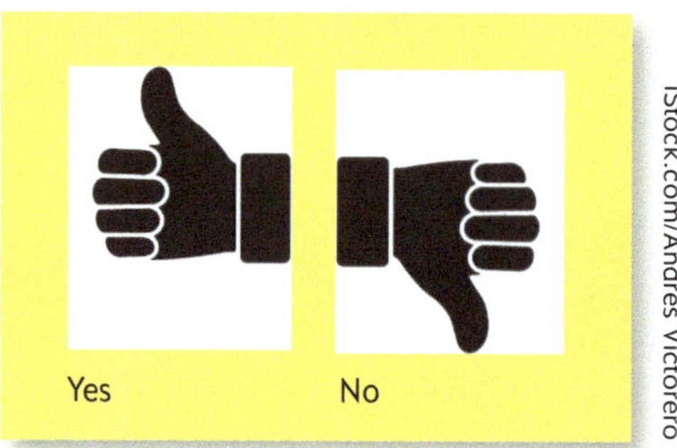

iStock.com/Andres Victorero

Using Yes/No cards can make the task tactile and fun for students.

Model/Do Together: Introduce the book. On a piece of chart paper or a whiteboard, write a couple of questions you are going to ask about the book when you are reading it. By frontloading the questions and explicitly discussing the questions prior to reading the text, students will be able to focus on the read-aloud. Encourage them to share their ideas, but don't push them to explain why, as they may not be ready to explain their thinking. Certainly, encourage them to talk in their heritage language with a partner about their deeper thinking, perhaps answering why they think what they do, but don't press them to do all of this discussion in English.

Sample questions might include:

Do you like the character?

Do you think the character did the right (or wrong) thing?

What prediction can you make about what will happen? Or what do you think will happen next?

Do you think the characters can _______________?

Release: Continue fostering discussion with students. Also continue to support as needed, by pointing to pictures in the book, the words you wrote on the chart, and so on.

Watch Fors and Work-Arounds

Students are not engaged in talking and thinking and are simply listening to you. If you notice students are passive,.that means they are not acquiring language through experience. Give them a chance to talk, gesture, or point. Encourage students to answer in any way that they can, which could be saying "yes" or "no" or answering in simple phrases (don't push for complete sentences; see the Scaffolds in the introduction, page 3 for more guidance).

13 Visual Vocabulary

Listening & Speaking

WHEN YOU MIGHT OFFER IT

When students are able to hold short conversations in class on social topics and get the gist of content lessons.

TARGET

Students will create a vocabulary bank (cards or notebook) by writing the word, drawing a picture, and writing a short definitional phrase in their own words.

Students need multiple exposures to new words through reading, writing, listening, and speaking for the concepts and terms to "stick." In this routine you use the target vocabulary of a unit (either from the vocabulary cards provided in a program or a textbook) as the jumping off point to a richer sequence of exposure to the word. The important thing to remember is to include explicit discussion and demonstration, collaborative work with peers, and multimodal experiences that include a lot of visuals. For example, students can look at several pictures, view a short video, move, make gestures, draw to help them learn vocabulary words, and write definitions of words in their heritage language.

Your Instructional Playbook

Materials: Target vocabulary. These words can come from your curriculum device for viewing multiple pictures or video, word journal.

Name It: We are going to learn new words today, but instead of just looking at cards we are going to get active with our brains and bodies!

What You Might Say Next: "We are going to do four things with each word we are learning. We are going to say the word, think about the word, and look at some pictures that show us the meaning of the word; we are going to act it out and finally we are going to write and draw a picture."

Model/Do Together: Showing and working on one word at a time, follow this sequence:

1. Write the word down and say it; students repeat.
2. Discuss the word's meaning. Show pictures—the more the better to build understanding of the word's meaning.
3. Ask students to think about the word and visualize the word's meaning in their mind.
4. Help student act out the word, or use hand gestures to remember the word.
5. Have students write the word in their journals and draw a picture.

iStock.com/aldomurillo

If the word you introduce is *misunderstand*, the hand gestures could be opening your hands out flat.

Release: Once students are used to the routine, encourage them to think of words that they want to work on together. As a group, you can facilitate the sequence for students as they work to develop their vocabularies.

Watch Fors and Work-Arounds

Some students may not be ready to act out the word. It is perfectly fine if they need more time before acting out words. Let them watch and enjoy the process. The same goes for students not comfortable or ready to draw the meaning of words on their own. If they want to copy a picture that you display, that would be a good way to support them. Students might be comfortable doing hand gestures or acting out the word with a partner. If they speak the same heritage language, they can discuss the word's meaning in their heritage language and say the word in English, working to make connections between the word and what it means.

Zoom the Room: Sound Walls

Listening, Speaking, & Reading

WHEN TO OFFER IT

Once students have learned a few of the sounds and letters in English. You will offer this task using the letters and sounds they have learned. Add additional letters and sounds as they learn them.

TARGET

Students can make words and sound out words with a partner.

Students need to develop facility in knowing letters and sounds. They need practice in decoding words, whether those are real words or nonsense words, to understand that if they know the sounds the letters represent, they can say the word. While sounding out nonsense words may seem like an odd thing to practice, students throughout their reading lives will encounter words they may not know how to say but sounding them out is a good first step in determining meaning. For instance, my husband speaks Farsi. While Farsi uses the Arabic alphabet, often words in Farsi will be spelled in the Roman alphabet on products in stores. The word for *bread* using the Roman alphabet is *naan.* I can read this word because I know the sounds and the double *a* signals me to not say the short vowel sound for *a*, but the alef sound. Being able to say the word, I can ask somewhat what the word means. In this task, students will randomly be paired, and depending on the pairing and the order they put their letter card in, the resulting word may be a nonsense word.

Your Instructional Playbook

Materials: Index cards with letters, digraphs, and diphthongs you have taught written on them. One per card. See appendix B for an example of a personal sound sheet for students to use and the different sounds to write on cards.

Name It: We are going to play our Zoom the Room game again today (see Task 7 for the other Zoom the Room activity). We will be putting sounds together to make words.

What You Might Say Next: "With your partner you will put your sound cards together in any order you want. You might find some of your words look funny. Some words will be real words, and some words will be nonsense words. That's ok—this is about making words today!"

Model/Do Together: Show a few of the letter cards you have and model sounding out the letters on each card separately, and then put the cards together to form a word and read the word. Reverse the cards and read the word the cards make. Model this a few times so that students can see the general steps for working with their partners.

Release: Set up expectations for the procedure. Each student holds a card that you have handed out, stands, and pushes in their chair. When given the signal, students carefully walk around the room, not touching anything or anyone, no talking. When given the signal (bell or chime), students are to get back-to-back with the nearest student. Those without a partner raise a quiet hand and the teacher pairs them. Students turn to face their partner, then they work together.

Here is a typical sequence:

1. Read their letter/letter combination.
2. Listen to their partner read their card.
3. Lay out the cards on a nearby desk or the floor and read the word.
4. Trade cards and wait for the teacher to tell them to start their "zoom" again.
5. Repeat several times to give students several letter combinations to practice.

Watch Fors and Work-Arounds

Students have difficulty with sounding out the letters on their card. Encourage them by reminding them what they know. Point to the sound wall you have up in the classroom (It's so helpful to display letters and sounds on a classroom wall!). Guide students through associating the letter and the sound and reinforce when they get it or approximate. It is important to celebrate their efforts to do it on their own rather than just simply waiting for you to tell them the sound the letter/letter combination makes. Of course, don't make them struggle or become extremely uncomfortable. If students are unable to figure it out for themselves, tell them the sound and encourage them to find the sound on the sound wall and make a mental note.

Bug:iStock.com/Victor Metelskiy; Duck:iStock.com/CSA Images; Fish:qiStock.com/vectorwin; Girl:iStock.com/Oxy D; Hat:iStock.com/Elena Platova; Jump:iStock.com/ChrisGorgio

Organize a sound wall with pictures to represent the sound

15 Shared Reading Predictable Text

Listening, Speaking, & Reading

WHEN YOU MIGHT OFFER IT

Once students are acquiring a few words in content areas, they will be ready to read more complex texts.

TARGET

Students participate in a shared reading of text that is a little harder than they can read on their own.

In a shared reading, students are encouraged to see, read, discuss, and interact with the text, not just listen. As students develop their vocabularies in English, they will be ready for shared reading experiences, where students are expected to read the text along with the teacher. The teacher supports the student's ability to read the text, in which I mean the students can decode the words and comprehend (at least getting the gist of the text). If students can already read in their heritage language, these reading skills will transfer to reading in English usually easily and naturally. If students are not already readers, try Tasks 15 and 16 first to help them learn sounds in English so that they can decode words. As in Task 16, you want to encourage students to discuss the text, even if they are saying only short phrases, or answering yes or no to questions you ask.

Your Instructional Playbook

Materials: Short predictable texts that have enough context and pictures to support language acquisition. Shorter texts are more effective as shared reading as they don't tax students during the reading. Use a document camera to display the book or text if you don't have copies for each student, but it's ideal that each student has a copy.

Name It: Today we are going to read together to develop your ability to decode words and understand what the story says.

What You Might Say Next: "We will also talk about the book and share what we think. I am excited to hear you share your ideas and thoughts."

Model/Do Together: In this context students will have the text in their hands during Shared Readings. This is a prime opportunity for students to practice in the moment with you modeling the "how." A couple of things to consider during your modeling:

Use "I" Statements when thinking aloud about the text: *I can make a prediction, I can visualize . . .*

Involve metacognition: Explaining the *because, why, or how of* our actions.

During the shared reading, you can also model skills and concepts such as:

Concepts about Print	Graphophonics	Fluency
Language Structures	Comprehension	Text Structures
Word Solving	Text Features	Visual Literacy

Using the text as your catalyst, you either introduce a skill or concept, or practice it. Generally, you introduce it during an explicit, brief lesson, and then practice it during shared reading time. And generally, you select one skill or concept as your main focus and plan the lesson around it.

Concepts to Model During Shared Reading

Concepts about Print	Print is organized in specific ways. Students learn that we read symbols for message, illustrations correspond to print, text in English goes left to right, we use return to sweep to the next line, and texts are organized with front and back covers.
Graphophonics	This is the symbol system used by readers that includes letter-sound or sound-spelling relationships of language. Student should know that are twenty-six letters with forty-four sounds in the English language and many ways to spell some of those sounds.
Fluency	The reading rate is an important consideration as students increase reading proficiency. Modeling fluent reading and taking about the strategies to read fluently is a critical consideration. Fluency includes pauses, inflections, intonations, and phrase boundaries.
Language Structures	Languages are structured in specific ways. Hearing a lot of language and internalizing structure helps build grammatical knowledge. (Why are verbs placed in a sentence as they are?; First, then, next, and finally cues readers by using organizational patterns.)
Comprehension	Readers use cognitive strategies to make sense of text. Strategies such as predicting, visualizing, monitoring, inferencing, making connections, and summarizing help students learn to understand and think through the words and their meanings they encounter.
Text Structures	Authors organize texts according to traditions, sometimes loosely. From expository text structures (problem/solution, cause/effect, and description) to narrative structures (story, grammar, plot, setting, characters, actions, conflicts, and resolution), all texts follow a pattern.
Word Solving	Contextual clues often help us understand meanings of words in a text. Sometimes, authors even insert misdirective or nondirective clues. Readers need to learn to recognize and analyze all clues for their usefulness. The use of affixes, suffixes, prefixes, bases, roots, or word families to help solve unknown words and make meaning.
Text Features	Graphs, charts, diagrams, illustrations, captions, bold or italicized words, and headings–all are meant to assist readers to deepen comprehension of the text.
Pragmatics	The ways in which context influences the implied meaning of the text, focusing on what people mean when they use language, and is useful in understanding characters and dialogue.
Visual Literacy	Picture books and graphic novels convey much of their information through nonlinguistic representations of information. How objects are positioned on the page and how they hang in the background or foreground often provide subtle information for the story within the pages.

Release: Encourage students to talk about the text. If they are not comfortable talking in the group, organize partners and have students pair/share first. Provide the text to them so they can read it on their own at a later time.

Watch Fors and Work-Arounds

Students struggle to read the words. During shared reading we want students to feel empowered to read along with us. Go slowly if you notice students are faltering. If the book is too difficult, stop the shared reading experience and read aloud the book or text instead. Remember that if students are not engaged in talking and thinking, and are simply listening to you, they are not acquiring language through experience. Give them a chance to talk, gesture, or point. Encourage students to answer in any way that they can, which could be yes or no, or answering in simple phrases. You can repeat this task multiple times with the same text, providing practice reading and checking understanding after repeated reading. You can also repeat this task with books and text that gradually increase in complexity.

Read Aloud and Partner Talk

Listening, Speaking, & Reading

WHEN YOU MIGHT OFFER IT

When students are able to comprehend short snippets of information read aloud.

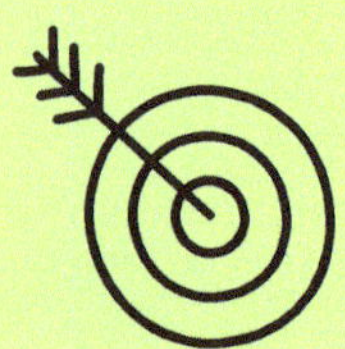

TARGET

Students can discuss information from a short read aloud, in fiction or nonfiction.

When you first start read-alouds with students, choose books that are short and with simple language to give students the greatest possible success in comprehending as you read. It is critical that the book or text have pictures as the pictures will help students with understanding. Be aware that students new to English are not going to understand every word you read but will get the gist of the story. To help students with comprehension of the read-aloud book, they can talk with each other to discuss either the literal comprehension of the text or, if they are ready, the deeper meaning of the text.

Your Instructional Playbook

Materials: Simple books with pictures that heavily support the text. Leveled texts are good for this; choose books at lower levels to ensure the language in the book is not complex. Students new to English are not yet ready for complex texts in English. Of course, as soon as they develop skills in listening comprehension, you can increase the complexity of the books.

Name It: We are going to work with a partner to talk about a story that I read aloud to you. By sharing with each other what we think, you can think together about the story to help you understand it.

What You Might Say Next: "We are going to think about the book that I have here. (Show the book.) As I read, I will stop and I want you to discuss the book with a partner to make sure you are understanding the story."

Conversation cards can help students talk with one another.

Cat:iStock.com/Mieszko9; Soldier:iStock.com/MariaArefyeva; Truck:iStock.com/Far700

Model/Do Together: Pair students up to be discussion partners before you read aloud. When you are first reading a story to students, stop in places in the book where you want to check student understanding. This could be after the characters are introduced or when the setting is described. Use the pictures in the book to help students understand what the words mean. Be careful not to do all the talking yourself. Instead, invite partners to converse by asking a sequence of who, what, why, and when questions and see if they can answer the questions.

Throughout posing these questions, provide visual support. For example, write the names of all the characters on chart paper. Draw or sketch a picture showing a moment of action to remind students of the story. Or go back to the book and point to the pictures. Give them time to process and revisit the book if they need.

Release: Give ample time for the partners to talk together to figure out the meaning of the book, or the answer to the who, what, why, and when question you have asked. End the session by facilitating a whole-group discussion about the meaning of the book.

Watch Fors and Work-Arounds

During the reading, students may feel lost and not understand what the book is about. Provide time for more discussion of elements in the text like the characters or the problem. Encourage students to talk with one another to develop understanding of the text. You can also encourage students to share their thinking by simply pointing to a picture in the book or on the chart you created. Once you have completed several read alouds with students, they might be ready for practice with text elements.

Some Text Elements to Explore in Shared Reading and Discussion

- Story elements (character, setting, plot)
- Character traits (nice, mean, unfriendly, caring, etc.)
- Main ideas in nonfiction text
- Details, events, timelines in nonfiction text

Daily Activity Sequencing

Listening, Speaking, & Writing

WHEN YOU MIGHT OFFER IT

When students begin speaking, or writing, in short phrases.

TARGET

Students can complete procedural writing by writing steps in short phrases.

Students acquiring English benefit from opportunities to write with focused teacher support. That's why guided writing, when you teach students with similar needs, is so valuable. After a brief explicit lesson targeting the skill, each student works independently, applying the technique in their own writing. In this twist on guided writing, each day you gather kids in needs-based groups, give the explicit instruction on a single skill, but then turn it into a *collaborative* writing session. Working together provides students with the extra scaffolding they often need. The most important thing to remember is to keep it simple, focused on one teaching point. For example, subject-verb agreement could be one focus.

Your Instructional Playbook

Name It: We are going to be writing about things we do every day before school, at school, and after school. Some of these things we do are called routines. The reason we are writing these routines about our classroom is so we can post them as helpful reminders for all of us. For example, what are the steps you take to sharpen your pencil? Let's think about that.

What You Might Say Next: Explain what a procedure is. For example, you might say, "When we brush our teeth, we get our toothbrush. Put the toothpaste on the bristles. Wet the toothpaste. Put the toothbrush in our mouth and move it back and forth. Watch me write out these steps." You will then write out the steps on a chart paper or whiteboard, and number the steps 1-4. Add pictures to the chart to help students comprehend the steps. If you have a specific way you want students to sharpen pencils or line up in class, that is another example of a procedure. When you do things the same way all the time, that is a routine. Brainstorm with the class all the different routines they know. Record ideas and information in a notebook.

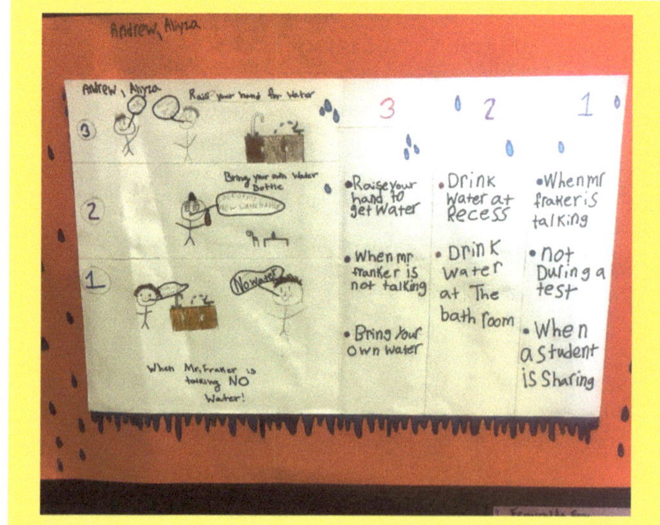

A class-created chart on how to go to get a drink of water.

Model/Do Together: After students brainstorm, have them select one routine off the wheel map for collaborative writing. Then ask students to say each step in the process. Invite discussion and write key words you hear on chart paper as you listen. (For example, *First . . . Second . . .*) The sentences don't have to be polished sentences just yet! Read the words and phrases aloud to students. You can sketch pictures for each step or add photos later. Write the label *Word Ban*k at top of chart paper and tell students that they can refer to this as they write.

Now, introduce a few sentence frames to help students get started with their writing. Show how they will start with a sentence frame and then how they can choose words from the word bank you've created to help them with their writing.

Ideas for sentence frames:

How to______________________________

To ________________, first you ________________.

Second you ________________. Provide frames for the number of steps needed)

(or) Next you__________________________.

It is important to remember to ________________.

Finally, you will ________________________.

Release: Invite students to write on their own using the sentence frames and word bank. It's good to provide fifteen minutes for writing. Move around the small group table, providing support as needed. Also use it as a chance to take note of possible teaching points for the next day's work. (You also collect other informal assessments you've given students to know which skills need additional support.)

Watch Fors and Work-Arounds

Look for students who need greater challenges. For some learners, the sentence strips will be too restrictive. They can compose their own sentences. To support them, carry a small whiteboard or small sheets of paper, and when a student asks for the spelling of a word or two, write it down for them. Your goal is not to give them correct spellings for everything, but to stoke their momentum as they write their own sentences.

Be ready to do-on-the-spot modeling. For example, you may see a student(s) isn't yet using the correct verb tense. Model it for them, which in directive sentences is an imperative. Remember, though, that students acquire language in the order they are ready for, based on their individual progression. So, in this example, even if they are then able to write the imperative tense in these sentences after your modeling, they haven't necessarily acquired the ability to use the imperative tense in all instances.

18 Teaching Sounds and Reading Decodable Text

Reading

WHEN YOU MIGHT OFFER IT

Once students are starting to read independently during shared reading opportunities and get ahead of the teacher.

TARGET

Students will decode words to read a text independently.

Students new to English will need to be systematically taught the letter names and the corresponding sounds for each letter, and letter combination. Begin by focusing on what the students already know; students bring a wealth of information with them to the classroom, and it is important to first assess what sounds they know and if they can hear the sounds in English. An effective sound-letter assessment is in appendix B on page 197. While this is an ELD task and not a whole- or small-group reading lesson, it is important to weave language development into the sound-symbol work you are doing. For this task, focus on teaching the sound or sound pattern that appears in the decodable text you have chosen, and then support students as they read the text and sound out the words.

Your Instructional Playbook

Name It: We are going to read a book today where you can work on sounding out the words. Then, we will talk about what is happening in the book and the meaning of the book.

What You Might Say Next: "We have worked on the sounds in this book before, but don't worry if you don't remember, we will practice first."

Model/Do Together: To use decodables as a language development experience, try these steps.

1. Begin by reviewing any sounds or sound patterns that you think students may need to work on before reading the text.
2. Lift out one sentence from the text (a short one) and write it on a whiteboard and practice sounding out the words together.
3. Discuss the meaning of the text. Decodable books tend to not have a lot of context with pictures, so you will need to discuss the books' meaning and draw or show pictures (use a device) to build understanding.
4. Move to the book and choral-read a page or two together. Stop and discuss what was difficult and what they think the text was about. Provide explanation and context as necessary.

Release: Support students as they read through the remaining sections of the book on their own. Emphasize students' efforts as they sound out the words. After reading, discuss the book as a group, pointing out the meaning of the text and what the text was about. Invite students to share their thinking. Encourage them to hear the words they are reading and think about what the words mean.

Watch Fors and Work-Arounds

Students are struggling to decode. You may have chosen a book that has letters and sounds that the students do not know. Rather than limping through the book, stop the reading and switch out the book. Celebrate any efforts students make to decode; don't worry if they are not perfect at first.

Students show readiness for additional experiences with decodable books. Find decodable texts that are also available as audiobooks. Students can listen to them during center time.

iStock.com/Polina Ekimova

Using picture cards to represent sounds with letters superimposed on top helps students learn words and the sound at the beginning of the word.

19 Word Manipulation With Onset and Rhymes

Reading

WHEN YOU MIGHT OFFER IT

Students are starting to read independently during shared reading opportunities and get ahead of the teacher.

TARGET

Students can hear sounds in words, change initial sounds, and read words created by adding new initial sounds.

Students acquiring English will need support during phonics activities to understand the meaning of words that they are sounding out. Onset and rhymes provide the opportunity for students to learn word patterns and then generalize decoding or spelling new words once they see and recognize the rhyme. For instance, if you know *map,* you may also know *cap*. This can be very helpful in building students' confidence when they are new to English and ready to start reading or spelling words on their own.

Your Instructional Playbook

Materials: Pre-organize the letter tiles or magnetic letters you are going to use based on the rhyme and sound substitutions you are planning to make. It is helpful for each student to have their own set of tiles and magnetic board.

Name It: Today we are going to work with some letters and sounds to practice decoding words. You are going to see that once you know how to decode and also spell some words, you will be able to sound out or spell other words because you are familiar with the pattern.

What You Might Say Next: "Check out the letters I have on the board." Organize your letters to look the same way (you would lay out letters for only the rhyme that you have chosen to work on).

Model/Do Together: While there is no exact way this works best, when working with students new to English, it is very important to discuss the meaning of each word after the students sound it out. Just because they can say a word, doesn't mean they will know what it means. Have picture cards, a device, or a whiteboard to draw on handy in order to bring meaning to each word.

1. Encourage students to sound out the rhyme, for example *-an*. Have them reread it a couple of items.
2. Add a letter in front of the rhyme, emphasizing the sound the letter makes and encourage students to sound out the word.
3. Discuss what the word means that they just sounded out. Provide context as necessary.
4. Change the initial letter and say, "I am going to change just one sound in the word. What's the new word?" Encourage students to sound out the new word. Reinforce students as they sound out and then blend the sounds into a word. Don't let students guess. If they cannot remember a sound, point to a sound spelling chart you may have available in the room and remind them what sound the letter makes.
5. Always take time to discuss the words' meanings each time you make a new word, providing context as necessary with pictures, photos, or drawings.

Release: After guiding the routine aloud a few times, begin to hand students letters or tiles and have them sound out the words on their own. Each student will go at their own pace. After they have built and sounded out numerous words, revisit the words they made and discuss the words' meaning.

Watch Fors and Work-Arounds

Students may not yet be ready to sound out words using different onset and rhymes. If the activity seems laborious, you may need to go back to teaching sounds until students know many sounds.

Students who are ready to extend the activity. Have students build the word, sound it out, and then write it down on a whiteboard or on a piece of paper. As they write, encourage them to listen for the sounds in the word they hear. (Adapted from Spear-Swirling, 2011.)

As students acquire language, they will develop the ability to read in English. If students can already read in their heritage language, these reading skills will transfer to reading in English. If students are not already readers, try Task 18 first to help them learn sounds in English so that they can decode words.

20 Writing Dialogue Journals With Sentence Frames

Writing

WHEN YOU MIGHT OFFER IT

When students are able to write short phrases and follow along with directions you give orally using pictures, gestures, or other supports.

TARGET

Students can write short phrases or add short phrases to a sentence frame.

As students are able to write more, dialogue journaling becomes a powerful routine. These brief, student-and-teacher exchanges of news, thinking, and feelings can be done at a pace that works for you and learners. This routine develops the teacher/student relationship and helps you model for learners how to write about an event and reflect on it. To support writers new to the English language we provide sentence frames. Why? Because composing in one's head in a heritage language and then translating to English is a tall order, involving meaning, words, syntax and semantics, and phonics. The sentence frames support students' efforts, building their confidence, too, as they express themselves and share their ideas in English.

Your Instructional Playbook

Materials: Composition notebooks or spiral-bound books for each student. Photocopies of sentence frames.

Name It: We are going to start writing in journals. You are going to write to me, and I am going to write back to you. We will do it once a week. It will be fun for me to learn more about you. We will write about different things throughout the year. (Show a variety of sentence frames and have these available for students to use.)

What You Might Say Next: "I realize writing in English may still be difficult, so we are going to use a variety of sentence frames to help you share your ideas. You can also draw or sketch in your journal and label the drawings if you wish. You might also want to decorate the cover of your journal. You each have your own notebook, so you can give it a personal title too! We can write about fun things we did outside of school, people, and activities we are looking forward to, favorite things. We can write about how we feel too."

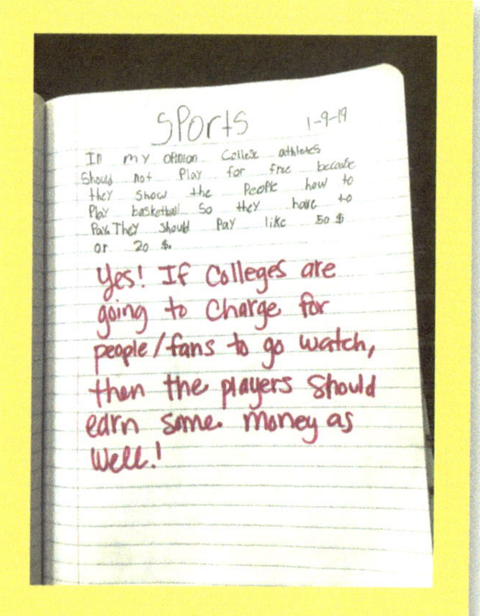

In this example of a student journal, notice how the student wrote her opinion and the teacher added his thoughts.

Model/Do Together: Open to a journal page and demonstrate how you want students to set up the page, with date at the top. Write a couple of sentences about something you know your students will enjoy, using sentence frames you have written on a whiteboard or displayed. Think aloud while you write so students can understand your thought process. Also think aloud why you are choosing a particular frame. You might quickly model two topics, so students get a feel for the possibilities, which can range from funny to sad. For example, I might say, "Today, after school, I am taking my dog to the groomer. My dog is a tiny little dog but he thinks he's the boss. He howls all the way to the groomer. The minute he sees the door, he tries to run away." Another one might be something like: "Last night I talked on the phone with my friend who lives far away. We shared news and laughed. But it made me feel sad that we can't see each other often."

Release: Introduce the frames and encourage students to choose the one that makes sense to them. Provide about ten to fifteen minutes for students to write in the dialogue journal, helping and supporting as needed. You want to ensure that they are selecting their own topic and words, not just copying what they heard you say. Write a sentence or two back to students so that they can read your response. If you are moving about the classroom and helping students, and you can fit it in, you can write a sentence back as a response right then and there. Otherwise, you can collect the journals and write the sentence later.

Watch Fors and Work-Arounds

Students aren't ready to write out sentences. One way we communicate with writing is by combining one or two words with a picture. Think about all the signs we see every day! Donut shops, exit signs, pizza places. It's all labels and pictures. Students can draw pictures, diagrams, or graphs, or take photos. Then they will label them so others know what we are trying to communicate about the image. You can comment on the images and ideas they present. You can create models so students know how to communicate through labeling.

A teacher-created chart based on a class's science topic. Pictures and sentence frames support students' writing.

20 (Contined) Writing Dialogue Journals With Sentence Frames

Offer a variety of sentence frames to help students. Students need access to lots of sentence frames of varying levels of complexity, as students are not in the same place with language acquisition. You can generate more as you notice your students' progress.

Look for when to phase out the frames. Like any learning tool, frames can get stale. Look for students who you know are ready to generate sentences on their own and nudge them to do so!

Examples of sentence frames:

Last night, I ______________________. (past tense writing)

Yesterday______________________. (past tense writing)

In class I am ______________________. (present tense writing)

Today, after school I will ______________________. (future tense writing)

More difficult frames

Last night, I ______________ and I felt ______________.
I felt this way because ______________. (past tense writing)

I used to ______________ but now I ______________.
I changed because ______________. (past tense writing)

In class, I am ______________ because I enjoy/dislike ______________ and I want to ______________.
(present tense writing)

I am going to ______________ because ______________.
(future progressive tense)

iStock.com/ChrisGorgio

SECTION THREE

iStock.com/simon2579

TASKS

for Students at the Developing Level of English Language Proficiency

Section III ● Tasks for Students at the Developing Level of English Language Proficiency		
21.	Giving and Performing Two-Step Directions	Listening & Speaking
22.	Personal Dictionaries	Listening, Speaking, & Writing
23.	Shared Reading: Ask-and-Answer Questions About Text	Listening, Speaking, & Reading
24.	Language Experience Approach	Listening, Speaking, Reading, & Writing
25.	Choral Reading: Readers' Theater	Reading
26.	Beginning to Write in English: Opinion Writing	Writing & Speaking
27.	Beginning to Write in English: Information Writing	Writing & Speaking
28.	Beginning to Write in English: Personal Narrative	Writing & Speaking
29.	Building Simple Present Tense Sentences	Writing
30.	Building Sentences: Add in Adjectives/Adverbs/Articles	Writing

Overview

When students are at the **developing level** of acquiring English, they are acclimated enough to learn language to communicate for social and personal purposes. This proficiency level is a gateway into using language for academic purposes, and so it's critical to make the most of it in the classroom. To communicate well, one must know the social register or the social setting in which the language is used (Wright, 2019). *Communicative competence* was the term coined by Dell Hymes in the 1960s (Hymes, 1971). To foster this competence, offer daily opportunities for students to speak and write.

In this set of tasks, we continue to provide interactive experiences with language that support students' risk-taking with expressing themselves. We focus on supporting students to say and compose meaningful messages, thoughts, and ideas. Students will learn how to:

- carry on conversations (both social and academic)
- develop their vocabulary, especially interpersonal language
- write in at least three genres (opinion, narrative, and informative)

When students progress from understanding English for social uses to also developing academic knowledge in English, we say they are moving from the **developing** level of English language acquisition to the **expanding** level. The tasks in this section reflect this movement. They all invite you to use interesting, grade-level content for the tasks so we knowledge-build while we language-build. Or put another way, because it takes one to two years for students to become fluent socially (Cummins, 2008), students should learn content the entire time they are learning English. We cannot hold off on content for two years!

And it really isn't as simple as students learning social language for two years and then starting academic language development (Fillmore, 2009; Valdes et al., 2015). Students are immersed in academic learning because they are in classrooms where kindergartners are studying bugs, or 8th graders are studying types of cells. The social contexts students learn are both academic and social settings. Their success depends on the development of prior knowledge.

Connect to grade-level content: All effective ELD instruction occurs through content. Integrate science and social studies as much as possible and give all students access to grade-level texts as much as possible, so no child feels "tracked" on a lower level. So, for instance, when teaching Task X Learning to Use Conjunctions, you might use a compelling, current topic as the heart of the lesson. Look for angles that your students seem jazzed about—thunder and lightning in a weather unit, or a heated debate about if great whites really are the most dangerous sharks. Content is what will make these ELD tasks pop for students and increase their desire to work with the language, talk about topics, read, and write to share ideas.

Use an Addictive Approach: Your students may continue to speak their heritage language to communicate and often use both. This way of communicating should be encouraged. Students will not get "mixed up" between the languages. What they are doing is communicating by translanguaging, the term for the holistic, dynamic notion of bilingualism developed by Garcia and Lin (2016). Translanguaging are multiple practices in which emerging bilinguals and multilinguals engage with language to communicate and make sense of their bilingual world (Garcia & Lin, 2016). Students don't need to speak solely in English to communicate with you or the class. The best instruction for multilingual learners sees the dual language as an asset and supports children using the language skills in their primary language to express themselves in English.

To refresh your memory of what to expect of learners at this stage, the following is information from WIDA.

WIDA's Descriptors for English Language Proficiency Level: Developing

Developing	What Students Are Able to Do
Listening	Follow multistep oral directions one step at a time.
	Understand questions and prompts when repeated words and phrases are used.
	Categorize or sequence oral information using pictures, objects.
Speaking	Speak in short sentences.
	Begin to communicate more often socially.
	State personal opinions simply.
	Retell events.
	Respond orally to show agreement or disagreement.
	Communicate orally about content by describing procedures (how to do something).
	Make frequent grammatical and pronunciation errors.
	Use of verb tenses is expanding and beginning to try irregular conjugations.
Reading	Identify details and main or key ideas in texts and make simple comparisons about text and story elements.
	Students will be able to connect causal- or content-related relationships in texts together.
	Make predictions.
	Retell stories.
	Use context clues to determine meaning of words that are not complex.
Writing	Begin to write using sentence starters and drawings.
	Write simple sentences.
	Describe events, people, processes, procedures.
	Write statements about books read and connect ideas together.
	Produce bare-bones expository or narrative texts.
	Compare/contrast information.

Source: WIDA Consortium (2012); WIDA Consortium (2020)

10 Tips for Success

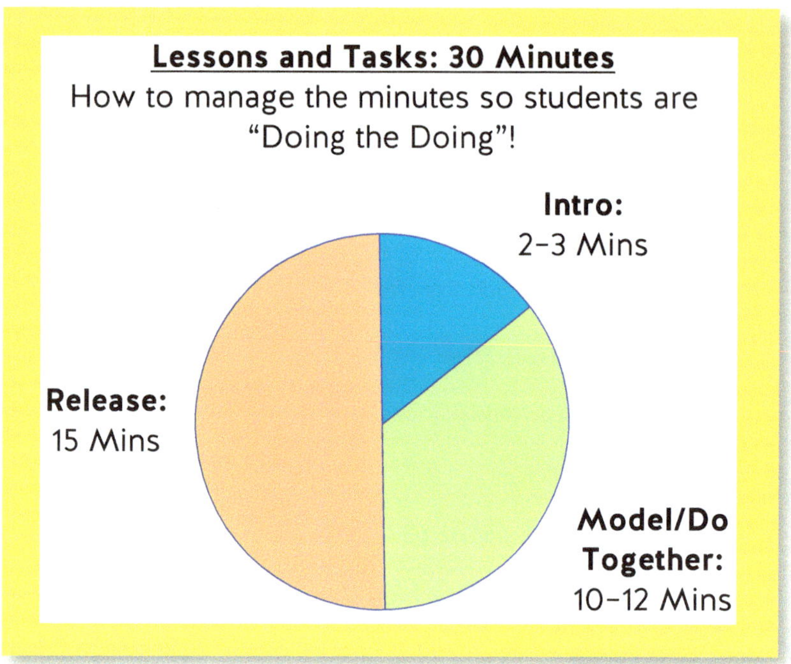

1. I recommend **three minutes max for your introduction** to the lesson. Be sure to state the purpose of the lesson and task.
2. Reassure students that you are going to show them how to do everything that is asked of them. Tell them you will do much of the work together but that they will be doing more and more work on their own.
3. **Model for nine to ten minutes.**
4. Use visuals to ensure that students understand. Real objects, videos, pictures—anything you can do to make the content comprehensible.
5. Pantomime, gesture, movement, extra explanation, and slower speech—all are good techniques to scaffold students' understanding.
6. **Plan on fifteen minutes at least for peer work and guided work.**
7. During peer work, look for signs that the work is too hard and pull students back together and model the work more if needed and offer more guided work time.
8. **Altogether, including release—plan for thirty minutes per task.**
9. As students work, and when and if you bring them back together, look for those students who you can tell are still shaky with it. Perhaps sit side by side with those students and provide additional support, or buddy them up with a partner.
10. At the developing level, students will be doing more shared reading with you. As you are presenting content in nonfiction texts, or books with complex language in picture books, use shared reading until learners are ready to be reading on their own.

iStock.com/simon2579

Giving and Performing Two-Step Directions

Listening & Speaking

WHEN TO OFFER IT

After students are following your directions fairly well.

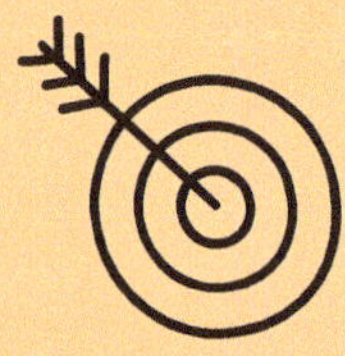

TARGET

Students can give or respond to directives.

In this version of Simon Says, students practice giving and responding to two- or more-step directions with a partner. Students enjoy giving commands to a peer and taking directions, so you'll find students are easily motivated. Start out by doing this task with total physical response (see Task 1 on page 18) where students are moving their bodies to the directions. After much practice, you can move to a drawing activity where a student draws a picture, hides it behind a book, and then tells their partner how to draw the same picture. You can also have students give directions on how to do something, like stacking blocks in a certain order, or using classroom objects to create a still life.

Your Instructional Playbook

Name It: We are going to play a game in which you give directions to a partner. At first, we will practice together and I will give directions, but after that, you will do work in pairs.

What You Might Say Next: "Learning how to follow directions is an important skill. Whether you are watching a video on how to scramble eggs or asking someone to tell you which way to go when you are lost, listening and recalling steps is helpful in life. I am going to lead the game a few times, and then it will be your turn to be the leader and give directions. We are all going to take turns being the leader."

iStock.com/PeopleImages

Giving and receiving directions develops listening comprehension and oral language.

Model/Do Together: Act out one set of directions yourself by saying a directive out loud, and then doing it yourself. Next, have students follow your directions a few times. Make sure the directions have at least two steps. For example: Stand up, push in your chair. Walk to the left five steps.

Release: Pair up students. Encourage them to take turns giving and carrying out directions.

Watch Fors and Work-Arounds

A pair is stuck and neither student is saying anything. Encourage one student to be the leader and ask them what they want to say. Give them a two-step direction and ask them to repeat it—to build confidence. Then ask them to give directions to their partner. Work with the pair a few more times before moving on. Make the point that it's okay if they don't know all the words. They can say half the directions and then act out the other half.

Personal Dictionaries

Listening, Speaking, & Writing

WHEN TO OFFER IT

Once students are moving into greater levels of English acquisition, they will be ready to maintain a personal dictionary.

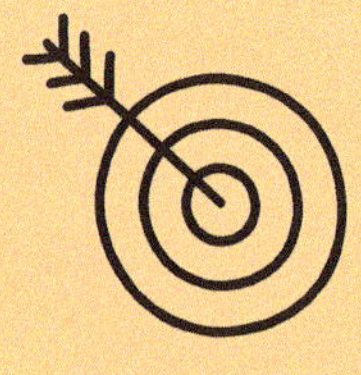

TARGET

Students will write words in a personal dictionary.

You will work with students to put the basic vocabulary in the dictionary that the group has been learning together. As students progress, they can use the book as a place to keep track of new words without your guidance. Across the school year, continue to talk explicitly about personal dictionaries, and how readers and writers use them. Demonstrate the possibilities! Dictionaries can house words students may want to use in their fiction and poetry writing one day or nonfiction words they want to learn more about. They can be handy references to check spelling or recall word meanings. The point you want to emphasize is that students don't have to worry about writing full complex definitions.

Your Instructional Playbook

Materials: composition books or spiral bound books for each student segmented out with sticky tabs labeled with the alphabet. (You can find printable personal dictionary pages on the companion website at **resources.corwin.com/bigbookELD**.)

Name It: You have learned a lot of words, and I am noticing many of you want to keep track of them. So, I have a new notebook for each of you that you can use to create your very own dictionary.

What You Might Say Next: "To begin your dictionary, think of some of the words we have learned together that you want to remember. You can also look at our word banks around the classroom. Ask me about words and I will tell you how to spell them. We are going to practice writing a few words and definitions together, and then you will have time to get your dictionary started."

Model/Do Together: Think aloud as you write a word on chart paper and think aloud about its spelling and meaning. If appropriate, connect it to other words, and say why you want to add it to a dictionary. Get across the idea that these dictionaries entries are to support pronunciation, spelling, and recalling meaning. No lengthy definitions required! They may even draw a picture or write definitions in their heritage language if they are able to.

Release: Facilitate time for students to choose words and record them in the dictionaries. Provide assistance as needed. When you are starting a new unit in science, social studies, math, or ELA, it is a good idea to have students record a few of the most important words to know.

Word banks can help students record words in personal dictionaries. Brevity and simple pictures will suffice.

A seventh-grade student writing in her word journal. Writing notebooks and journals become a lifelong tool!

Shared Reading: Ask-and-Answer Questions About Text

Listening, Speaking, & Reading

WHEN TO OFFER IT

Once students are participating in shared reading in class, they are ready to go deeper in comprehension work.

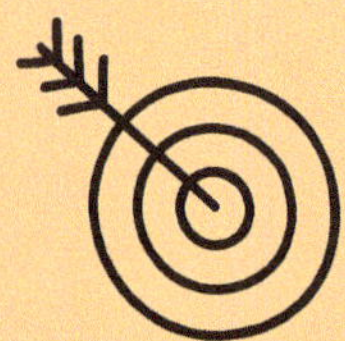

TARGET

Students can ask questions and answer questions about complex text with the support of the teacher.

Shared reading is when the students can see the text clearly and can read along with you. They may have a copy of the book or text, or you may be projecting it with a document camera. The shared aspect of the reading means that students are able to work through the words and think about what they mean with your voice guiding the reading and providing support. This task begins the experience of shared reading. As they build confidence, encourage them to talk more about the text and ask questions about it. Oral language experiences such as this provide students the opportunity to delve into topics, formulate their own ideas, and then try sharing their thoughts in English (or a blend of heritage language and English).

Your Instructional Playbook

Materials: A text your students can read with your support or use a picture book or a nonfiction text with lots of picture and text feature support; sticky notes, chart paper, and markers

Name It: Today when we read together, we are going to focus on asking and answering questions about the text.

What You Might Say Next: "What kinds of questions do you notice I ask you when we are talking about the text? What questions do you have when you are reading? Let's brainstorm some of those questions and ideas." (Write out their ideas on a whiteboard or chart paper.)

Model/Do Together: Hand out copies of the book, and front load its meaning. You can do this through a book walk, pointing out features, discussing challenging vocabulary, and so on. Building this understanding with this initial book grazing helps students to predict the main ideas. With students who are reading in a language that they are still acquiring, this frees up their minds to make connections between what they know will be in the story and what the words are saying.

Start the shared reading, inviting students to read aloud along with you. They can also read silently, but hearing them is preferable, as it gives you an instant assessment of who is able to pronounce the words and follow along, and who might need support. Stop where the beginning of the book ends and talk about the characters, who they are, and what they are doing. Do the same in the middle and also at the end. Stop in appropriate places in the book and ask them what they are thinking and what questions they might have. Hand out sticky notes and have them write down at least one to two questions about the text that all of you can discuss after you finish reading.

Release: Ask students to share their questions. Put their sticky notes on the chart paper as students take turns. Encourage them to answer one another's questions, going back into the text to find support. Your role is to facilitate. As students respond, guide students to help you collaboratively compose an answer. Write it on the chart paper. Don't rush this phase! Keep opening the question up to the entire group. This creates rich, varied oral language that every learner benefits from hearing.

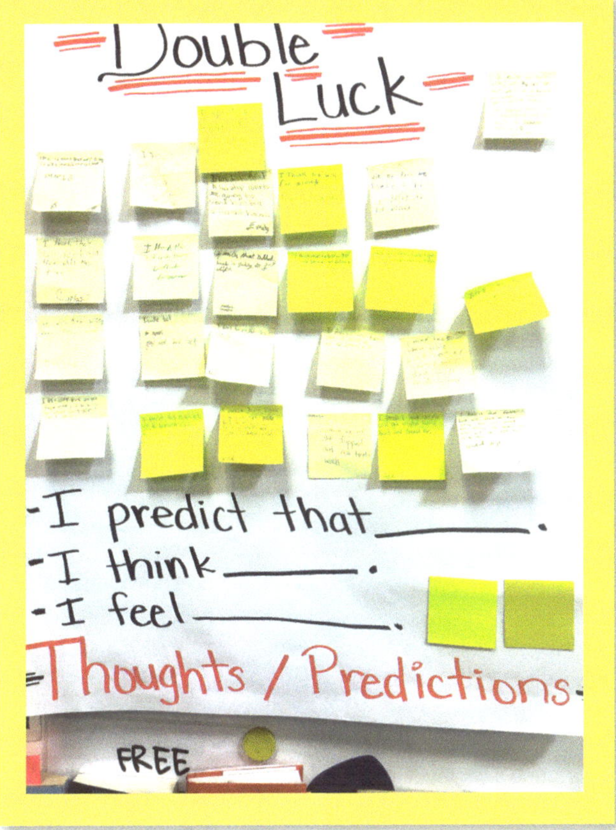

This example is organized around asking and answering prediction questions.

Watch Fors and Work-Arounds

Students may not be ready for a complex text. Watch for learners who seem to struggle to figure out (decode) the words. You can do a quick check with one sentence and ask everyone to do choral read. Listen in to see if a student is frustrated or is simply reading silently. If the student is overly frustrated, slow down the reading, taking it line by line. Read each line twice. You can also read the line aloud once and have the students choral read after they have heard you read the sentence first.

Students may not have the words in English to appropriately express all that they want to say about the story or the text. If they cannot write out the full question, encourage them to write a question mark on the sticky note with a bullet point and then put the sticky note on the page where they had that thought. After you finish reading together, encourage students to revisit the page with their question. They can say the bullet point and point to lines or pictures in the text to help them communicate what their question is. You can gently model and encourage them to say the words. Use prompts like the following to draw out their thinking:

What do you think the story was about?

What else do you think about the story?

Did you like it? Dislike the book?

Sentence Frame to Try:

I have a question on page . . .

I wonder

I think

I want to know why/if

Language Experience Approach

Listening, Speaking, Reading, & Writing

WHEN TO OFFER IT

Once students can say a few phrases on their own.

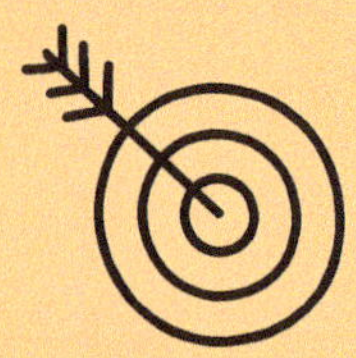

TARGET

Students can compose orally with teacher support and the teacher will write the sentences.

While this task looks like a writing task, it is really an oral language development task and vocabulary development task. You lead conversations with students about shared experiences, building in new words, phrases, and techniques for communicating well. It's called the language experience approach, and its premise is that students can write more—and more fluently—if they write based on firsthand experiences. It makes intuitive sense, and there are decades of research supporting its efficacy. To put it in action, have students participate in a collaborative writing process. The experiences might be something special you did in class, revising a science experiment, having lunch in the cafeteria on pizza day, or any other shared experiences. Because students have lived the topic, they have the memory to lean on as they work to find the best words.

Your Instructional Playbook

Name It: We are going to write together today so we can write a longer piece. This will be a narrative story about something we have all experienced. To make it fun, we will add in our thoughts and our feelings.

What You Might Say Next: "Let's think of things we have all done at school together. What are some experiences we have had? (Provide examples as necessary to get students thinking.) I am going to jot the ideas here on chart paper, and then we can select a favorite to write about."

Model/Do Together: Based on the topic the students pick, discuss with them what they did, as well as their thoughts and feelings. You could write this brainstorm in any order on a whiteboard. After collecting ideas, ask students what sentence they believe they should write first. As they say the sentence, count the words in the sentence and model writing the sentence on a large piece of chart paper. Continue in this manner, facilitating the conversation so that students are brainstorming the sentences. If some students are ready, invite them to come to the chart and write the sentence, or part of the sentence.

Watch Fors and Work-Arounds

You may need to guide students to talk and write in past tense. You will be modeling in past tense, so students may be giving you ideas in present tense if they have not yet acquired facility in past tense. Model the correct verb tense and point out you are changing the verb because it is past tense since it is an experience from the past.

Students in the group may be at differing levels of language proficiency. Ensure that all students have a chance to think and brainstorm a sentence; due to excitement, more proficient students will take over, and less proficient students won't get to practice with you. This is natural when the energy is flowing in your classroom. Just be aware of it and make space for all students to think through a sentence or add to the group sentence.

Students are ready to write longer pieces. Rearrange students to sit in their groups. Based on the topic the students pick, discuss with them what they did, and their thoughts and feelings during the experience. Guide them to talk in past tense. You could make a word bank on a whiteboard that they refer to when they are writing in their groups. Explain that each of them will write at least one sentence strip and preferably two. Their goal is to talk together and collaboratively plan their story. Prompt them if they get stuck. For example, *Where did you go? What happened first? What happened next? How do you feel about that day, moment, or experience?*

We ______________________________.

First ______________________________.

Second ______________________________.

Next ______________________________.

Finally ______________________________.

Things we did:

We______________________________.

Then, we ______________________________.

Something fun was ______________________________.

What we liked most was ______________________________.

In the end ______________________________.

Choral Reading: Readers' Theater

Reading

WHEN TO OFFER IT

When students can read simple texts. Make sure to choose text complexity that is in their zone of proximal development.

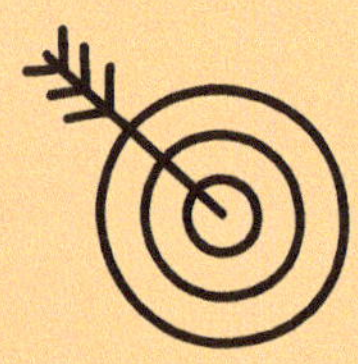

TARGET

Students can read parts in a play.

Readers' theater is a type of shared reading where students take on a role during the recital of a script. In pairs, or alone, students read one specific part of a play. It's a popular, engaging activity for students and develops their reading, writing, speaking, and listening abilities. With this task, I encourage you to have students read in pairs, as it supports each learner with decoding words. Reading aloud together also helps the less confident child feel braver. For students who are expanding their language acquisition, keep the text easy. There is a sample text labeled Readers' Theater in Appendix B, beginning on page 209. If you have time, you can adapt favorite stories that are dialogue-driven (Mastrothanasis, 2023) to use for Readers' Theater.

Your Instructional Playbook

Name It: We are going to read today, but this book is a bit different. It is a script. In a play, TV show, or movie, actors memorize a script. We won't be acting, but just reading each part pretending to be a character in the story.

What You Might Say Next: "You don't need to be worried about figuring out all the words on your own. We will practice together a few times, and you are going to be reading with a partner."

Model/Do Together: Model with one of the scripts in Appendix B (see page 209 for script examples for Readers' Theater). Read aloud one character's part. Then read aloud another character's part, explaining to students that they will work with their partner to read with expression. Hand out the scripts and have student pairs choose characters. Before they begin rehearsing, read the script together. You can lead them in a choral reading, or you can read each line, and then students can repeat. Check with students after a few lines to talk through unfamiliar vocabulary. If needed, stop and discuss meaning as often as necessary. Remind them to notice question marks and exclamation marks, as these punctuations help them know how to say the line.

Release: Invite student pairs to practice their parts. Give them enough time for them to say each of their lines several times until they are reading the line fluently or fairly fluently. After practice, perform the script by everyone taking turns reading their lines. The students might enjoy this enough that you read it more than once! Once students feel confident, they can "perform" their script to other groups or students in other classrooms. If you want to make it even more fun, easy-to-use props can be ordered online—look for photo book props.

Watch Fors and Work-Arounds

Students may struggle with comprehension. If you notice learners who are reading aloud adequately but may not understand what they are reading, step in to support. Sit with the pair of students and break down the sentences with them to ensure they get the meaning. Provide context for them about what is going to happen or has already happened in the script so that their parts make sense to them.

Students who are quiet. Some students are too shy to read or seem reluctant to speak aloud. You may make groups of three if necessary and encourage the student who is reluctant to speak aloud to mouth the words and practice in their head.

Beginning to Write in English: Opinion Writing

Writing & Speaking

WHEN YOU MIGHT OFFER IT

When students have basic vocabulary somewhat developed in English and know most of the letters and sounds in English.

TARGET

Using sentence frames, students can write an opinion statement.

As is the case in teaching all genres, opinion writing needs to be foregrounded by lots of shared opportunities to listen to you read aloud examples. Also provide lots of guided discussions after each reading. This immersion phase is so key, and it can take several days, but the payoff makes it worth it. Read aloud published opinion pieces (movie reviews, etc.) and picture books in which someone is making a case (*I Wanna Iguana* is one of many!). Invite ideas about what students notice and like. Read funny ones, feisty ones, moving ones, conveying the idea that the writer has to have a strong connection to the topic.

Your Instructional Playbook

Name It: We are going to write about a topic for which we have a strong opinion. An opinion is our thoughts and feelings about something. We say why we like it or don't like it. An opinion might state why something is good or bad. We might be talking about an idea, a book, a movie, a new flavor of ice cream! We say our opinion when we believe something and we want others to know our thinking.

What You Might Say Next: "As writers, we can share our opinion about things we believe or know. For example, I think tacos are the best food. That's what I think! I am going to write that down, and I'll show you how I do that." Keep the opinion statement short and simple. Don't teach other parts of an opinion (reasons, conclusion, etc.) just yet.

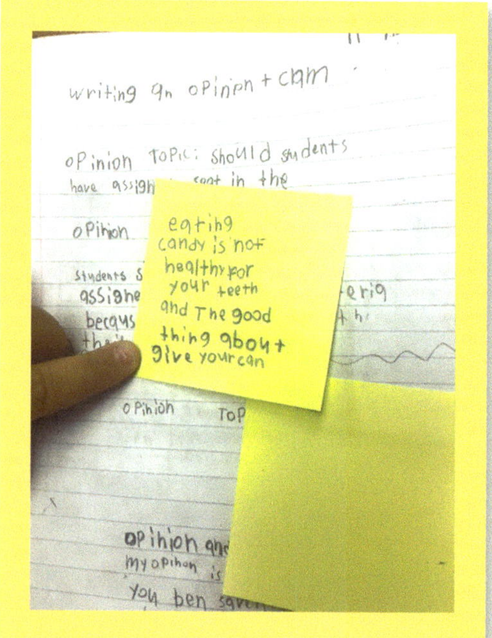

A student opines about candy! An opinion can be written as a simple statement. Learners at the developing level begin to get the hang of connecting ideas in their writing.

Model/Do Together: Using a sentence frame such as the following: __________ is the best ________. Model your process on chart paper or the smartboard. Point out to students that they can look at the letter/sound chart as they listen to you think aloud your process of spelling words. Say, "When you write, listen to the sounds in the word you are writing down. Think about which letter represents what you hear." It's important to model this encoding action because while the words might be simple, it will likely not be easy for students to spell. When you are done, invite students to read the sentence aloud. *Tacos are the best food.*

Brainstorm topic ideas. You can either write an opinion as a class or go immediately to having each student write on a topic of their choice. When students work on their own, they should first select a sentence frame. Then guide them to orally say the sentence they are thinking of.

I believe __________ is the best __________.

The worst __________ is __________.

__________ is better than __________

I like __________ the best.

__________ is the best __________.

I don't think __________ is __________.

My favorite __________ is __________.

Release: Guide students as they write their opinion sentences. Encourage them to think of the corresponding letter or letter combinations that make the sounds they are hearing in the words. Talk to them to draw out why they have the opinion they do. Even though at this stage they are only writing the statement, it is motivating and helpful for them to share their bigger idea.

Watch Fors and Work-Arounds

Students may need access to a sound/letter chart (see Appendix B, page 197) to help them make connections between sounds and letters. If they don't know the word for what they want to write, help them discover the word by looking at a book that they are reading or have read with you or by checking a website. You can always tell them the word but focus first on helping them be resourceful.

Students may be ready to add reasons to their opinion statements. You have a range of readiness levels in your class, of course, so differentiate as needed. For example, students who are ready can add "because" to their sentence and write their reason for their opinion. Students can write more than one reason, write a concluding sentence, and jazz up their statement to make it more attention-grabbing–opinion-writing; and this can be done often, and you can layer in more complexity over time.

27 Beginning to Write in English: Information Writing

Writing & Speaking

WHEN YOU MIGHT OFFER IT

Once students have basic vocabulary somewhat developed in English and know most of the letters and sounds in English.

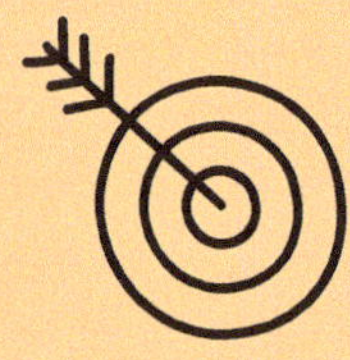

TARGET

Students can write an information sentence by using a sentence frame and spelling words by hearing sounds in words.

Build up to information writing with lots of read-alouds and discussions of the genre. Strong examples develop students' "ear" for the genre. Curate a collection of mentor texts and have them in plastic tubs so students can study them. Cocreate an anchor chart as you read aloud and talk about these texts, so that the characteristics of information writing are on display. Consistent read-alouds and shared writing experiences provide learners with empowering, enjoyable group experiences that help support them as they do the hard work of writing on their own.

Your Instructional Playbook

Name It: We are going to write about a topic, thing, or idea that interests us. When we share information, we do it for various purposes. For example, sometimes we share news about a local event or an event in the world. Sometimes we share information to help someone, like when we give directions. There are many reasons. Because information is often factual—things that are true—we want to make our writing clear.

What You Might Say Next: "As writers, when we write about a topic we know a lot about, it can be hard to share all we know, because we could write an entire book! So, it can be helpful to focus on two or three important things. For example, I love frogs. I am going to write about three facts I want people to know. Frogs live in water and on land. Frogs are often green. They eat flies."

How to End an Informative Essay

1. Use a transitional phrase
2. Summarize your subtopics (don't repeat)
3. Call to action (tell your reader to do something)

Leave steps such as this displayed, so students can refer to the information as they write.

Model/Do Together: Write the sentence frame on chart paper before you begin demonstrating. Keep your sentences short. As you think aloud and write, model the process of looking at the sound chart to help you spell. Also tell students that you listen to the sounds in the words and think about which letter represents what you hear. You need to explicitly model this encoding action because while the words might be simple for you to spell, it will likely not be easy for students to spell. Remember, you want a swift, engaging pace so there is plenty of time for students to write; your modeling shouldn't exceed ten minutes.

Brainstorm with students about what they know about. You can revisit topics you have studied as a group. If you need to develop a topic, choose one students are interested in, obtain a short book, or visit a website and pull facts out. Write the facts on a chart or slide. Using sentence frames, guide students to orally say the sentence(s) they are thinking of. Reinforce that they are writing facts in informational writing, not opinions. Repeat this type of writing often, drawing from what you are studying in science and social studies.

> ____________ is/are/has/does ____________.
>
> ____________ (fill in subject you are studying with them—for example, buildings) can be ____________.
>
> In addition, ____________ is/are/has/does ____________.
>
> Also, ____________ is/are/has/does ____________.

Release: As students write their informational sentences, help them stay focused on their main idea. Ask, "What are three things you want to share about your topic?" Have students orally share their writing with partners.

Watch Fors and Work-Arounds

Students may need access to a sound chart (see Appendix B, page 197). The sound chart supports them as they make connections between sounds and letters. If they don't know the word for what they want to label, help them discover the word by looking at a book that they are reading about their topic or have read with you, or look at multimedia support.

Some students may be ready to write more than a couple of sentences. Invite them to add details to their sentences or additional sentences. These students might also enjoy using a four-square map in which they write four attributes about the topic. This tool is terrific for the planning stage; students can fill it out and then write four sentences on a separate paper.

28 Beginning to Write in English: Personal Narrative

Writing & Speaking

WHEN YOU MIGHT OFFER IT

Once students have basic vocabulary somewhat developed in English and know most of the letters and sounds in English.

TARGET

Using sentence frames, students can write a short personal narrative.

Students can begin writing in various genres once they have acquired some basic vocabulary and have had lots of shared opportunities to listen to you read aloud, and to write group stories and texts. Personal narratives are inherently appealing to your learners, as they like to tell stories about their lives, and they can draw from their experiences to help them select events, vocabulary, and meaning. As you talk about published personal narratives that you read aloud (or passages from longer works), point out what you notice about them. Create an anchor chart listing characteristics of the text, such as the following: *an event, how the character reacted to that event,* or *the author's use of temporal words*. Keep it simple so students don't feel overwhelmed as they set out to write.

Your Instructional Playbook

Name It: We are going to write about something that happened to us, something we did or remember. I call this a memory moment. It doesn't have to be anything big like a trip or a birthday party; it could just be going to the store or eating your favorite breakfast in the morning.

What You Might Say Next: "Memory moments are little stories we want to share with others. It's a moment that is special to us, even if it's something simple we do every day. I. have a memory moment from yesterday when Mrs. Corcoran gave me a hug in the hallway. She had listened to me share that my dog was sick and she gave me a hug to help me feel better. I could write about that."

This chart helps students remember parts of a narrative. For students acquiring English, charts like this function as word banks as well, providing support for spelling and meaning.

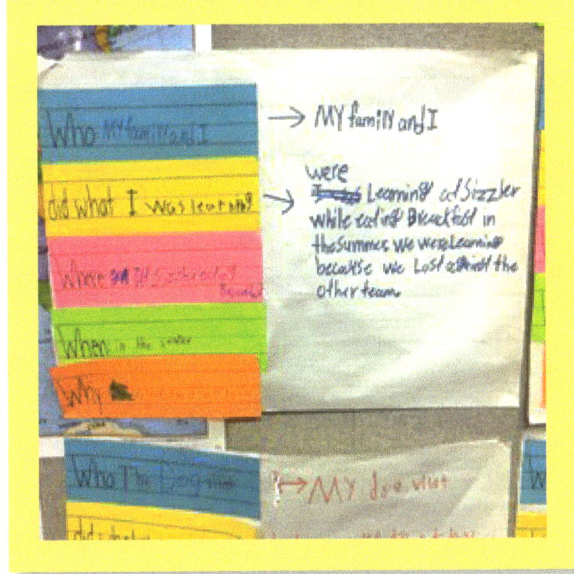

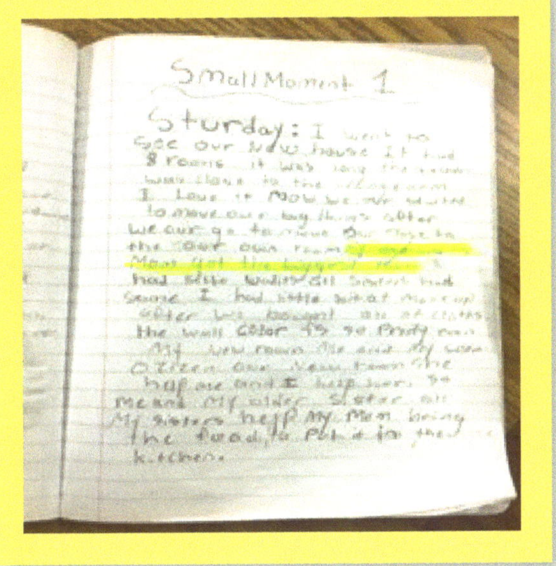

These two examples of a student's writing show how much growth occurs during the developing into expanding proficiency phase. This student has developed much more language in a few months.

Model/Do Together: Model writing the memory moment that you just shared. Keep the example to two to three sentences. You will also want to demonstrate using supportive tools. For example, use the sentence frames for personal narrative writing and talk about how they help you. Model how you are listening to the sounds in the words and thinking about which letter represents what you hear.

Invite students to brainstorm about memory moments they have. You might have students turn to a partner and share an idea they want to write about. Once they are ready, send students off to write.

A few sample sentence frames:

Once ________________.

Last night/week/year ________________.

What happened next was ________________.

Also ________________.

In the end ________________.

28 (Continued) Beginning to Write in English: Personal Narrative

Release: Guide students as they write their memory moments. Help them to stay on topic and figure out how to write the words in English as best they can. Remember you want to empower them to use strategies and tools independently. For example, facilitate their using the letter sound chart rather than just providing the spelling for them. You want to encourage them to be able to hear the word, break it up into syllables, and then spell each syllable. Students may be able to only write two or three sentences. Support and celebrate their efforts. As they acquire more language, they will be able to write longer pieces.

Watch Fors and Work-Arounds

Students may need access to a sound chart (see Appendix B, page 197) to help them make connections between sounds and letters. You can always tell them the word, but focus first on their empowerment and help them figure it out rather than just telling if possible.

iStock.com/simon2579

Building Simple Present Tense Sentences

Writing

WHEN TO OFFER IT

Once students have been immersed in weeks of shared writing, guided writing, and independent writing experiences.

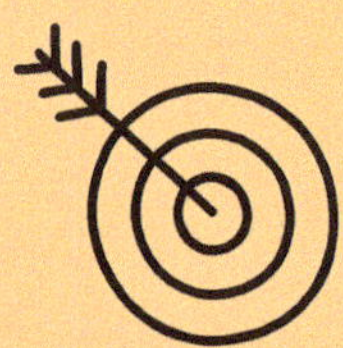

TARGET

Students will write a sentence with a subject, a verb, and an object.

Students learn to put sentences together properly by building them with you. They should feel confident in writing a couple of sentences with your support before you introduce rules of language, like subject, verb, and object. We want students to always have a sense from us that learning English is about using the language to express self, to communicate, and to understand others. If our instruction focuses on grammar rules too much, and before students are ready for it, it's counterproductive. Rules about language can be taught once students are fluent enough to immediately apply them to their own writing.

Your Instructional Playbook

Materials: Sentence strips in three colors, or small pocket charts in three different colors and plain-colored sentence strips. (One color sentence strip or pocket chart will represent the subject, one color will represent the verb in the sentence, and one color will represent the object.)

Name It: We are going to work together to build some sentences. These sentences will have a subject, a verb, and an object.

What You Might Say Next: "This is going to be fun because we get to color-code our sentences to make sure we are writing them correctly. We've talked about how a sentence is complete if it has a subject—something doing the action. A verb—a word that describes the action. And the object—the thing/person the action is done to. Watch this! 'Mrs. Akhavan (point to yourself) drops (drop a pen) the pen.' (Write *Mrs. Akhavan drops the pen* on chart paper.) So in this sentence, I am the subject, doing the action. What is the verb? What is the object?"

Model/Do Together: Write another simple sentence on a chart. Avoid pronouns because students may not yet be ready to learn what pronouns stand for. Also, use present tense if you have students at the emerging level of language proficiency, as they have not yet mastered multiple verb tenses. Following are highlights of what to say and do:

- Underline in green the subject, the verb in yellow, and the object in red. Explain that the subject is a noun. Explain the function of the verb and that the object is the taking the action. For example: *Roberto climbs rocks.*
- Brainstorm another sentence with students and write it on a sentence strip, either color-coded or plain.
- Put each part of the sentence in the correct location in the pocket chart and reinforce the idea of the subject (noun), the verb (present tense), and the object (the what).
- Describe the subject as the "who" or "what" of the sentence, the verb as the action, and the object as the item, person, or thing that receives

the action. For example, *Marlea sings songs, Jaime jumps rope, N'dea kicks (the) ball.*

- If you add in an article like *the*, or *a*, describe why you are adding it in. Give your explanation in a way that will make sense to students.
- Brainstorm a few additional sentences with students orally, to help students begin to think of what they will write on the sentence strips.
- When students have their sentence decided, guide them to count the words in their sentence. (Counting words is a way of scaffolding the writing. They can count how many words they plan to write so they don't forget them as they work through composing their sentences.)
- Remind them they will write the subject on one sentence strip, the verb on another, and the object on the third.

Release: As students start writing, remind them of their sentences and how many words they will write on one sentence strip. Guide them to ensure the verb is present tense. After they write, gather back together as a group and have each student put their sentence strips into the pocket chart. Have each student read aloud their sentence, supporting as necessary.

Watch Fors and Work-Arounds

Students may not have all the vocabulary they need. If they can describe what they are thinking, then tell them the words that they are looking for, so they can work on their writing. For example, a student might say "My sentence is I play . . . You know that thing, with the (and then the student gestures playing a guitar)." In this instance, tell them *guitar*.

Students can brainstorm but cannot get the words on the page. Guide students to count the words. Also help them to plan to write the subject on one sentence strip, the verb on another, the object on the third, and the adjective on the fourth. If they need to add an article, like *a* or *the*, just have them write it with the subject or the object. For example, *the girl, the rope, a book,* and so forth.

Building Sentences: Add in Adjectives/Adverbs/Articles

Writing

WHEN YOU MIGHT OFFER IT

Once students know the basic building blocks of sentences.

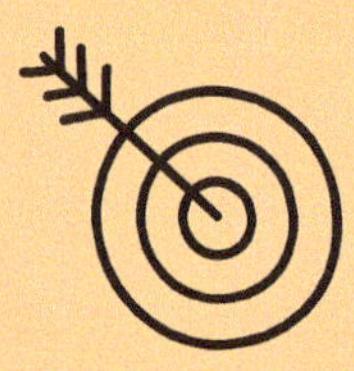

TARGET

Students can add adjectives to the sentences you are creating with them.

Now that students can learn to put sentences together properly by building them with you (see Building Simple Present Tense Sentences, Task 29), they will be ready for more. Remember that acquiring language is about authentic language experiences. This type of task, which is a task about how English works, should be taught when students are ready for it and can immediately apply the new knowledge to relevant writing experiences. You can do this task with any genre—personal narrative, opinion, and informative writing. And as always, connect the task to your curriculum content, so you are always accelerating grade level goals.

Your Instructional Playbook

Materials: Four sentence strips of different colors or four-color small pocket charts and plain-colored sentence strips. One color sentence strip or pocket chart will represent the subject, one color will represent the verb in the sentence, one color will represent the object, and one color will represent the adjective.

Name It: We are going to work together to build some sentences. These sentences will have a subject, a verb, an object, and also an adjective. Remember, the subject is the person or thing doing the action. The verb is the action. The object is the person or thing being acted upon. "The wind blows the kite." "The mother hugs her baby." Now we are going to add in an adjective.

What You Might Say Next: "We are going to do more work, color coding our sentences to make sure we are writing them correctly. We are going to use a different color for each part of the sentence. Today we are adding to what we know by adding an adjective. An adjective adds a detail to the sentence. It helps our readers picture what we say. 'The *strong* wind blows the kite.' 'The mom hugs her *cute* baby.' Okay, let's practice together."

Model/Do Together: Write a simple, present-tense sentence, with an adjective, on a whiteboard or chart. Avoid pronouns because students may not yet be ready to learn what pronouns stand for. Following are highlights of what to say and do:

- Underline the subject with a green marker, the verb in yellow, the object in red, and the adjective in blue.
- Explain what an adjective is and how it modifies the nouns. You can demonstrate with the adjective modifying the subject and also the object; you may have to add an article with the noun. For example, *The dog jumps the fence* becomes *The smart dog jumps the fence* when we add the adjective "smart." Or *The bird is red* and then say, *The bird is bright red.*

- Together, come up with another sentence, and this time write it on a sentence strip, either the color-coded one or the plain one.
- Put each part of the sentences in the correct location in the pocket chart and reinforce the idea of the subject (noun), the verb (present tense), and the object (the what), and place the adjective in the correct location (the modifier).
- Brainstorm a few more sentences with students orally.
- Have each student come up with a sentence they want to write. Guide them to count the words to help them remember them and ensure they have a complete sentence.
- Remind students they will write the subject on one sentence strip, the verb on another, the object on the third, and the adjective on the fourth. If they need to add an article, like *a* or *the*, just have them write it with the subject or the object. For example, *the girl, the rope, a book,* and so forth.

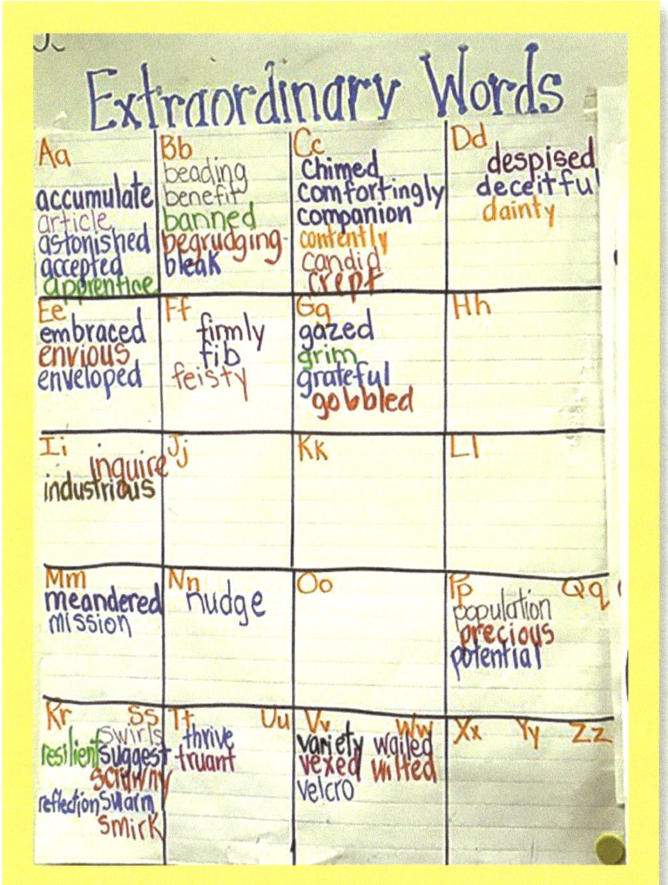

Word walls of any kind are living documents of learning! Keep adding to them, and have students help make decisions about what goes on them.

30 (Continued) Building Sentences: Add in Adjectives/Adverbs/Articles

Release: Encourage students to start writing; remind them of their sentences and how many words they will write on one sentence strip. Guide them to ensure the verb is present tense.

After they write, gather back as a group and have each student put their sentence strips into the pocket chart. Have each student read aloud their sentence, supporting as necessary.

Watch Fors and Work-Arounds

Students may not have all the vocabulary they need. If they can describe what they are thinking, then tell them the words that they are looking for, so they can work on their writing. For instance, a student might *say* "My sentence is 'The cat purrs today.'" You would gently guide the student to learn that instead of saying "today" the student might say "always purrs." Make use of word banks, continually adding to them, making new ones, and referring students to them to expand their vocabularies.

Students are ready for more. On subsequent days, you might model past tense verbs, helping them to correctly conjugate regular and irregular verbs. Continue using the sentence strip method, color coding the part of the sentence you are adding with different color sentence strips or using a different color marker. Other lessons include the following:

> **Teaching Adverbs:** Guide them to write the sentence with the correct order for the adverb and the object. For example: *The dog jumps the fence quickly*. Students might write *The dog jumps quickly the fence.* You will need to explain that when there is an object that receives the action of the verb, the adverb moves to the end of the sentence.
>
> **Teaching Articles:** Articles can be tricky for students acquiring English to learn because their heritage language may use them differently. Discuss with students how articles are used before nouns. There are three articles in English: *the* (used before a singular or plural noun), *a* (before a singular noun beginning with a consonant sound), and *an* (used before a singular noun beginning with a vowel sound).

Note: There are other ways articles are used than what I am sharing here, but because you are teaching an ELD lesson to students who are increasing their language acquisition, who are not yet fluent, keeping the objective basic will help them grasp the idea. Write a simple sentence with the article *the* in it. Then write one with the article *a* in it and a third one with the article *an* in it. Talk about the three sentences and the use of the three different articles. As students acquire English, they will acquire knowledge about when to use an article or not. Not all students will simply pick up this knowledge, and explicit instruction can help. Repeat these lessons and practice until students regularly apply them in their writing.

1. Write out another sentence: *There was a drop of water on the table.* And *There was water on the table.* Discuss how in the first sentence the noun *drop* can be counted, and in the second sentence there is too much water to be counted. So, when a noun can be counted, the article to be used is *the.*
2. Write out two sentences: *I saw an eagle yesterday. The eagle was large.* Here, *an* is used to indicate the number of eagles (single) and the specific identity of the eagle is not known to me. For example, it is not the same eagle that lives in the trees near my house. *The* is used in the second sentence to indicate the specific identity of the eagle. It was the eagle I saw.
3. Write out another sentence: *Some of the apples fell off the tree.* Some is the plural form of *a* or *an;* use *some* when there is an unspecified, limited amount of something (but more than one).

SECTION FOUR

iStock.com/danielfela

TASKS for Students at the Expanding Level of English Language Acquisition

Section IV ● Tasks for Students at the Expanding Level of English Language Acquisition		
31.	Cognates Help Students Learn Vocabulary	Listening & Speaking
32.	Discuss Text During Read-Alouds	Listening & Speaking
33.	Recounting Stories Read Aloud and Together	Listening, Speaking, & Reading
34.	Match Vocabulary Words With Definitions	Listening, Speaking, & Reading
35.	Ask and Answer Questions During Shared Reading: Informational Texts	Listening, Speaking, & Reading
36.	Dialogic Instruction: Main Idea and Theme	Listening, Speaking, & Reading
37.	Act Out Concepts of Tier 2 Words	Listening, Speaking, & Reading
38.	Write Short Answers to Text Questions	Listening, Speaking, & Writing
39.	Building Sentences: Pronouns and Prepositions	Reading & Writing
40.	Building Sentences: Conjunctions With Subordinate Clauses	Reading & Writing
41.	Practicing Verb Tenses	Speaking & Writing
42.	Practicing the Perfect Verb (Past, Present, and Future) Form	Speaking & Writing
43.	Read, Stop, Think, Say During Shared Reading	Speaking & Writing
44.	Independent Reading: Visualizing and Asking Questions About Text	Speaking & Reading
45.	#HUE During Reading Strategy: Informational Texts	Reading
46.	Writing Paragraphs	Writing
47.	Writing Longer Pieces: Personal Narrative	Writing
48.	Writing Longer Pieces: Information	Writing
49.	Writing Opinion Pieces: CREW	Writing
50.	Writing Longer Pieces: Procedural	Writing
51.	Writing Longer Pieces: Book Reviews	Writing

Overview

When students are at the expanding level, an important part of their continuing development is to have them produce language daily for as much time as possible. By producing, I mean they are involved in productive talk. In this section, the tasks often involve tools that help students engage in discussion that gets them talking, reading, thinking, and reasoning together (van der Veen et al., 2017; Zweirs, 2014). These tools include graphic organizers, pictures, carefully chosen texts, and the classroom time to explore ideas.

There are five talk moves that encourage productive talk (Chapin et al., 2009). These talk moves are as follows:

1. **Revoicing:** The teacher repeats some or all of what a student says. You would use this move when what the student said is unclear. After revoicing, the teacher asks the student to confirm if the message in the revoicing was correct. It might sound like "So, you are saying that it's a plant cell."
2. **Repeating:** One student is encouraged to restate another student's reasoning. You would use this move when you want students to listen closely to one another and be able to state what another student said. The first student can confirm if their intended message was correctly repeated. It might sound like "Can you repeat what she just said but in your own words?"
3. **Reasoning:** The teacher asks students to apply their own reasoning to someone else's reasoning. You would use this move when you want students to expand on each other's thinking, or when you want them to explain their thinking. The teacher focuses on facilitating respectful discussion among students, helping students to agree or disagree and explain why they think as they do. It might sound like, "Do you agree or disagree? Why?"
4. **Adding on:** The teacher prompts students to participate further in the discussion. You would use this move to increase student engagement in the classroom discussion by asking them to give further input. It might sound like, "Would someone like to add more to this idea or thought?"
5. **Waiting:** The teacher uses wait time to ensure students have the time to gather their thoughts and prepare to make a statement or answer. It might sound like the teacher saying, "Wait, just think. Think about . . . " and then the teacher would glance at a watch or clock to time the "waiting."

As you teach the tasks, use the five productive talk moves. These moves will help you guide students to higher engagement with any topic. You may notice that the tasks in this section require more cognitive lift by the students. They can do it! It's important they do the reading, discussing, and writing with greater independence now.

To refresh your memory of what to expect of learners at this stage, following is information from WIDA.

WIDA's Descriptors for English Language Proficiency Level: Expanding

Level 4	What Students Are Able to Do
Listening	Compare/contrast functions, relationships from oral information
	Analyze and apply oral information
	Identify cause and effect from oral discourse
Speaking	Discuss stories, issues, concepts
	Give speeches, oral reports
	Offer creative solutions to issues, problems
Reading	Interpret information or data
	Find details that support main ideas
	Identify word families, figures of speech
Writing	Summarize information from graphics or notes
	Edit and revise writing
	Create original ideas or detailed responses

Source: Adapted from WIDA Consortium (2012); WIDA Consortium (2020)

10 Tips for Success

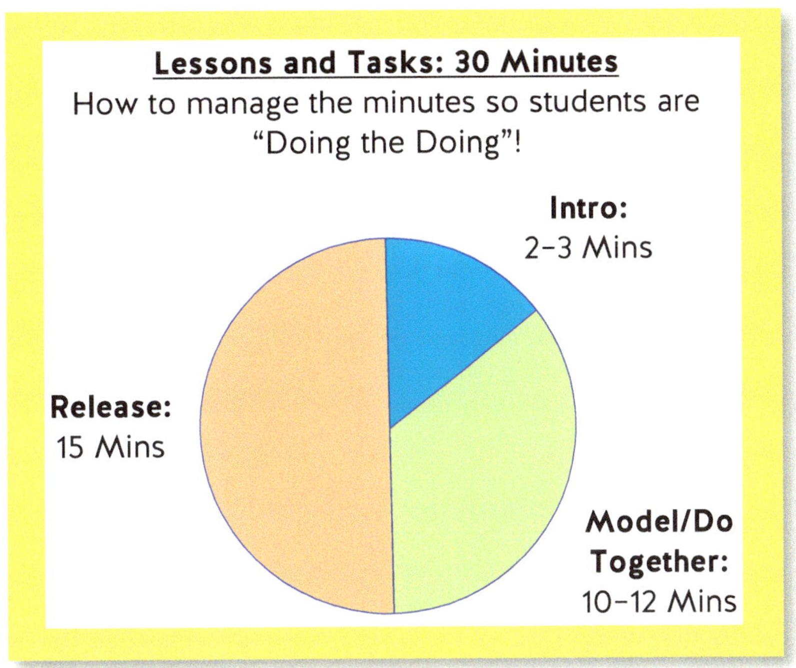

1. I recommend **three to four minutes for your introduction** to the lesson. Be sure to state the purpose of the lesson and task.
2. Before modeling, preteach the **most important** vocabulary for students to know. Don't just teach a list of words. Consider the concepts that will be introduced in the task and preteach the related vocabulary.
3. **Model for nine to ten minutes.**
4. Use visuals to ensure that students understand. Use videos or pictures from the Internet. Draw pictures if you need to make the content comprehensible.
5. Use extra explanation and repeated speech to make sure the content related to the task is comprehensible and makes sense for students. Remember that good ELD lessons are focused on ELA, math, social studies, or science content.
6. **Plan on sixteen or seventeen minutes at least for peer work and guided work.**
7. During peer work, look for signs that the work is too hard, and pull students back together and model the work more if needed and offer more guided work time.
8. **Altogether, including release, plan for thirty minutes per task.**
9. As students work, and when and if you bring them back together, look for those students who you may need additional support and scaffolding to either understand the content or be able to express their thinking about the content.
10. At the expanding level, students will be launching into independent reading and only be doing shared reading with you or peers using complex text. As you are working with students during independent reading, and if they seem to be struggling to comprehend, move back to shared reading whole group or with partners.

31 Cognates Help Students Learn Vocabulary

Listening & Speaking

WHEN TO OFFER IT

Any time after Spanish-heritage language learners understand some spoken English, or when they are reading.

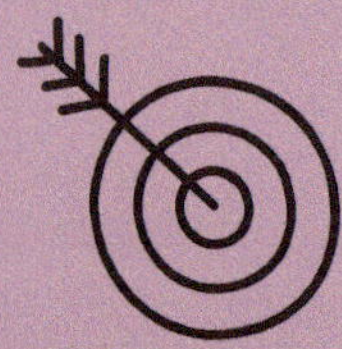

TARGET

Students will use cognates in Spanish to understand the meaning of words in English.

This task is for students who speak Spanish as a heritage language. It advances what they have already discovered—that Spanish and English often have similar words and meanings, because the two languages share cognates. Cognates are words that come from the same root and have similar meaning, spelling, and pronunciation, so if a student knows a word in one language, they can figure out the meaning of the word in English (Freeman & Freeman, 2014). Because many English academic words have a Latin base, students who speak languages derived from Latin may already know the words, and the meaning can just transfer to English (Montelongo et al., 2011). There are about twenty thousand English-Spanish cognates, and 30–40 percent of English words have cognates in Spanish.

Your Instructional Playbook

Name It: You know a lot of words that are nearly the same as words in English. We are going to check out some of these words and create a word bank to help us remember the new pronunciation of the word. We call these words *cognates*.

What You Might Say Next: "How many of you know the word *activo*? What does it mean? What is an English word that sounds like it?" When students hear this activo/active connection (or you can use another word you know they know), continue, "It is easy to connect the meaning of these two words because of cognates. Cognates are words that have the same meaning and nearly the same spelling and pronunciation. There are slight differences, but if you work to remember the cognates you can learn a lot of words very quickly."

Model/Do Together: Write a handful of words from the cognate list (see Appendix B, page 203) on a chart/whiteboard. Put two words side-by-side so that students can see the words/spelling similarities. Model and guide along these lines:

1. Pronounce the two words and have students discuss the similarities.
2. Read aloud a few of the cognates from the list and invite students to pick out about ten cognates. (Student choice is key here.)
3. Next, create a word bank together with the cognates. Make sure you list the two words side-by-side so that the students can see the similarities between the words in both languages and also see the spelling and pronunciation differences. You don't need to put the definitions of the words on the cognate word bank because the students know the word in their heritage language.
4. Select a handful of words from the bank to use in writing a paragraph together consisting of three to four sentences. This can be a fun and silly activity so don't make the meaning of the paragraph too serious. The activity is about having students play around with language in order to recognize cognates and begin using them.

Helpful tips for cognates in Spanish:

- *-ity* in English becomes *-idad* in Spanish (e.g., difficulty = *dificultad*)
- *-ous* in English becomes *-oso* in Spanish (e.g., curious = *curioso*)
- *-ance* in English becomes *-ancia* in Spanish (e.g., ambulance = *ambulancia*)

Release: During shared reading with the class, stop when a cognate appears in the text. Discuss the word with students and encourage them to make a note in the margin or in their personal word dictionaries regarding the word in English, its spelling and pronunciation.

Watch Fors and Work-Arounds

Students may over identify cognates when reading and identify false cognates. False cognates look and sound similar but have very different meanings. Encourage students to stop reading when they don't understand the text and take a close look at the sentences. Point out that there is a false cognate and it may be confusing them as they try to figure out the meaning of the sentence. Read aloud the sentences before and check the sentence after, and then ask the student predict what they think the actual meaning of the word is. After predicting by using the meaning of the sentences, they can also look up the word.

Cognate Bank

Cóntrólár
Ácción
Celebráción
Náción
Pánicó
Mápá
Ámbulánciá

Discuss Text During Read-Alouds

Listening & Speaking

WHEN TO OFFER IT

Once students can get the gist of short sentences and phrases during read-aloud, they are ready to listen with levels of comprehension beyond surface understanding.

TARGET

Students can pick up plot, theme, and big ideas and share their thinking about the book.

Your goal is to have students thinking about a text and having a productive discussion about it. However, the big difference here is that students will not be reading—they will only be listening. This frees up their brains to develop academic listening comprehension. They will need many opportunities to listen to more complex texts read aloud, and time to think about the meaning of the text. *Your goal is to keep instilling in them that they need to know what they think, and they need to know and name what questions they have*. It's through this dynamic interrogation of text and their own thinking that they become active, rather than passive, readers.

Your Instructional Playbook

Materials: a fiction or nonfiction book students would enjoy. If fiction, ensure that the literary language is not overly complex. If nonfiction, choose a text with visuals that you can display with a document camera.

Name It: We have an interesting topic to read about today. (Name it and describe the topic.) In this task, I am going to read it aloud—and your job is to listen really well. I like to think of it as super-alert listening. When you do that, then it teaches you how to read with the same active brain.

What You Might Say Next: "When we read a story, our minds are doing a lot. We are imagining the scene and the characters. We are constantly trying to picture the scene. This picturing of the scene happens in two ways, right? For example, we think about Little Red Riding Hood going through the woods to her grandmother's house. We picture that red cape she is wearing. We wonder where the story is taking place. But we may also be thinking: *Is something going to happen? What is the grandmother like?*" (Next, you might do a visual tour of the book, looking at pictures, diagrams, charts, or other media to ensure students seem primed to start reading.)

Model/Do Together: The work together with a read-aloud (and it's similar with a shared reading) generally follows these steps. Notice that you are intentionally building background knowledge and oral language.

1. Build background knowledge about the text and topic. If you are using a novel, give a bit of background knowledge about the characters, conflict, setting.
2. Read aloud, reading in smaller segments than you would normally.
3. Stop reading often to check for literal understanding as you progress through text.
4. If students can retell what the sentences said, then ask a more thoughtful question and encourage students to discuss their answers.
5. Stop and discuss difficult vocabulary as often as needed.

6. Continue reading, stopping at appropriate spots to ask questions that invite students to predict, infer, make a comparison, analyze, and other higher-order thinking.
7. After reading, discuss the text, the meaning, and the main points. Help them tease out the details the author intended them to think about.

Release: Once you have the routine down, encourage students to do nearly all the talking during the discussion of a read-aloud text on a subsequent day. You focus on facilitating and avoid talking and rescuing! In the beginning you may pose questions and need to answer them by pointing to parts of the text, but don't do this for too long. Students will get used to you doing the work and they will become more reluctant to participate.

Watch Fors and Work-Arounds

Students are quiet and won't discuss the text. Students may not have understood what you read. Prod a bit to see if that is the case. If so, reread and then stop again for discussion. If they have literal understanding but are unable to answer a question with more depth, do a think-aloud so students can see your thought processes on answering the question.

Students understand the text well but are struggling to make deeper connections. Often these students don't seem to make connections between the chapters or draw inferences about character actions. They may need additional tools for tracking their understanding. For example, teach students to take jot notes (I call them *jot dots*). Jot notes are little bullet point notes they write in a reading notebook to record what has happened in a story. They can write when you stop and discuss or check for literal understanding. Then, when it's time for a larger conversation, students can use their jot notes to help them converse.

After discussion of a text about sharks, students wrote down their thinking on index cards and affixed them to a chart their teacher had made.

33 Recounting Stories Read Aloud and Together

Listening, Speaking, & Reading

WHEN TO OFFER IT

Once students are able to retell stories with facility, offer this task so they can begin to share big ideas and their own thoughts about the book.

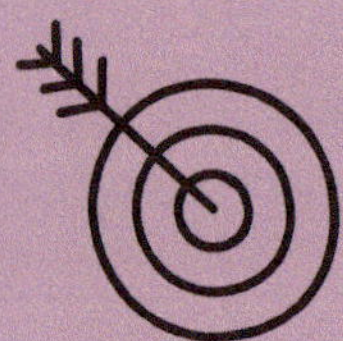

TARGET

Students can give an account of a story read aloud.

Task 10 involved students in retelling stories that had been read aloud. Now that students are listening to you read aloud more complex stories, and they are participating in shared reading with you of narratives, you can focus on having students describe significant events in the story. Giving an account of a story is different than a retelling because the student is not focused on telling events in exact order but rather focused on conveying the major events and ideas. (Giving an account is not quite as succinct as giving a summary, but it's a step toward that.) An account involves the big ideas, as well as a reader's own thoughts and ideas about these big ideas.

Your Instructional Playbook

Materials: a picture book rich with literary language, or a short novel, poem, or other narrative text.

Name It: In this task, we practice the skill of bringing our experiences to the text. Things happen in the text—and we have our own responses to it.

What You Might Say Next: "Today we are going to read a book about___________." (Introduce the book and discuss the topic of the story. Your goal here before reading aloud is to build background knowledge. In essence, you are freeing up their brains ahead of time so they have more cognitive space to do the deeper, less literal connecting. You can review pictures, or show pictures, diagrams, charts or other media. With fiction, it's even okay to share the plot ahead of time.)

Model/Do Together: Read the story aloud or conduct a shared reading, stopping often to restate what is happening. Students can take jot dots in their reading notebook on story elements, plot points, ideas they have, and any connections. After reading, ask students to tell their account of the story. Encourage them to add in their ideas, their connections, and to point out the meaning of the story for them. You want more than a retelling. Use a sentence frame if students need one to get started.

The characters in the story are ____________ and they had a problem with ____.

The problem in the story was ____________ because ____________.

In the end ______________ happened because ____________.

This part reminded me of ____________ because ____________.

I thought ____________________ about ____________________.

Another thought I had was ______________________ because when ____.

Additionally, ______________ was ______________ and this was similar/unlike ____.

The meaning for me is ________________ because ____________.

Use sentence frames if students need support in learning to articulate an account of a story.

Watch Fors and Work-Arounds

Students may get stuck in retelling. Model giving an account of a story, adding in your thoughts and feelings. Be deliberate in what you say and stop and tell students why you said what you did. For us, the thinking we are going through when recounting is natural and may come easily, but students may not be aware of how to think like this or understand that their thoughts and ideas about the story are important. It's possible you might also think aloud about some of the details you *didn't* include, so students begin to develop a sense of unimportant/minor details.

34 Match Vocabulary Words With Definitions

Listening, Speaking, & Reading

WHEN TO OFFER IT

After you have begun a unit of study in science, social studies, math, or English and you have explained, defined, and worked with key words.

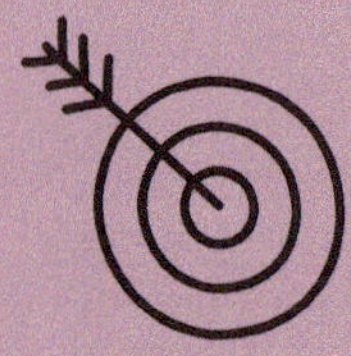

TARGET

Students can match words with their definitions.

Students at the expanding level of English language proficiency can hold personal conversations with other students. This fluency signals they are now ready to work with the intention to learn academic vocabulary. As students acquire content area vocabulary, they are developing cognitive, academic language skills that go beyond social language skills. Starting slow with vocabulary games can be helpful and fun. Pull words from readings, or other material students are studying so the words have context.

Your Instructional Playbook

Materials: You can do this with apps like quizlet, or you can create game pieces using index cards. Use individual whiteboards for students for the model/do together phase.

Name It: We are going to play a game today where we must match words with their definitions.

What You Might Say Next: "The words are from the unit we have been studying in ___ (science, social studies, our novel, etc.). Playing this game will help you remember what the words mean."

Model/Do Together: First, introduce the words and discuss their meanings. Use pictures, video, or other media to support students. Next, ask students to write each word on a whiteboard, and with a partner, write the definition. Then, run through the words once before starting the matching game. Say a word, and see if students can remember the meaning of the word without looking at their whiteboards. Then, play one matching game together using words and definitions written on index cards or an online application.

Release: Invite students to play the matching game in partners or individually to check their understanding. Don't change out words until students are confident with the word set and only introduce words *after* providing meaningful context.

Watch Fors and Work-Arounds

The word-matching game may be too easy for some students. Challenge these students to use each word in a sentence. Working in pairs, they can write the sentences on a whiteboard.

In this example, students made clue cards that matched the vocabulary.

35 Ask & Answer Questions During Shared Reading: Informational Texts

Listening, Speaking, & Reading

WHEN TO OFFER IT

As students begin to understand more language as you are reading, you can organize time daily for shared reading of texts of interest to students.

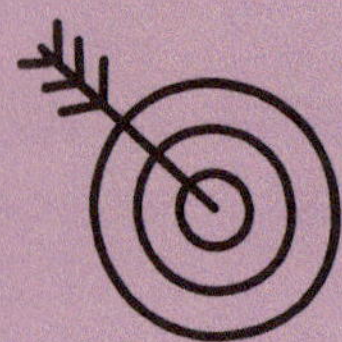

TARGET

Students can discuss text during shared reading.

When choosing a shared reading text, don't choose a text so complex that students won't be able to work through the reading of the words along with you. Also ensure that the text is not overladen with pronouns as pronouns can be difficult for students to map back to the noun without stopping and rereading sentences a few times. You want the language in the text to be *just right* so that the reading experience is enjoyable and students are engaged.

Your Instructional Playbook

Materials: A copy of the text for each student; or students should be able to see the text displayed clearly.

Name It: Today we are going to read about an interesting topic. (Describe the topic briefly.) As I read, you are going to be learning new facts. Listen actively, and we will talk about what we are learning along the way. We are going to stop and wonder and ask questions, too. This helps us to understand all along the way.

What You Might Say Next: "Before we read this text together, let's do a sneak preview of it, okay?" (Focus on building background knowledge for students before embarking on the text. Can review pictures, show pictures, diagrams, charts, or other media.)

Model/Do Together: Remind students how to do a shared reading and that they will be following along with you as you read. Encourage them to read the words also (reading aloud is preferred so you can listen in and ensure students are successfully saying the words). Stop in appropriate places to discuss the meaning of the text. First focus on literal meaning. If students understand the literal meaning (they can repeat what the sentences said), ask more meaningful questions of the text. Focus on students thinking more deeply about the text, perhaps making a prediction or an inference about what they have read.

Release: Once you have the routine down, encourage students to do nearly all the talking during shared readings. You focus on facilitating only. You can guide and support students to do the talking by posing questions that encourage students to share their thinking. The first few times, students may not be talkative. That is perfectly natural. Encourage them to share their thoughts. They may need to pair-share first or write their thoughts down on a whiteboard to feel stronger about sharing their thoughts.

Steps to a Shared Reading to Develop Oral Language:

1. Build background knowledge about the text and topic.
2. Invite students to read aloud with you.
3. Stop reading to check for literal meaning first.
4. Ask a more thoughtful question and encourage students to discuss their answers.
5. Continue reading.
6. After reading, discuss and compose a question or two students might have about the text or the topic.

Watch Fors and Work-Arounds

Students who are quiet and don't discuss the text. Students may not know how to ask a question of text or go back and look at the text to support their answer to questions that arise in group discussion. Model this process of pausing and puzzling over something in a text. Think aloud—giving students the blow by blow of your questioning and problem solving—so students can get a concrete sense of what it means to reread and check assumptions about meaning and other acts of monitoring one's comprehension.

36 Dialogic Instruction: Main Idea and Theme

Listening, Speaking, & Reading

WHEN TO OFFER IT

Once students can discuss complex text and identify the main idea in an information article or portion of a nonfiction book.

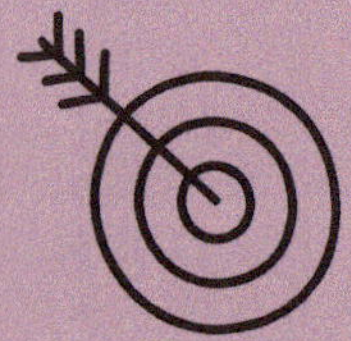

TARGET

Students can discuss the main idea of a text from shared reading.

Dialogic instruction is a conversation you facilitate *with* students. It is not teacher-led, but to the greatest degree possible, student-led. In this task, your instructional focus is on promoting talking to learn. This type of dialogue honors that the struggle to organize thoughts is part of content acquisition. Students come up with words to shape an understanding, and together with peers, grow their knowledge (Britton, 1972; Min-Young & Wilkinson, 2019). In this sense, language development and content learning are inseparable. The talking to learn can occur after a shared reading, or you might wish to discuss after a video or reading digital content together.

Your Instructional Playbook

Name It: We have been exploring texts together during shared reading, and today I want to think more about the ideas in the text. In doing so, we can also learn from one another about how we comb through words and sentences to figure out what's essential for us to know.

What You Might Say Next: "We are going to (read/explore websites/watch video) and then talk about what we think is most important in the material and why."

Model/Do Together: Introduce the text that you are reading together. Provide background information just as I suggest in Task 23. Conduct these as shared reading experiences so that students have support when reading and can focus on comprehending the text. You'll want to stop often and chat about what each paragraph or part means. This will help them later when they discuss the big ideas.

Define and discuss the main idea (the most important points made in a text or medium). In this lesson and in five-minute lessons on subsequent days, use passages of the text or whole texts to model all you wonder and notice as you deduce the main idea. This way, students will know to look at headings, words in bold, first and last sentences, pictures and captions, and so on.

Release: As you facilitate students' discussion, ask questions such as the following:

> What is important in this text/material? Why?
>
> What do you think about it? Why?
>
> What seems to matter most to the author?
>
> Why do you think the author is sharing this information?
>
> How is this text different from another text we read on this topic?
>
> How does this text help us understand the world?

During dialogic instruction students will and should struggle to wrap their minds around the meaning. This is when the big understanding comes to students that will cement together new learning with the language they are acquiring. You can end a dialogic task by facilitating a shared writing stating the big points they have learned and what they think about it.

Watch Fors and Work-Arounds

Students who have developed interpersonal language skills may appear more fluent than they actually are. (See my language tips on page 97 at the beginning of this section on expanding language proficiency). The reason they appear more fluent is that they have developed interpersonal language, but they are still developing academic language proficiency. To support students, draw pictures, use diagrams, and silently point to text features and other visuals that can help them comprehend.

Students who want to speak but are reticent. Talk with them about what they want to say and then write their idea on a sticky note. The student can use the note as a support to help them speak.

Students are ready for more. Read a longer story, perhaps a short novel, and focus on the theme. (I suggest selecting a text at the Grade Two/Grade Three level or a graphic novel for any age.)

In this example, students were working to identify the theme of the text they read.

Act Out Concepts of Tier 2 Words

Listening, Speaking, & Reading

WHEN TO OFFER IT

Once students are reading texts with more complex language, they need to know vocabulary words that appear frequently in these texts.

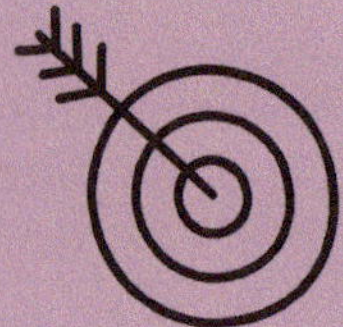

TARGET

Students know that to learn more challenging, abstract words, they may need to use various tools to help them get the full meaning.

Tier 2 words (Beck et al., 2013) are high-frequency words that are used often across content areas. Some examples are *responsibility, addition, respect, evaluate, unite, industrious*. In this task, we harness the power of Total Physical Response (TPR, see Task 1) to support students' grasp of them.

Your Instructional Playbook

Name It: There are many words that take a while to learn. Some of these words describe a thinking process, like *evaluate*. Some Tier 2 words are fancier ways of saying words we know, like *briskly*, which means to move fast. We are going to work on some of those words today by acting them out.

What You Might Say Next: "It might seem weird to act out words, but I think this activity will help you get the meaning of words that are hard to understand. I will act them out with you. We can have fun together, but we won't make fun of each other. Sound good?"

Model/Do Together: Explain define Tier 2 words further and display a list of common Tier 2 words (see Appendix B, page 201). Use your judgment about how many words to tackle during this first collaborative work. Three or four is often enough. Using pictures, diagrams, video, and other media, show what the word means in the best way possible. Tier 2 words are not always easy to explain, but finding an idea that students can make connections to will help them grasp the idea of the words. For instance, the word *responsibility* is a Tier 2 word. You could show a father caring for a young child to get the meaning across. You can discuss the word meaning and elicit ideas from the students.

Release: Working in pairs or trios, have students choose a word from a list, or a pile of words cards, and have them pantomime the word meaning. They can help each other decide how to pantomime the word. Encourage them to practice a few times, so that they can remember the routine and show others in class.

Watch Fors and Work-Arounds

Students remain confused about word meaning. Students may need additional explanation. It can help to teach the word's concept. For instance, if the word is *responsibility*, show short videos or pictures found on the Internet with students doing typical chores or doing something nice for others. Discuss the concept of the word and then help students name the actions they are seeing in the video or pictures in any way they can describe the word's meaning. Discuss at length in a way that makes sense to the students, and then, reintroduce the new word again, connecting it to the context you have provided.

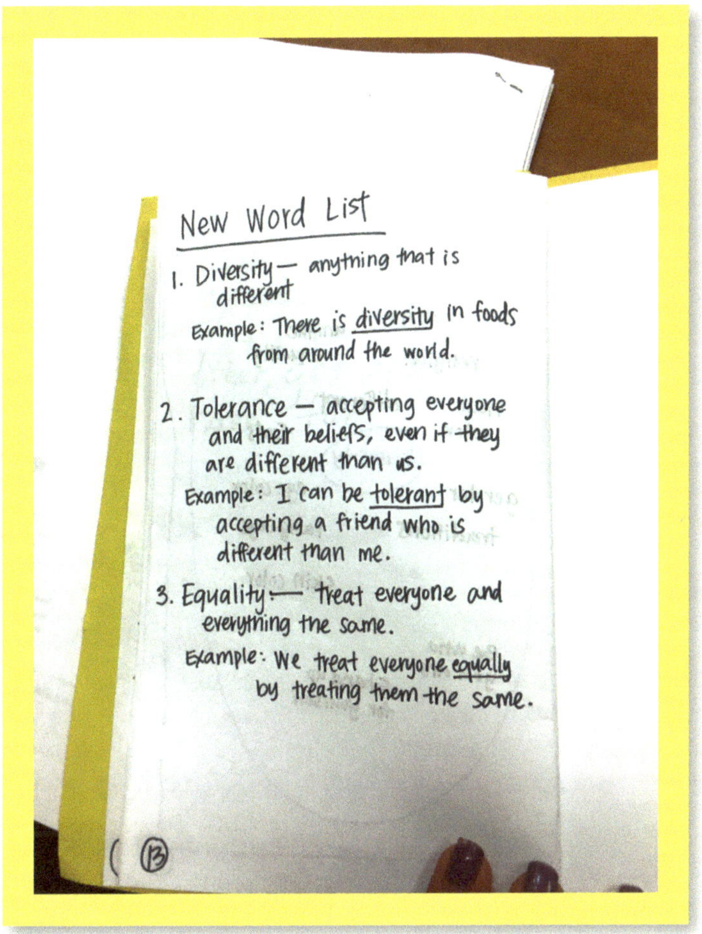

Keeping vocabulary notebooks helps students learn new words.

38 Write Short Answers to Text Questions

Listening, Speaking, & Writing

WHEN TO OFFER IT

Once students are reading simple informative texts.

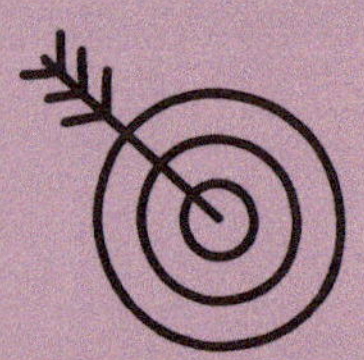

TARGET

Students can answer text-dependent questions about simpler informative texts.

Part of learning to read in school involves answering text-dependent questions. These questions are crafted specifically to compel a reader to recall a text accurately. These questions are a good way for a teacher to assess a student's comprehension. Another benefit of working with them is that it reminds readers that as they read, they can monitor their understanding by asking themselves these types of text-related queries. When working with students who are acquiring English, begin by reading simple texts without complex language. This affords them cognitive space to learn strategies for answering text-dependent questions.

Your Instructional Playbook

Materials: Short nonfiction/informational text on an interesting topic, one copy for each student; sticky notes; pencils.

Name It: Text-dependent questions are questions usually answered during your reading or after you finish reading. These questions can only be answered by information in the text, or ideas you draw from the text (inferences).

What You Might Say Next: "It is important for us to share our thoughts in writing as well as when we talk together. Sometimes on tests, you will be asked to write answers to questions after you read. When I think about answering questions about the text, I use what I call the 'I Spy' strategy."

Model/Do Together: As students learn to work with text-dependent questions, it can help to start with shared reading rather than an independent read. (Students need to access the text, so a read-aloud, where the teacher only sees the text, is not appropriate in this situation.) The collaborative work goes along these lines:

1. Before reading, frontload for students the meaning of the text and review vocabulary that may be difficult.
2. Ask students to share what they know about the topic and what they are thinking the text might be about. Help them make predictions that align with what you have shared and the key words or vocabulary in the text.
3. Begin the I Spy strategy by reading the question at the end of the text. Think aloud to model how to determine keywords in the question. For instance, a keyword is not in the sentence stem; it is in the part of the sentence that directs them back to the reading. For example, in this text-dependent question, the key words are in the middle and end. *Why do you think Ruby felt scared when she got off the bus?* So the question is asking why, which is important, but all questions are going to ask something of students: who, what, why, when, or how. What is important is to spy the *content* keywords,

Ruby felt scared . . . getting off the bus. So the key word is *scared* and I would underline it for students. I know this is a keyword because it appears in the question and I have to figure *why she felt scared.*

4. Once you practice a few times finding the key words in the question, show students how to then go back to finding the key word in the text, *get off the bus, scared, Ruby.*
5. Then demonstrate how to reread the sentences around those key words to find the answer. Students can write notes about their thinking on sticky notes or in a notebook. If they use sticky notes, they can "flag" the point in the text that reveals the answer and has the keyword.

Release: To set up students to try the I Spy strategy, tell them you are going to do a shared reading together. They will use their pencils to underline key words in the questions and use their sticky notes to write what they think the answer is. Together, read the text, stopping in appropriate places to check that students are comprehending. Read the question together and have students spot the key words. Guide the discussion so the correct words are known. Then students, independently, reread to find the key words and write their answer on the sticky note. Come back together as a group and discuss what everyone wrote. Discuss what is the most appropriate answer and highlight how the text helped them answer the question.

Watch Fors and Work-Arounds

Students are struggling to understand the text. Reread the text together, stopping frequently to discuss challenging vocabulary, meaning, and so on.

Students are unable to identify the correct key words in the question. Write the question on a whiteboard and analyze it. Circle the first part of the question that is asking who, what, why, when, or how, and have students say which of the "w"s the question is focused on. Point out it's helpful for them to know this, but the important clue to "spy" is the word or words pertaining to the story/text. Encourage them to find the key word. Don't just do it for them. Teach them how to find it for themselves.

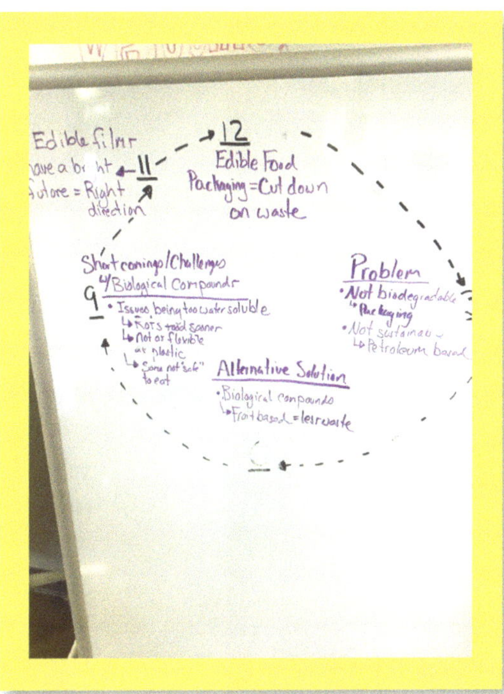

Students practiced the I Spy strategy and the teacher wrote out their ideas and thinking.

39 Building Sentences: Pronouns and Prepositions

Reading & Writing

WHEN TO OFFER IT

Once students start using pronouns orally or in writing but may need help with accuracy.

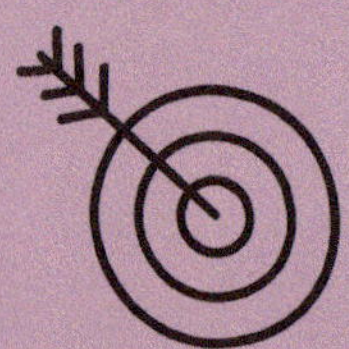

TARGET

Students can correctly substitute a pronoun for a noun in a sentence.

Pronouns can be tricky for students acquiring English because there are so many of them, and they may function differently in English than they do in a student's heritage language. In my experience, the most common challenge is that students struggle to identify what noun the pronoun is standing in for. In this task, you teach students to backtrack to previous sentences to determine the noun. Over time, and one pronoun at a time, you will teach nine types of pronouns: personal, possessive, indefinite, relative, interrogative, reflexive, intensive, demonstrative, and reciprocal. There is no fixed order for teaching them; highlight one when it has fit and meaning for students. For example, you might notice students beginning to use a particular type in their peer talk or in their writing.

Your Instructional Playbook

Name It: We are going to build sentences that substitute a pronoun for a noun. This will help us with our reading, so we know how to map pronouns back to the noun that they represent. It will help our writing flow as we use different types of sentences.

What You Might Say Next: "Pronouns are words that substitute for nouns. Some examples are *he, she, it, they*. Pronouns can be tricky, right? It's easy to wonder if we should say, 'My brothers and me are going to the movies' or 'My brothers and I are going to the movies.' We are going to work together on all this pronoun use, and that will help you in your talking and in your writing."

Model/Do Together: Your demonstration and guided work can go something like this:

1. Begin by choosing one type of pronoun (see chart that follows).
2. Show a couple of sentences using the pronoun and show how the original sentence changed because of the pronoun.
3. Write an additional sentence on a whiteboard and have students help you select a pronoun to substitute for a noun based on your lesson objective.
4. Then have students restate the sentence and rewrite the sentence on their own whiteboards. Pronouns become easier for students with practice. It is also helpful to pause when reading aloud, note the pronouns, and trace the pronoun back to the connecting noun to check for student understanding.

Types of Pronouns

Type	Definition	Example
Personal	Substitute person's name, third-person noun in a sentence (I, you, he, she, it, we, they); replace name of object in a sentence (me, you, him, her, it, us, them).	My teacher went to the office. He went to the office. The dog wants a bone. It wants a bone. Go play with Sara. Go play with her.
Possessive	Show that noun owns or possesses something. Possessive pronouns do not need an apostrophe+S to show possession (mine, yours, hers, his, its, ours, theirs). There is no apostrophe in its.	That book is N'hia's. That book is his.
Indefinite	Used when the noun isn't specific. Singular indefinite pronouns function as singular pronouns in a sentence (anybody, anyone, anything, each, everybody, everyone, everything, little, much, nobody, no one, nothing, one, somebody, someone, something). Plural indefinite pronouns function as plural nouns (both, few, many, several). Some indefinite pronouns function as both singular and plural (all, any, more, most, none, some, such).	No one is helping. Many are helping. None are helping. All bring lunch.
Relative	Connects a clause or phrase to a noun or pronoun; they add information to a sentence. Some refer to a specific noun and act as the first word in a noun clause (who, whom, which, whose, that). Indefinite relative pronouns have -ever at the end and describe general or unknown nouns (whoever, whomever, whichever, whatever). You can use relative pronouns to introduce adjective clauses. They connect dependent clauses to independent clauses to create complex sentences.	Look for the boy who took the ball. The toy, which was Sara's, was red. The girl that lives next to the school plays on the playground. Thank whoever sent the cookies. Whichever you choose will be great. We should play whatever game comes next.
Interrogative	Used for asking questions.	Who (subject) Whom (object) Whose (possessive, when referring to people) Which and what (people or things)

(Continued)

39 (Continued) Building Sentences – Pronouns and Prepositions

(Continued)

Type	Definition	Example
Reflexive	Used when the subject of the sentence is also the object of the sentence: Singular: myself, yourself, himself, herself, itself Plural: ourselves, yourselves	Singular Kyle burned himself on the stove. Jamie enjoyed herself at the concert. Plural We've made ourselves something to eat. They helped themselves to more cake.
Demonstrative	Used in place of particular things to show what's being discussed.	This and that refer to specific things in relation to the speaker. These refer to nearby things. Those refer to things far away.
Reciprocal	Express a mutual relationship or action. The pronouns show the relationship between nouns.	Each other One another

Release: Using the chart that you brainstormed together, have students work in pairs. Give them two sentence strips. On the first sentence strip they will write a sentence (you can provide the sentence if it is easier for them to copy than compose) with the nouns named, for example, Ali went to the store. On the second sentence strip they rewrite the sentence using pronouns in place of the nouns, for example, He went there. Gather students back together and have them put the sentence strips in the pocket chart and share what they combined together and why. Talk through any of the sentences that don't properly substitute pronouns for nouns and coach the students on how to fix the problem.

Watch Fors and Work-Arounds

Students may feel frustrated in figuring out which pronoun to use. Have them read each sentence and circle the noun and write the pronoun above it that they think is appropriate. Then, have the student reread the sentence but substitute the pronoun. You can give the student a copy of one or two paragraphs of text and continue this practice: Tell the students to circle the nouns and write a pronoun above the noun and reread for accuracy.

Students are ready for more. Teach students to use prepositions. Tell students that prepositions are important in helping make our sentences clear. I'm *in* the classroom. Nigel is *at* the movies. The phone is *on* the table. These three examples are prepositions related to time. There are many types of prepositions in English. *Go on to name the type you have chosen to teach—check out the chart that follows.* Follow the same lesson sequence as for pronouns.

Prepositions of Time

Use these prepositions when discussing when events take place. They can also be used to talk about multiple events happening at the same time.

Preposition	Sentence Structure	Example
in	in + a specific month in + a specific year in + the morning, afternoon, or evening	My birthday is in February. I was married in 1992. I have to go to school in the morning.
at	at + a specific time at + night	I have to go to school at 7:45 a.m. tomorrow. I can watch TV at night.
on	on + a specific day of the week on + a specific date	I do not go to school on Saturday. I was born on July 29, 1995.
for	for + a duration of time	I have gone to Hamilton School for a year. I have been in Mrs. Candor's classroom for five months. I have been studying for one hour.
during	during + the time something happened (a noun)	It snowed during the night. The teacher took roll during class. He played video games during lunch.

40 Building Sentences: Conjunctions With Subordinate Clauses

Reading & Writing

WHEN TO OFFER IT

Once students can write a narrative, informational or opinion piece, teach this task as part of the revision process.

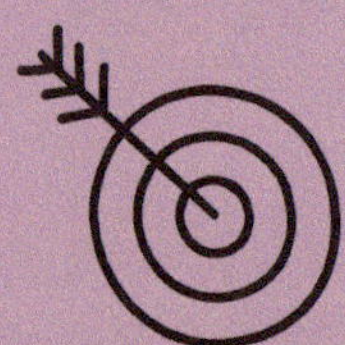

TARGET

Students can add detail and description to sentences.

As students develop language proficiency, you need to ensure their academic language skills continue to increase. Knowing how to properly add information to sentences can help students include more content in their writing. In this task, we help writers add rich detail to sentences, while avoiding run-on sentences. Develop students' facility with sentence writing takes time. Don't rush it, and even though grammar and punctuation come into play, you want to present it to students as opportunities to communicate. As you offer demonstration lessons and collaborative writing practice, keep celebrating and analyzing sentences from all your reading. Published authors are masters of clear, colorful sentences of varying cadence, lengths, and clauses!

Your Instructional Playbook

Materials: Three colors of sentence strips, or three-color small pocket charts and plain colored sentence strips. One color sentence strip or pocket chart will represent the first sentence, one color will represent the conjunction, and one color will represent the phrase or subordinate clause being attached to expand the sentence.

Name It: We are going to work together to build longer sentences that provide more information about our topics. We are going to work with dependent clauses and many different conjunctions.

What You Might Say Next: "Dependent clauses are phrases that are not sentences. They don't have an active verb in them to help them stand alone as a sentence. We have lots of choices in how to connect these types of phrases to sentences to make our writing interesting."

Model/Do Together: Begin by showing sentences from mentor texts you have gathered. You can use fiction or nonfiction. The sentences you choose need to be complex sentences with an independent clause (a simple sentence that can stand alone), a dependent conjunction, and a dependent clause (a phrase or group of words that cannot stand on their own as a sentence; there is no active verb). Write out a few of these sentences on a chart paper with the students helping you circle the independent clause and underline the dependent clause.

Brainstorm information students know about and create a t-chart. Use information from an inquiry study you have done together or a book that you have read. Following is an example; you will want to make sure your chart has many options for students to combine phrases.

Mammals are animals that give birth.	comfort finds them
Mammals are warm-blooded.	with blood rushing through their veins.
There are many types of mammals in the world.	tall ones, short ones and small, tiny ones.

Introduce a handful of subordinating conjunctions like the following: after, although, as, as if, as long as, as though, because, before, besides, despite, even if, even though, if, if only, in order that, now that, once, provided that, rather than, since, so that, that, though, unless, until, when, whenever, where, wherever, whereas, whether, while, without.

You will need to explain the meaning and use of the subordinating conjunctions. Use the examples from *the* mentor text to assist.

Model how to combine two of the clauses with a subordinating conjunction. For example, *With blood rushing through their veins, mammals are warm-blooded.*

Release: Using the chart that you brainstormed together, give pairs of students two sentence strips to combine the independent clause with the subordinate clause using the subordinate conjunction. Remember it doesn't matter if they learn the titles of these parts of speech; what matters is they learn how language works so they can expand their ability to write. Gather students back together and have them put the sentence strips in the pocket chart and share what they combined and why. Talk through any of the sentences that don't properly combine clauses.

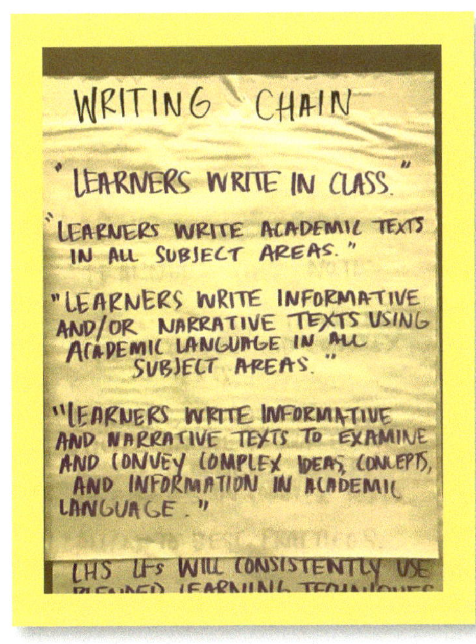

(Continued) Building Sentences: Conjunctions With Subordinate Clauses

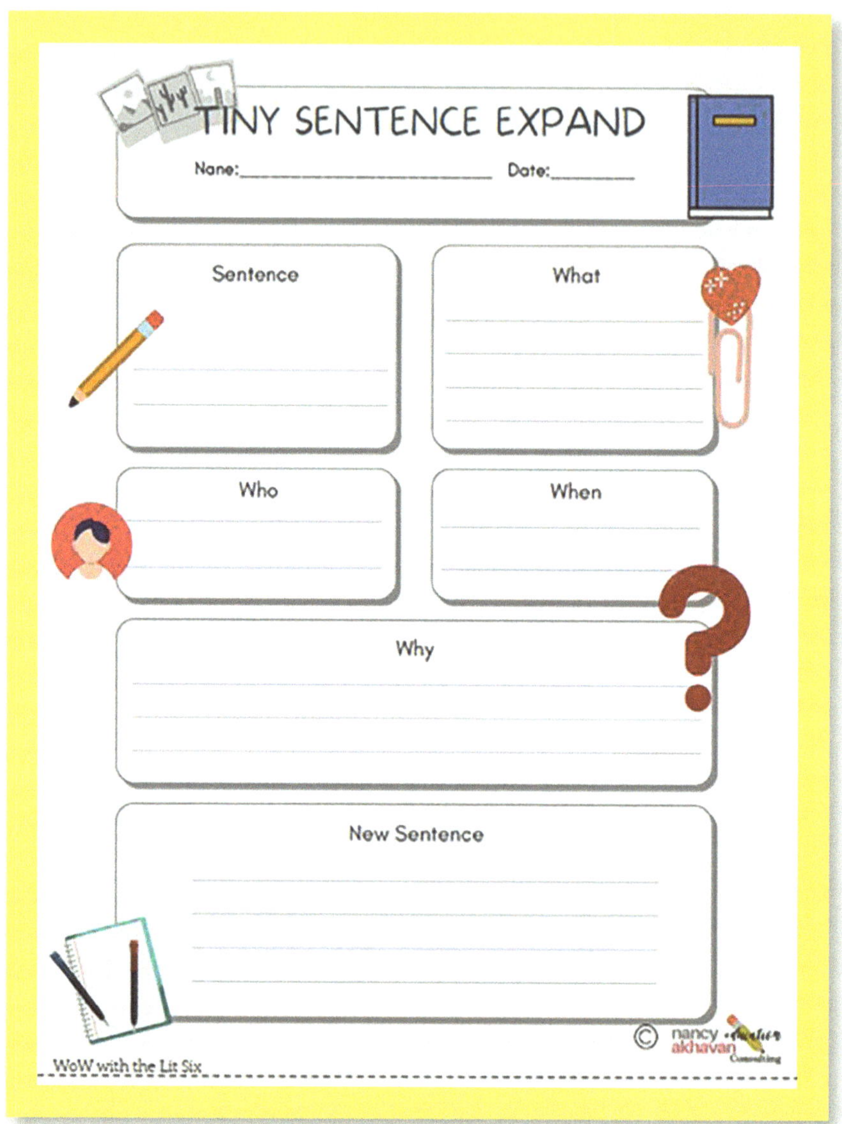

Watch Fors and Work-Arounds

Students struggle to figure out what clause is independent and dependent and what can connect. Have them read each clause and circle it if they think it stands alone and underline it if it cannot. Then guide them to choose a subordinate conjunction that would make sense. Knowing what conjunction to pick will get easier as students continue to read more complex text *and* as you stop as a class to discuss complex sentences when reading.

iStock.com/danielfela

Practicing Regular Verb Tenses

Speaking & Writing

WHEN TO OFFER IT

Once students are talking and writing more and more, but continue to use incorrect verb tense even after repeated modeling from you.

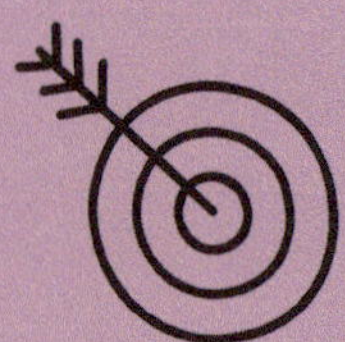

TARGET

With support from the teacher, students will be able to write or say a sentence using the correct verb tense. (Start with regular verbs and move to other tenses once students show that they are ready for working on additional tenses).

Learning the correct verb tense takes time and practice. It's not an overnight thing! Understandably, teachers sometimes feel students aren't "getting" their lessons or their lessons aren't clear. The truth is, along with explicit lessons, students need many opportunities to talk and write to increase their facility with tenses. Remember that students acquire language in a predictable order, so you want to provide opportunities for students to learn about verbs and verb tenses and keep circling back to them over time. I've found it helps students tremendously when I cluster a lesson on a verb tense with a mentor text read aloud, and then have students talk and write using the verb tense. When learners see authors use verbs, it's motivating, because it's in a compelling context.

Your Instructional Playbook

Name It: Verbs are the "doing" word in a sentence or the action word. The verb form changes based on the subject of the sentence we say and write, as well as the tenses of the verbs we use (which is when something is taking place or happening). We are going to work on present, past, and future tense today.

What You Might Say Next: "Let's practice a few verb tenses together. I am going to give you directions, and as you follow them, I am going to emphasize when the verb changes tense." Make up what you want to say—but a routine can go something like this:

Say: We walk

Say: We will walk

Have students walk around their tables or desks.

Say: We walked.

Ask: When did the verb change tense?

Example of regular verbs:

Dress, need, fix, act, want

Model/Do Together:

Have a stack of sticky notes handy and write the regular verb tenses on the sticky notes. Invite students to categorize the verbs with you as you model. Make columns on a whiteboard or chart paper labeled first, second, or third person.

After the introductory example, invite students to follow your directions and emphasize the verb tense change. Following is an example of what to say and do:

We are students.

I am a student. (point to self)

You are a student. (point to another person)

They are students. (point to three to four students)

Repeat these steps to teach present tense, simple past, past participle, and future tense.

Continue playing other language games. For example, have students act out the actions you command like "play the guitar." Try to use regular verbs so that students can get the hang of acting out present tense. Then give commands for the verb in other tenses: -ed and -ing endings (play, played, playing, will play).

After playing a few games, using Total Physical Response (TPR) (see Task 1, page 18), shift to modeling what the word looks like in writing.

Prepare a chart with three columns showing how verbs show time: Past, Present, Future.

Past	Present	Future
Liked	Like	Will like
Talked	Talk	Will talk

Have a stack of sticky notes handy and write the regular verb tenses on the sticky notes.

Ask students to categorize the verbs with you, placing each one in its correct column.

Release: Hand out to each student a copy of the graphic organizer you used above. Also provide them with a list of regular verbs conjugated in the tenses you have been practicing. Guide learners to get in groups of three or four and have them put the verbs from the list in the correct column.

Watch Fors and Work-Arounds

Students may get the verb tenses confused. Help students check the ending of the verb first to decide what tense the verb is (-ed, -ing). If they notice that the verb doesn't have an ending (it is the present tense form), have them check if the word *will* is in front of the verb so they can decide if the verb tense is present or future.

Practicing the Perfect Verb (Past, Present, and Future) Form

Speaking & Writing

WHEN TO OFFER IT

Once you notice students using different tenses of verbs orally and in writing. Offer this task after students have a lot of experience with the verbs in Task 41.

TARGET

Working in groups, students will categorize verb tenses for past, present, and future form.

As adults, and especially if English is our heritage language, we speak and write in the past perfect, present perfect, and future perfect verb tenses effortlessly. What makes teaching it tough, though, is that we may ourselves struggle to explain it. So here's a refresher:

- Verbs describe an action, occurrence, or state of being.
- The perfect form of the verb tense is used to talk about a completed action or condition and always has a form of the word *have* or *had* connected in front of the past participle.
- The participle is a word made out of a verb but is actually used as an adjective.
- Present perfect tense indicates an action that began in the past and is completed in the present. *(I have been swimming.)*
- Past perfect tense indicates an action that began and was completed in the past. (*I had been studying* or *I had lost my keys, so I got new ones.*)
- The future tense indicates an action that will be completed by some specific time in the future connected by the verb *will, shall* + have. (*The students will have eaten lunch by 12:30.*)

Your Instructional Playbook

Name It: Verb tenses take time to learn. Today we are going to talk about some that are tricky because they have other words connected to them in order to express time. I don't want you to be discouraged if you get confused. You will pick it up! Verb tenses help you clearly express when something is occurring or has happened.

What You Might Say Next: "Some tenses use *have* or *had* in front of part of the verb (participle), and others use *will* or *shall* **and** *have*. These verbs indicate things that began in the past but finished before or after something else occurred. Or, something that looks like past tense (have eaten) but has the word *have* in front of it—telling us it is happening in the future."

I have read my book.

Sara threw away her paper because she had torn it.

We will have played soccer by noon on Saturday.

I would have cut up the vegetables to make dinner, but I had cut my finger on the knife.

Model/Do Together: Invite students to brainstorm with you actions that started and finished in current time. (e.g., We played video games.). Then brainstorm together actions that started in the past and finished during the current time (e.g., We have been playing video games.). Or, *We have been playing soccer since morning.* Write students' ideas on a whiteboard, thinking aloud as work and discussing with them how to phrase past tense actions by using the present tense of *have* + past participle (the present perfect tense).

So, if students say, "we played video games," you would guide them and together you would write "We have been playing video games."

Make a "phrase" bank instead of a word bank, brainstorming the different ways that the present perfect tense can be used in sentences.

Example Phrase Bank:

Have been playing

Have been eating

Had been playing soccer

Have torn

Have played

Then, perhaps on another day, repeat the process using the past perfect tense (past tense of *had* + past participle) and the future perfect tense (*Will* or *shall* + have + past participle). Create anchor charts like the one that follows for students to use as a reference.

Present tense of *have* + past participle = present perfect tense

Past tense of *had* + past participle = past perfect tense

Will or *shall* + have + past participle = future perfect tense

Release: Provide three-column note-taking graphic guide (see Appendix B, page 215) for each student. Also distribute a list of present, past, and future perfect verb tenses you have been practicing. Encouraging students to work in small groups, have students put the verbs on the list in the correct column. They can also use the verb tenses you have provided and write out a few sentences.

Watch Fors and Work-Arounds

Students may get the verb tenses confused. Point out the "I Spy" words to look for to help students categorize the type of verb tense they are looking at. The "I Spy" words are the helping verbs that indicate that the action started in the past and ended in the present. Notice the "I Spy" words underlined in these sentences:

Present perfect will have present tense of *have* + past participle.

Past perfect will have past tense of *had* + past participle

Future perfect will have *Will or shall* + have + past participle.

If students are up to a challenge, encourage them to write a paragraph using a couple of the tense forms in the paragraph.

43 Read, Stop, Think, Say During Shared Reading

Speaking & Reading

WHEN TO OFFER IT

Once students are able to decode what they are reading, and are ready to focus on comprehension of the text.

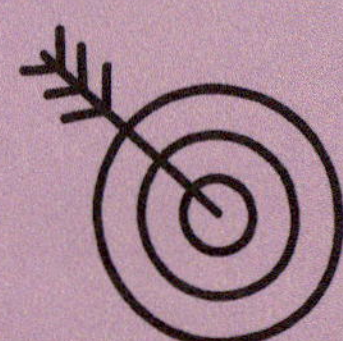

TARGET

Students will be able to monitor their own reading for understanding.

As students progress in their reading abilities, they will be ready to read more and more on their own. Providing students help with learning independent reading strategies will put them in control of their own reading. This shared reading task develops their ability to check their own comprehension as they read independently.

Your Instructional Playbook

Name It: When you are reading, it's important to check your own understanding. We are going to practice a strategy that will help you do that.

What You Might Say Next: "When you read, you can stop and think about what you are reading. You do this pausing naturally when you get a feeling the text isn't making sense. But as you become a strong reader, it's good to deliberately practice stopping from time to time and saying aloud what you understand. Then you can start reading again."

Model/Do Together: Thinking aloud, model the steps of the strategy shown below with a shared reading of a compelling text. Ensure that you go slow and *talk* about your thought processes as you reflect as you read. You are deconstructing a complex process, and your goal is to let students know that good readers do not just speed through text. They are pausing a lot to check understanding. They are rereading. They are asking themselves questions.

1. Before the modeling, select a text and decide where you are going to stop to think aloud and talk with students.
2. Read aloud the designated sentences in a chunk of text (maybe sentence by sentence, a couple of sentences, or a paragraph).
3. Stop reading and reflect.
4. Think about what you just read, what it said, and how it relates to previous sections of text that you read.
5. Say what you think the text says aloud to your partner.

Release: During different times of the day, incorporate paired reading into the activities. Having students work in pairs, have them practice Read, Stop, Think, Say together.

Read to where you sense your understanding/attention getting shaky.

Stop and reflect on what you just read.

Think about how it connects to the text so far.

Say what you think the text says.

iStock.com/guru86 iStock.com/Victor_85 iStock.com/Fourleaflover iStock.com/robert6666

Display the Read, Stop, Think, Say steps as a wall reference and make it into bookmarks for your students.

Watch Fors and Work-Arounds

Students read large chunks of text before they stop to check comprehension, and then they don't know what they read. Have students stop reading in smaller chunks of text and then check their understanding. If the text is a bit more complex than they can handle in large chunks, have them read line by line.

44 Independent Reading: Visualizing and Asking Questions About Text

Speaking & Reading

WHEN TO OFFER IT

When students are reading a lot in and out of class but are not comprehending what they are reading at a deeper level.

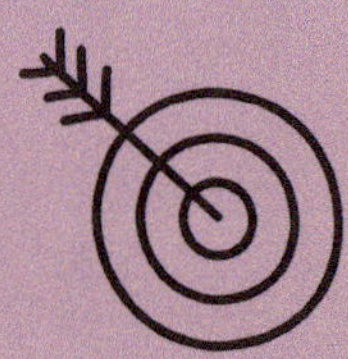

TARGET

Students can see a movie in their minds as they read and are able to ask questions of themselves about the text to sharpen comprehension.

Students began learning to ask and answer questions during shared reading, but they need to begin to transfer that skill to when they read independently. In a large study I conducted that included one thousand middle school age students, I found that there were a couple of strategies students didn't use often. One of these strategies was visualizing, and another strategy was asking questions about the text and the author.

Your Instructional Playbook

Name It: When I am reading, I use a couple of strategies that help me get involved. I think in my head and ask questions while I am reading and I also have a movie running in my head about the story that is happening.

What You Might Say Next: "Sometimes I 'talk' to the author while I am reading, or I 'talk' to a friend about the book, but I am doing this in my head. I might say, 'Check this out! Why did the author do that!' I also see pictures in my mind that I create based on what I am reading. This 'movie' helps me think about the book more deeply."

Model/Do Together: Offer variations on the following steps, using different, engaging texts:

1. Start by reading a text aloud, pretending as if you were reading independently.
2. Stop in a logical place and share your thoughts.
3. Discuss in depth the "movie in your mind." Share the sentences that gave you the details to form that picture in your head. You could talk about what you think the character looks like too.
4. Ask students to share what they were thinking based on the passage you read.
5. Talk about how the "movies" are the same and different, emphasizing that there is no single correct "movie" but that what we see in our mind shouldn't conflict with the story world the author created.
6. Think aloud what you are thinking and feeling so far, and what questions you have. When it's natural, provide an example of when you aren't sure you like the author's choice. For example, when J.K. Rowling chose to kill Dumbledore, I said to myself, "NO! What are you thinking!!"

Release: Encourage students to use these thinking moves during independent reading.

Watch Fors and Work-Arounds

When you check in with students, they are not using the strategies. You can gently model and encourage them to say the words. Read a sentence with them and say what you are thinking. Ask them about their thoughts. If they have trouble articulating themselves, a sentence frame might help:

I have a question on page . . .

I wonder . . .

I think . . .

I want to know why/if . . .

#HUE During Reading Strategy: Informational Texts

Reading

WHEN TO OFFER IT

Once students are reading informational text often.

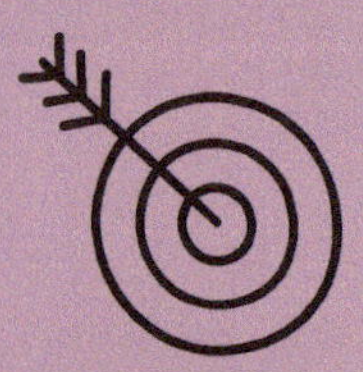

TARGET

Students can annotate text to help them focus their attention to comprehend.

Strategies that set students up for comprehension are great supports as students read more and more texts and books independently. Our goal is always to have students take these tools and use them on their own, without us. With this strategy called #HUE (number, highlight, underline, explain), students have a tangible process for checking their understanding.

Your Instructional Playbook

Name It: We are going to practice a strategy that can help you as you read nonfiction texts.

What You Might Say Next: "You can use this strategy when you are reading informational text in books, but you can also use it when you are reading with an e-reader. With an e-reader, you will need to use the in-text citation tools like underlining and highlighting. You can underline and highlight when reading texts on paper also."

Model/Do Together: Thinking aloud, model the steps of the strategy:

#HUE (Highlight, Underline, Explain)

= number the paragraphs

H = Highlight important vocabulary words

U = Underline the main idea and most important details

E = Explain; write a margin note stating what the text says

Release: Once students can independently use the strategy, encourage them to do it often when reading informational text. You can make a poster of the strategy to remind students and post it in a visible place in the room.

Watch Fors and Work-Arounds

Students are going through the motions but are highlighting everything in the text. Help students identify the main idea by spotting words that repeat and information that seems to explain other information (then trace it back to the first mention of it—that's the main idea).

Students are not writing margin notes. Students may not know what to write in the margin. In the margin they practice stating the main idea in their own words. They will need some support to do this as they may just want to rewrite what they read.

46 Writing Paragraphs

Writing

WHEN TO OFFER IT

Students are ready for this activity when they are writing longer pieces of writing.

TARGET

Students work in small groups to write a paragraph about the topic you brainstorm together.

As students are able to write more text, they can begin to form paragraphs. And as you notice this readiness for conceptualizing a paragraph, teach into it—but with a light touch. Emphasize that paragraphing is how we organize our ideas. We shape paragraphs to make our communication easily understandable. What we want to focus on when students start writing is the purpose behind the effort: communication. Once students can communicate their ideas and feel strongly about what they have to say, that's my cue that they have the will and the skill to learn additional paragraphing techniques. A word of caution: when we push paragraphing too soon and get into the weeds of particular sentence types, we overwhelm students. And it also sets them up to think that all "good" writerly paragraphs are built the same way, which isn't true.

Your Instructional Playbook

Name It: Today we going to look at how writing is organized into paragraphs. We are going to look at an example of an author's paragraph and talk about how the paragraph helped the author say what they wanted to say.

What You Might Say Next: "I am going to read aloud a paragraph from a book we all have enjoyed together. I'll read it aloud a couple of times, and then we are going to notice how the author developed it."

Model/Do Together

1. Display under the doc camera an engaging, clear example of a paragraph from a magazine or a book with which students are already familiar.
2. Read it aloud and ask, "What do you notice about the flow of it?"
3. Listen to students' answers, guiding them to notice indenting, number of sentences . . . any aspect of it that contributes to the sense that one idea flows nicely into the next.
4. Next, or on another day, read the paragraph aloud a second time, asking students beforehand to listen for the ideas they are hearing.
5. Point out that the author grouped together like information to build the paragraph. Ask, "Why might the author do that? How does it help us as readers?" (When the details are organized, it helps the reader understand the big ideas of the piece. A paragraph holds information together around a central idea.)

On Another Day:

1. Cocreate a paragraph together with students. It works best when you select a general topic from a current content area. Then, to give

students a choice, invite them to brainstorm a narrower topic they want to write about, for example, the hunting habits of sharks. Work together to list the information they suggest and have books about the topic on hand if you wish.

2. Teach students the elements of a paragraph. Create an anchor chart all students can see easily. Provide examples of each element from books; you can also invent sentences on the spot related to your chosen topic that illustrate a topic sentence or two sentences that create a sense of cohesion. Your chart might include *unity, coherence, topic sentence, adequate development.* (See the box example, below.)
3. Convey that these elements make a paragraph clear and interesting. Reassure them that when they write, they don't have to think about all these elements as separate things to do—they often overlap with one another.
4. Turn back to your brainstormed info about the class topic. Using a whiteboard, draft a paragraph, modeling the process of writing and pausing to make decisions about a first sentence, sequence of information, and so on.

Unity: one idea = one paragraph. The paragraph has one singular focus, and it does not include extraneous information.

Coherence: paragraphs hang together to be understandable. A writer uses bridges to connect information together. The bridges include:

- **Logical bridges (Topic):** Same idea carried from sentence to sentence.
- **Verbal bridges (Language)** includes use of key words, synonyms, pronouns, transition words.

Topic Sentence: Indicates the general idea of a paragraph. It isn't always the first sentence!

Development: the topics are discussed fully. Some techniques to use:

Description, examples, facts, statistics, details, stories, definitions, compare and contrast, cause and reasons, consequences and effect.

Transitions: linking words that help the paragraph move forward. Transitions can be words, phrases, and full sentences. Transition sentences are often used at the end of a paragraph to transition to the next paragraph.

46 (Continued) Writing Paragraphs

Release: Organize students into small groups to write the next paragraph about the topic you brainstormed. Ask them to start with their topic sentence, and then add two to three sentences with detail. The last sentence of their paragraph can be a transition sentence or a closing sentence (if it's the end of the piece of writing you close, not transition). Have students choose roles. For example, one student will write the topic sentence, another student will write the first supporting sentence, and the third student will write the second supporting sentence.

Watch Fors and Work-Arounds

Some students would benefit from additional modeling or demonstration. Gather students around a pocket chart, and model/write together a new paragraph, but this time write each sentence for the paragraph on a separate sentence strip and put the strips in the pocket chart. If using the pocket chart, you can reorder the sentences to model and discuss the best order of the sentences to meet the elements of a paragraph.

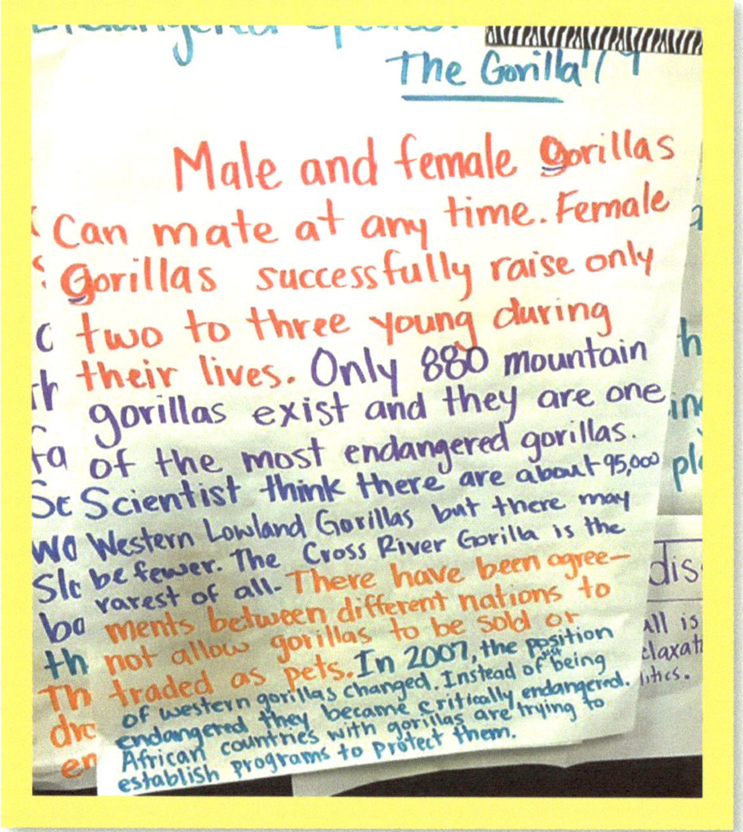

Learning to write paragraphs takes time and practice.

iStock.com/danielfela

47 Writing Longer Pieces: Personal Narrative

Writing

WHEN TO OFFER IT

Once students are able to write narratives and are ready to write longer pieces.

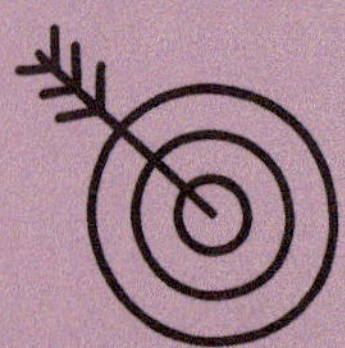

TARGET

Students can write a longer personal narrative that includes detail, dialogue, character action, and a closing.

At this level of language acquisition, students have gained lots of social language and are developing academic language skills. They are ready to write longer pieces. They will still need scaffolds to support them, but the scaffolds are no longer simply sentence frames. Students need many opportunities to explore mentor texts (published texts that you "unpack" with students so they can see what choices the author made in writing). This task is not a one-and-done task. You want students writing daily if possible. This task is more of a troubleshooting task you can use when introducing writing longer pieces or use when students need additional support.

Your Instructional Playbook

Name It: I am noticing how much you have been writing and it is time for us to think more about what goes into our narrative stories. I am noticing how you are adding more details. Personal narratives need details that make us want to keep reading. We can add in dialogue, sensory details (meaning what we hear, taste, smell or feel), and reflections.

What You Might Say Next: "To help us learn how to tell a good story, let's look at a story we all will like and talk about what makes it so enjoyable." Show a published narrative and point out some of the features in the narrative. You could point out how the story begins, how characters are introduced, and so on. (Check the Narrative Writing Genre Map shown below to choose an idea or two to point out.)

Model/Do Together: Write a part of a narrative, highlighting a genre feature that you are focused on (see below). Model writing the trickiest part so that students can see how you are applying your thinking to the writing and still focusing on the writing technique. For example, you may be writing an engaging beginning or showing students how to add dialogue. If students need support, you can use some of the sentence frames in the chart based on the writing technique you are modeling. Remember the sentence frame is designed to support the students in getting started with their writing, but if they don't need that support, don't use the frame.

Narrative Writing Genre Map

	Description
Purpose of narrative	*Tells a story. A personal narrative is autobiographical writing that shares a specific moment and reflection with the reader.*

Narrative Writing Genre Map	
	Description
Characteristics	*Has story structure* *Has clear beginning, middle, and end* *Characters are well developed (in personal narrative character includes the self)* *Personal narrative shares a memory experience, including thoughts and feelings* *Characters have thoughts and feelings* *May include dialogue* *Focuses on a specific experience or an extended period of time in a fictional or real story* *Personal narrative has a narrow focus; it is written about a small scope of time* *Engages the reader* *Establishes a situation, plot, point of view, setting, and conflict* *Includes sensory details and specific language to develop plot and character* *Conclusion follows logically from the plot; personal narrative ending includes a reflection*
Uses/types	*Story* *Personal narrative* *Memoir* *Autobiography*
Organization	*Beginning, middle, end* *Uses temporal words to show passage of time* *Has engaging beginning to hook the reader* *Satisfying ending brings closure to the piece* *Dialogue can be between people, things (fantasy), or writer's inner thoughts* *Includes writer's thoughts and feelings* *Presents information chronologically* *Ending can include a reflection* *Longer pieces may have chapter*

(Continued)

(Continued)

Narrative Writing Genre Map	
	Description
Techniques	*Personal story tells story from one's own life* *Follow a timeline in the story* *Can use flashback memories to provide detail* *Stories from own life are often told in first person* *Stories told through observation, or another's perspective, are told in third person (he/she/they)* *Use dialogue to show action, thoughts, and feelings of characters* *Include writer's thoughts and feelings* *Develop content through descriptive techniques* *Exclude extraneous detail* *Develop pacing through sentence variety* *Show, don't tell, to develop detail* *Use sensory details to create emotion and mood* *Magnify the moment to slow down narrative action and create visual picture in reader's mind*

Source: Adapted from Narrative Genre Map, Nancy Akhavan, Heinemann, 2009

Release: Guide students as they write their narratives. Help them to stay on topic and figure out, as best as they can, how to write what they are trying to express. Remember to support and facilitate helping them think through what they want to say. You can refer them to mentor texts to check out authors who handle a particular writing technique, or you can brainstorm with them how they might try something. You can write an idea or example on an individual whiteboard for them. Encourage students to share with one another, check their work against what you have modeled that day and in the past, and help each other.

Students finish writing but are anxious that it isn't correct and perfect. Caution: *Do not* over edit their work. Celebrate what they can do and don't look for perfect writing. They are in the intermediate phase of language acquisition, and they may not always write with correct verb tense or put adjectives and nouns in the correct order. When you feel a student is ready to revise their work, choose one or two things to focus on and *let the rest go.*

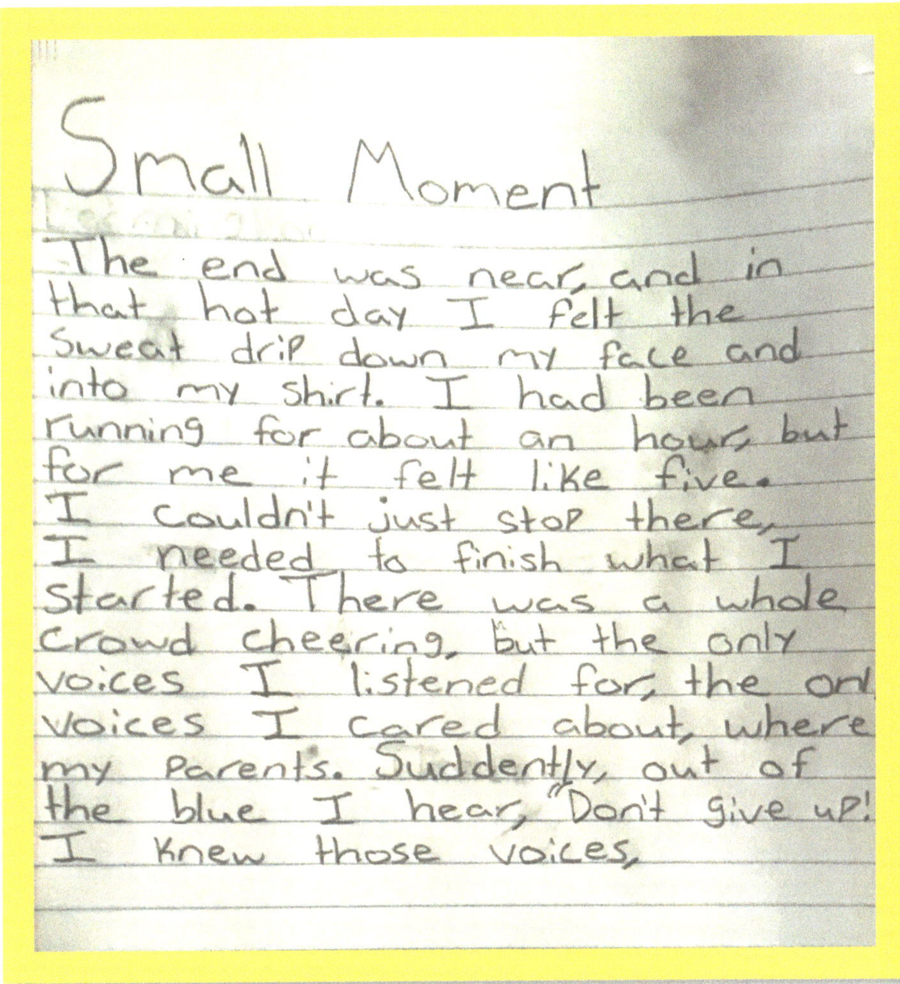

Small Moment

The end was near, and in that hot day I felt the Sweat drip down my face and into my shirt. I had been running for about an hour, but for me it felt like five. I couldn't just stop there, I needed to finish what I started. There was a whole crowd cheering, but the only voices I listened for, the onl voices I cared about, where my Parents. Suddenly, out of the blue I hear, "Don't give up! I knew those voices,

Students will develop voice as they write and use picture books and novels as examples of how authors use language to engage readers.

48 Writing Longer Pieces: Information

Writing

WHEN TO OFFER IT

Once students are writing more or writing longer pieces, or when students need additional support.

TARGET

Students will organize ideas in longer informational reports.

Having students write informational reports can be fun and exciting. You will bring together students reading or researching and taking notes and writing tasks like this one. During an informational unit (perhaps on butterflies or the reduction of bees in our world?), students learned information and vocabulary related to all the concepts you taught. You will now have students use these notes, information banks, and vocabulary definitions to write an informational report. I often see students bloom during informational writing. They share what they know, see their words on paper, and it is exciting for them. They can see their own growth.

Your Instructional Playbook

Name It: I am noticing how much you have been learning about topics we are exploring in class and it is time to write a report about what you have learned. In this task, we are going to learn how to organize our ideas to write the report.

What You Might Say Next: "Writing a piece of nonfiction can seem really hard. The important thing is to rely on how other writers have done it. It's also helpful to focus on one technique at a time. Then you can add in other features. And before you know it, your piece will sound great!" Show a published informational text and point out some of the features in the book, text, or report. You could point out how the information is shared, how the piece is organized, and how text features support the information the writer has included in the paragraphs. Check the genre feature list below to choose an idea or two to point out. (You can use the Informational Report Writing Genre Map to choose an idea or two to point out; try making such a chart with your students, as well, so they have something to refer to.)

Model/Do Together: Write a part of a report highlighting a genre feature that you are focused on (see chart below). Demonstrate—and think aloud—how you write the trickiest part so that students can see how you are applying your thinking to the writing and still focusing on the writing technique. For example, you may be writing an introduction and showing how to introduce the topic after the hook. If students need support, you can use some of the sentence frames in the chart based on the writing technique you are modeling. Remember the sentence frame is designed to support the students in getting started with their writing, not to hold them up. So if they don't need that support, don't use them.

Informational Report Writing Genre Map

	Description
Purpose of informational report	*Demonstrates ability to choose a topic, research it (or use provided information), organize information, and write about the information and data. Selects and uses appropriate nonfiction text features such as charts, graphs, bibliography, table of contents, and appendix.*
Characteristics	*Has clear organization including sections and section headers* *References text(s) or multimedia information* *May have a guiding question, or inquiry statement, that organizes information* *Topics are stated clearly. Students in grade four and above include topic sentences.* *Writing is based on information.* *As appropriate to grade level, sources are mentioned, quoted, and/or cited.* *Transition words and headings guide writing and create organization* *Writing in the middle supports the main ideas with facts and details* *Has labels and drawings that represent facts and details*
Uses/types	*Topic reports* *Informational reports* *All about books/reports* *Feature essay* *Newspaper stories*
Organization	*Has clearly developed organization and structure* *Structure may be patterned as topic headings, headlines, or topic chapters* *Communicates idea, theories, insights, and information* *Has concluding section or sentence* *Employs nonfiction conventions including diagrams, charts, table of contents, appendix and/or bibliography*

(Continued)

(Continued)

Informational Report Writing Genre Map

	Description
Techniques	*Show close reading and understanding of research topic or context* *Take notes by paraphrasing and write paragraphs based on notes* *Sentence variety develops pacing* *Develop context through descriptive and analytical techniques* *Exclude extraneous detail* *Quote directly from text (as appropriate to grade level)* *Synthesize information in own words* *Use organizational technique to research information and track research to create a comprehensive and clear paper* *Paraphrase information from reading/research* *Track thinking in logical order* *Use notes to organize information into sections, main ideas, and supporting details* *Give synopsis of research at beginning of report* *Include insights gained from research*

Source: Adapted from Narrative Genre Map, Nancy Akhavan, Heinemann, 2009

Release: Guide students as they write their reports. Support them in thinking about what they have learned about the topic, what they know, and how they can put that knowledge into words. Show them how to structure their reports. Don't get hung up on needing a certain number of paragraphs. Have students paragraph as appropriate to the amount they can write. The report can be succinct with one paragraph or be longer with two, maybe even three paragraphs. Keep your expectations appropriate for what they can do but also don't ask for only a paragraph because in my experience, I find we underestimate what students are capable of. Remember that the writing doesn't have to be perfect. Caution: *Do not* over edit their work. They are in the intermediate phase of language acquisition, and they may not always write with correct verb tense or put adjectives and nouns in the correct order. When you feel a student is ready to revise their work, choose one or two things to focus on and *let the rest go*. Celebrate their writing; don't have *inappropriate* expectations for perfection.

Watch Fors and Work-Arounds

Students are stuck and cannot write. Support students by suggesting they write their report with a partner. The partners can work together to put the information into paragraphs and keep the information organized. If you pair students together, pair students with fairly even abilities so one student doesn't just take over and the other student doesn't get as much practice with getting their ideas on the page.

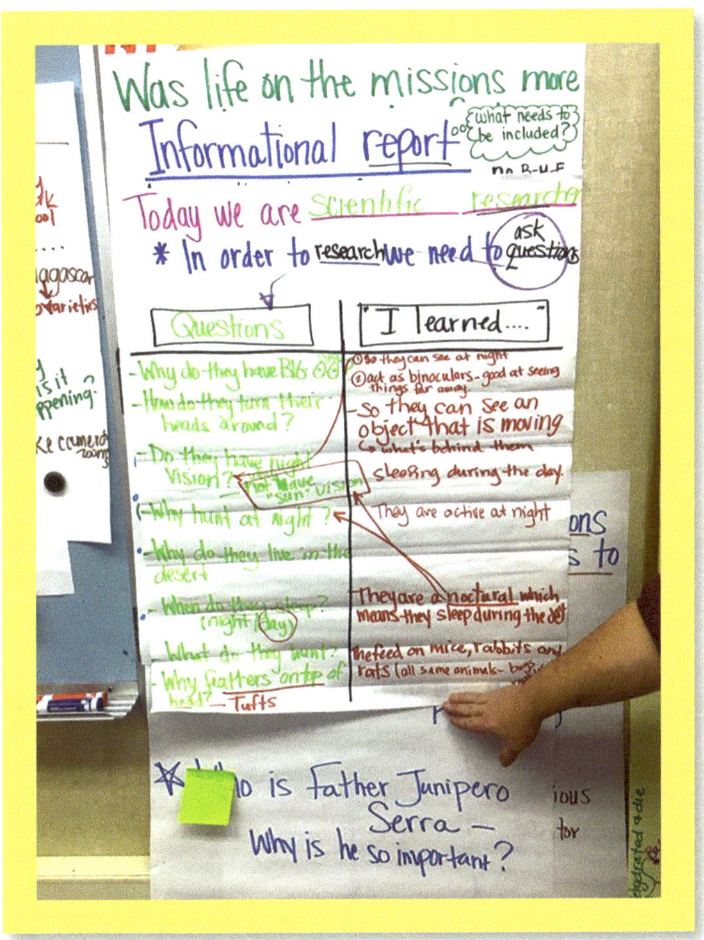

Students will become more proficient at writing in English as they study topics of interest; notice how the teacher is prepping students for their writing by recording their thinking.

49 Writing Opinion Pieces: CREW

Writing

WHEN TO OFFER IT

Once students are able to write short opinion paragraphs on their own, they are ready for this task.

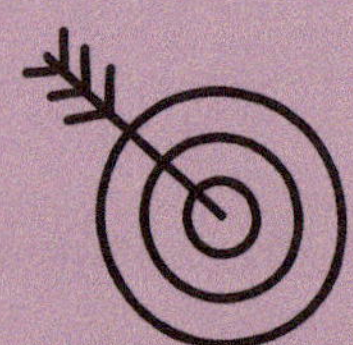

TARGET

Students are able to write opinion pieces with a claim, reasons, evidence, and a logical conclusion.

When it comes to writing opinions, I have found that giving students a mnemonic to remember what goes in an opinion piece is important. When writing in ELA or social studies, it is common for the reason to come before the evidence. When writing in this way, the reason connects the evidence to the claim. This is actually the same style when writing an argument; however, in argument writing there needs to be a buildup of reasons and evidence, mostly from accepted sources, where in opinion writing the reasons and evidence can come from students' thinking and feelings. It is good for students to learn the correct form for opinion writing so that when they begin writing arguments, the transition is easy. I see many teachers have students use a mnemonic that puts the evidence before the reasons, but this is more typical of scientific writing than writing in other genres.

Your Instructional Playbook

Name It: When we state our opinion, there is a way we can write our opinions to make strong statements.

What You Might Say Next: "Let's look at how one author accomplished writing a strong opinion. Let's look at exactly what made it work." Show a published opinion piece and point out some of the features in the opinion: the claim, the reason, and the evidence (if there is any evidence). You could point out how the opinion begins, if there is a hook to catch the readers' interest, and then how the topic is introduced with a claim. (Look at the Opinion/Argument Writing Genre Map shown below to choose an idea or two to point out.)

Model/Do Together: Model writing an opinion as a simple paragraph, highlighting a genre feature that you are focused on (see chart below). Model writing a claim first so students get used to stating their point, or *making a claim* about what they believe. After you write the claim, think aloud as you write a reason or two. If students need support, you can use some of the sentence frames in the chart based on the writing technique you are modeling. Remember the sentence frame is designed to support the students in getting started with their writing, not to hold them up. So if they don't need it, don't use it.

The mnemonic device I use all the time is CREW. I have found this to be very successful with students acquiring English as it gives them a frame to relate to. When students progress to writing arguments, the W stands for the warrant. The warrant reinforces the claim. It is an underlying belief that connects a reason to the claim. When students write opinions, I just call the W the *wrap-up*. (Find a printable CREW graphic organizer on the companion website, resources.corwin.com/bigbookELD.)

C.R.E.W. Device for Effective Opinion Writing

C claim

R reason

E evidence

W wrap-up

Opinion/Argument Writing Genre Map

	Description
Purpose of opinion/ argument	*Demonstrates ability to make a statement or claim, about a situation or issue, and provides reasons and textual evidence*
Characteristics	*Has clear beginning, middle, and end* *Makes a claim (statement), provides reasons and based on grade level multiple points of evidence* *Grades six and above write an argument, not an opinion leaving out writer's thoughts and feelings* *Opinion and argument essays give details to help the reader track the statement/opinion/argument* *Presents justifications through references to text or research* *Arguments present counterclaim* *Counterclaims include the claim, reason, and evidence*
Uses/types	*Opinion essays* *Argument essays*
Organization	*Clearly developed beginning, middle, and end* *Has engaging beginning to hook the reader* *Ending brings closure, restated the opinion/ argument in a new way* *Opinion includes writers' thoughts and feelings* *Presents information in logical order*

(Continued)

(Continued)

Opinion/Argument Writing Genre Map	
	Description
Techniques	*Show close reading and understanding of research topic or context* *Take notes by paraphrasing and write paragraphs based on notes* *Sentence variety develops pacing* *Develop context through descriptive and analytical techniques* *Exclude extraneous detail* *Quote directly from text (as appropriate to grade level)* *Synthesize information in own words* *Use organizational technique to research information and track research to create a comprehensive and clear paper* *Paraphrase information from reading/research* *Track thinking in logical order* *Use notes to organize information into sections, claim, reasons, and supporting details* *Give synopsis of research at beginning of report* *Include insights gained from research* *Writing strong claims* *Referring to evidence to back up reasons connected to the claim* *Set context through descriptive technique* *Quote directly from text* *Analyze big ideas and write them in own words* *Write clear reasons* *Concluding statement connects reasons and evidence to the claim*

Source: Adapted from Narrative Genre Map, Nancy Akhavan, Heinemann, 2009

Release: Guide students as they write their opinions. They can use the sentence frames to get started with the sentences. If they need a source for a topic, have them first brainstorm in a notebook to brainstorm things they know about and things they think and believe.

Sentence frames for opinion writing:

I believe/think that ____________________. (Claim)

__________ is the best/worst ____________________. (Claim)

_______________ is the most interesting _______________. (Claim)

Many people believe that ____________________. (Claim)

This is true/untrue because ____________________. (Reason)

One reason is ________________________. (Reason)

Another reason is _____________. (Reason)

The reason for this is ____________________. (Reason)

__________ discusses this point by saying ____________________. (Evidence)

In the article, the author says _______________. (Evidence)

Additionally, ______________. (Evidence)

Another point is ______________. (Evidence)

As you can see ______________. (Wrap-up)

Therefore______________. (Wrap-up)

The honest truth is ______________. (Wrap-up)

In closing ______________. (Wrap-up)

Watch Fors and Work-Arounds

Students are stuck and cannot write. It can help to complete one piece together as a shared writing. Focusing on one or two writing techniques, compose an opinion paragraph that has all parts of CREW. Work with your students taking turns writing the sentences (or typing on a shared document if appropriate) and thinking through the next reason or piece of evidence. Model for students how to tackle what seems to be the biggest roadblocks for the students.

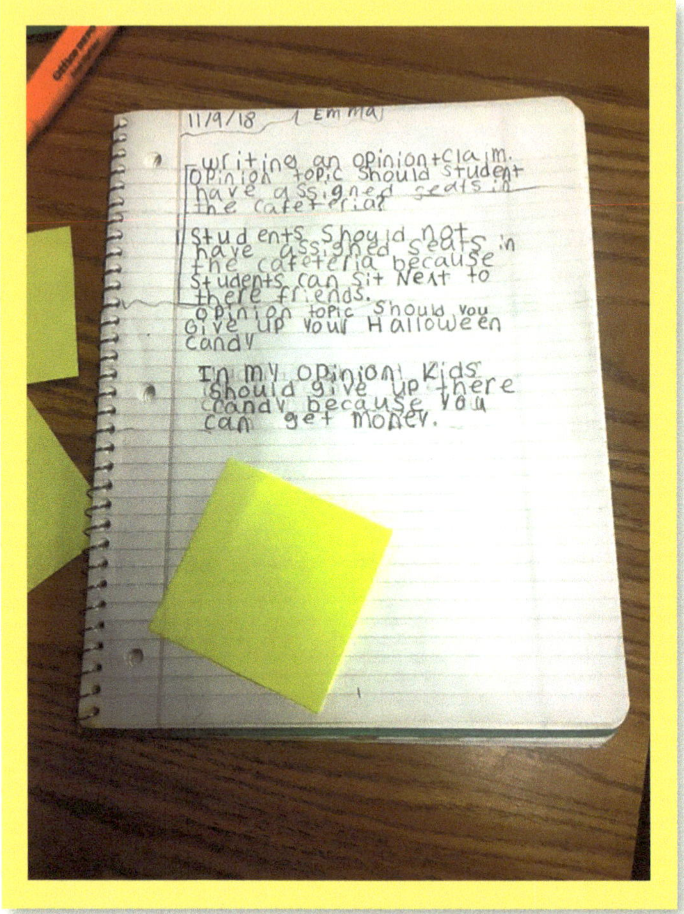

Students are able to use CREW to organize their ideas and make strong claims.

iStock.com/danielfela

Writing Longer Pieces: Procedural

Writing

WHEN TO OFFER IT

Students may have written many personal narratives, opinion pieces, or informational reports and are ready for a new genre of writing.

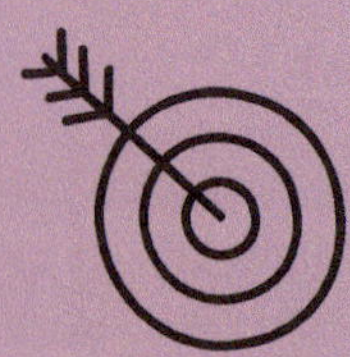

TARGET

Students are able to write a procedural piece as an expert on a topic.

Procedural writing can be validating for students when you ask them to write about something they know how to do. Students need to be honored for who they are and the knowledge they bring to the classroom. There are many things students learn at home and do with their families that they can share through writing. Personal narrative writing is one way students can share about their lives, but procedural writing helps them be an authority on a topic.

Your Instructional Playbook

Name It: We are going to write about how to do something. This is called procedural writing. You might know how to do something cool or great, and you can share it with the class in your writing.

What You Might Say Next: "The main thing to do with procedural writing is make sure you write in a way that is so clear, your reader can do it too. That's why it's also called how-to writing. You are writing directions for someone else to follow." Show a published procedural text (you can write a mock-up or show a cooking, craft, or automotive blog). Point out how the author is sharing the steps of how to do something but also sharing tidbits of knowledge, opinions, and ideas. Make sure and note how the piece is organized. There will likely be a section with steps (and pictures!) and also a few sentences woven into the steps stating tips that the author knows. Authors often also add in thoughts and feelings to each step as they share what works best according to them. (The Procedural Writing Genre Map shown below can help you choose an idea or two to point out.)

Model/Do Together: Write a part of a procedural report highlighting a genre feature that you are focused on (see chart). Model writing the introduction and the first couple of steps so that students can see how you are applying your thinking to the writing and still focusing on the writing technique. For example, you may be writing the introduction and sketching out a picture. You might then write out step one adding your thoughts and feelings to bring interesting information into the steps so that the piece reads more like a blog than an instruction manual.

Procedural Writing Genre Map

	Description
Purpose of procedural writing	*Provides an explanation. Describes how to make something, how to complete a task, how something works, how to get somewhere*

Procedural Writing Genre Map

	Description
Characteristics	*Clear and concise* *In logical order* *Easy to follow* *Avoids jargon language*
Uses/types	*How-to directions* *Recipes* *Annotated map directions* *Manuals* *Learn to . . . books (knit a sweater, play the piano)* *Craft magazines and websites* *Blogs on how to do things*
Organization	*Beginning identifies topic* *Middle includes a set of instruction* *Order of steps is organized by time, location, and need* *Steps are in logical order, beginning with first step and concluding with last step* *Middle steps include clear description of action and directions* *Clear outcomes described at the end*
Techniques	*How to guide readers to visualize each step* *Make the writing real* *Using simple easy-to-follow language* *Avoiding flowery language and jargon* *Revising actions to make ideas clear* *How to follow a timeline* *Using subheadings and bulleted lists to provide detailed explanation*

Source: Adapted from Narrative Genre Map, Nancy Akhavan, Heinemann, 2009

Launch students into the writing by having them brainstorm things they know a lot about. On the wheel map they can brainstorm things they know how to do, even if it is as simple as making a sandwich, tying shoes, or getting ready for school.

Release: Guide students as they write their procedural reports. Support them in thinking what they have learned about the topic, what they know, and how they can put that knowledge into words. Show them how to structure their reports.

Watch Fors and Work-Arounds

Students are stuck and cannot write. Support students by suggesting they write their report with a partner. The partners can work together to put the information into paragraphs and keep the information organized. If you pair students together, pair students with fairly even abilities so one student doesn't just take over and the other student doesn't get as much practice with getting their ideas on the page.

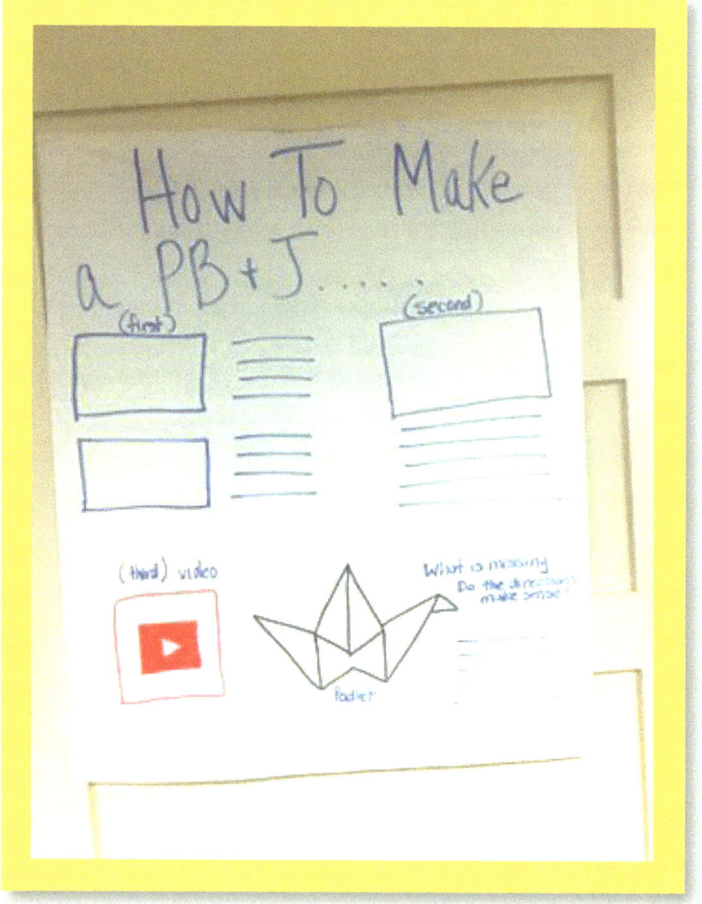

Here, the teacher created a visual reminder of the expectations for how they were to write their procedural papers.

iStock.com/danielfela

Writing Longer Pieces: Book Reviews

Writing

WHEN TO OFFER IT

Students are reading a lot in and out of class and want to share books with each other. Or, students are ready for a new type of genre writing.

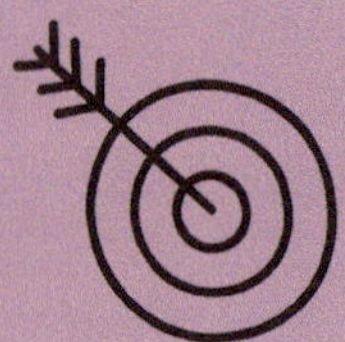

TARGET

Students are able to write a book report, sharing about a book, stating and claim and giving evidence.

Book reports are a fun way for students to write their opinions. They can write book reports based on books you've read aloud to them or books they have read on their own. You can organize books in your classroom library by book reviews. You can group reviewed books together or organize by the most popular book. It's fun for students to read each other's book reports. You can clip them to the inside cover of the book. Or put the book reports and the book in a Ziploc bag and store them together. You can also glue a paper pocket inside the book and store a few written on five-by-eight-inch cards.

Your Instructional Playbook

Materials: Books students have self-selected to read.

Name It: Readers recommend books to each other. We are going to begin recommending books to each other by writing book reviews sharing our opinions about books we've read.

What You Might Say Next: "Share a published book review that you find on the Internet or on an app like Instagram. Book reviews can be short snippets of information. The CREW format students learned when writing opinions can help them write a handful of short sentences sharing their thoughts about the books." (The Book Report Writing Genre Map may help you find points to share, too; try filling in a chart like the one below with your students.)

Model/Do Together: Launch students into writing book reports by having them share orally their thoughts and ideas about books they have read or are currently reading. Review the CREW (see Task 49) format with them and model how to write up a quick book review on something that you have read recently. (Find a printable CREW graphic organizer on the companion website, resources.corwin.com/bigbookELD.)

C.R.E.W. Device for Effective Book Report Writing

- C claim
- R reason
- E evidence
- W wrap-up

Book Report Writing Genre Map

	Description
Purpose of book report	*Demonstrates ability to make a statement or claim about a situation, book, or fact(s), and provides reasons*
Characteristics	*Has clear beginning, middle, and end* *Makes a claim (statement), provides reasons, and based on grade level identifies story's theme* *States judgment about the book* *Book reports give enough information to entice the reader* *Gives details to help the reader track the statement/opinion* *Presents justifications through references to text* *Provides synopsis of the story/book*
Uses/types	*Book report* *Favorite part of a book (for young children)*
Organization	*Clearly developed beginning, middle, and end* *Beginning may include a summary of the book for book reviews* *Has engaging beginning to hook the reader* *Ending brings closure, stating the opinion* *Opinion includes writers' thoughts and feelings* *Presents information in logical order*
Techniques	*Sentence variety develops pacing* *Develop context through descriptive techniques* *Exclude extraneous detail* *Quote directly from text (as appropriate to grade level)* *Paraphrase information from reading/research* *Track thinking in logical order* *Use notes to organize information into sections, claim, reasons, and supporting details*

(Continued)

(Continued)

Book Report Writing Genre Map	
	Description
	Writing strong claims
	Referring to evidence to back up reasons connected to the claim
	Set context through descriptive technique
	Quote directly from text
	Give synopsis of story

Source: Adapted from Opinion Genre Map, Nancy Akhavan, Heinemann, 2009

Release: Guide students as they write their book reviews. You can have them write on index cards so the card can slip into the book.

Sentence frames for writing book reviews:

_________ is one of the best/worst books I have read. (Claim)

One reason is _______________________. (Reason)

Another reason is _______________. (Reason)

The reason for this is _______________. (Reason)

The character changes/faces their problem by _______________.

The book was suspenseful/informative/reminded me of _______________.

Watch Fors and Work-Arounds

Students are stuck and cannot write. Support students by suggesting they write their report with a partner. The partners can work together to put the information into paragraphs and keep the information organized. If you pair students together, pair students with fairly even abilities so one student doesn't just take over and the other student doesn't get as much practice with getting their ideas on the page.

10/17/19 Shark lady

In my opinion, the book Shark lady was interesting because the book talk about somebody time life.

I thought, the Shark lady was boring because it was only talking about sharks only and not a person's life.

After reading, Shark lady, I was amazed that the shark lady went though all of this and met her d

Although unfinished, you can see here how this student began writing their book review with a claim.

SECTION FIVE

iStock.com/Nosyrevy

TASKS for Students at the Bridging Level of English Language Proficiency

Section V ● Tasks for Students at the Bridging Level of English Language Proficiency

52.	Ask and Answer Questions During Read-Alouds	Listening & Speaking
53.	Read and Discuss Content: Book Study	Listening, Speaking, & Reading
54.	Read, Stop, Think, Say: Independent Reading	Reading
55.	Write Lengthy Argument Paper	Reading & Writing
56.	Book Reviews: Evaluate a Novel or Nonfiction Text	Reading & Writing
57.	Paraphrasing Orally and in Writing	Speaking, Reading, & Writing
58.	Arguing a Point Orally	Listening, Speaking, Reading, & Writing
59.	Graffiti Notes	Listening, Speaking, Reading, & Writing
60.	Write Family History	Listening, Speaking, Reading, & Writing

Overview

As students grow and develop their language proficiency will advance. Once students are in fourth through eighth grade you can see large differences in students' acquisition levels. Some students who have been in school continuously since the primary grades may continue to be at the expanding level, while others are moving into the bridging level. As students reach and progress in the bridging level of English proficiency, their work should be conducted more and more often in content areas. There should be few lessons, if any, that are not connected to the broader social studies, science, and English language arts frameworks that guide your curriculum.

When students are learning language while learning content, it is best to shelter the instruction. Sheltered instruction refers to self-contained classes based on content domains. For instance, students in middle school typically have five to six courses throughout the day including English, math, science, and social studies. A high-quality sheltered classroom (grades four and above) provides numerous scaffolds to ensure students are learning the content in lessons presented in English. Additionally, good sheltered instruction also uses bilingual materials and encourages students to lean into their heritage language to express themselves, learn content, and make sense of the world (Wright, 2019).

When teachers use sheltered instruction, they are using multiple ways for students to understand content. Pictures, diagrams, web-based sources, and cooperative learning are used to ensure students understand the topics of study. Students read and write regularly and are provided the opportunity to express themselves and their learning.

Students at the bridging level will likely be ready for direct feedback on how to improve their language use in writing and orally. That said, feedback needs to be provided in a supportive manner and at a time that a student is ready to receive the feedback in order to learn. Feedback is given to help students reflect on what they are able to do in English and the adjustments they need to make to continue their proficiency development. This is best done through interactive, cooperative lessons where students are working together on projects that guide students' learning. Rote type lessons are less than ideal as repeated practice is rarely engaging and purposeful. Content learning and vocabulary instruction need to be focused on engagement and meaningful use (Akhavan, 2007).

To refresh your memory of what to expect of learners at this stage, the following is information from WIDA.

WIDA's Descriptors for English Language Proficiency Levels–Bridging

Level 5	What Students Are Able to Do
Listening	Draw conclusions from oral information
	Construct models based on oral discourse
	Make connections from oral discourse
Speaking	Engage in debates
	Explain phenomena, give examples, and justify responses
	Express and defend points of view
Reading	Read independently with an understanding of less complex text and a growing understanding of complex text
	Conduct research to glean information from multiple sources
	Draw conclusions from explicit and implicit text
Writing	Author multiple forms/genres of writing
	Apply information to new contexts
	React to multiple genres and discourses

Source: Adapted from WIDA Consortium (2012); WIDA Consortium (2020)

You may notice the book ends with stage five Bridging. Stage six, Reaching, mentioned in the introduction to the book, includes the lifelong growth a multilingual student will make as they use language throughout their school career and into adulthood. They will continue to develop an expanding repertoire of words and phrases that develops with precision over time (WIDA, 2020).

10 Tips for Success

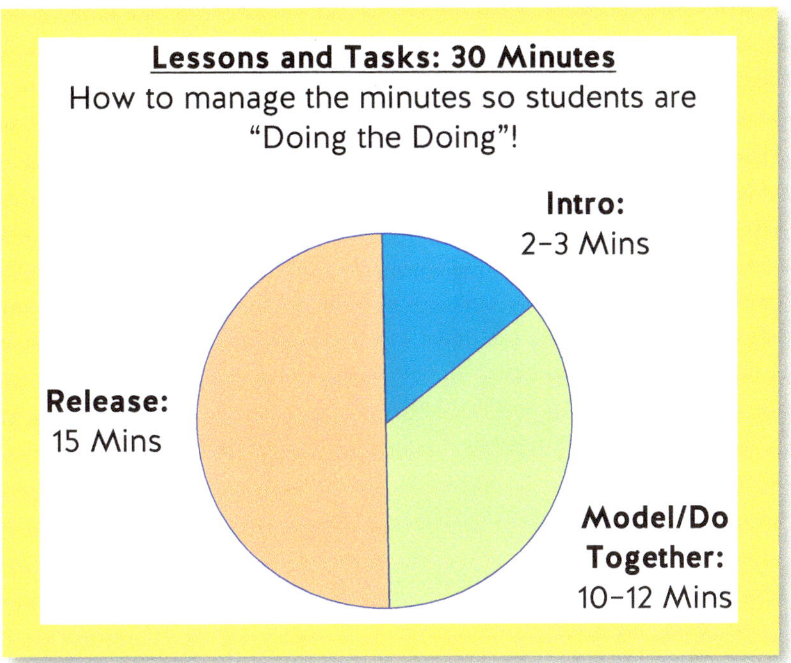

1. Focus on students reading more complex text. Provide support to scaffold their understanding.
2. **Keep your introduction to three to four minutes.**
3. State the purpose of the lesson and make sure students understand what the task is that they will be doing. At this level, students are doing more work independently.
4. Work with academic vocabulary. Provide extra explanation—anything you can do to make the word meanings comprehensible. Don't skim over words; provide context for the most important words for students to know how to be successful at the task.
5. **Model for seven to eight minutes.** Teach mini lessons before assigning the tasks. Don't just jump into the task. The mini lesson appears under the heading "**Your Instructional Playbook.**"
6. Use modeling time to ensure the content you are presenting is comprehensible; this is especially true for the academic language that will be in the texts students are reading.
7. **Peer work and independent work, plan on seventeen to eighteen minutes at least,** but look if the work is too hard and you need to pull students back together and model the work as students work with you.
8. **Altogether, including release—plan for 30 minutes.**
9. Encourage students that they can do the work on their own. They can use the skills they have learned to ensure they are comprehending as they read and listen.
10. Provide lots of listening experiences of academic texts. Students' listening skills need to grow into understanding complex discussion and information.

Ask and Answer Questions During Read-Alouds

Listening & Speaking

WHEN TO OFFER IT

When students can say short sentences or phrases during academic lessons where they listen to information presented, they are ready to work on saying more during read-alouds of complex text.

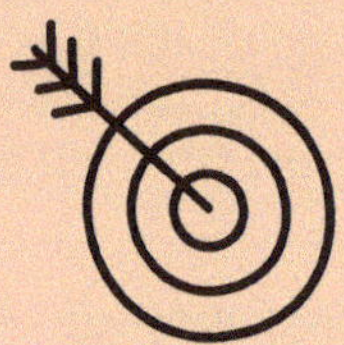

TARGET

Students can ask and answer questions during and after a read-aloud of complex text.

This task continues the experience of students asking and answering questions during reading, but instead of reading with you in a shared reading, or reading independently, students are listening to you read, or a recording, and then asking and answering questions of the text. This task is a listening comprehension task using complex text. As in Task 35, oral language experiences provide students the opportunity to delve into topics, formulate their own ideas, and then share their thoughts in English. In this task, students will be reading the complex text on their own. They will be working independently to ask and answer questions to monitor their own comprehension.

Your Instructional Playbook

Materials: Complex text assigned to class as part of regular curriculum instruction.

Name It: You have been working with me to ask and answer questions during reading so that you can comprehend what you are reading. Now, I want to make sure you can ask and answer questions while you are reading on your own.

What You Might Say Next: "If you remember, when we have read together, we have lots of questions and ideas that pop up. Some of the answers to the questions we can find in the text, so we reread it. Some of the answers we could not find in the text, so we had to connect ideas from the text together to answer those questions. Now, you are going to work on this same kind of thinking, but you will do it while reading on your own. It can help to write your questions and thoughts in your reading notebook."

Model/Do Together: As in Task 45, it will help to front load the text for the students. This is extremely important as students will be reading the text independently and need context to make sure that they have some connections to connect to as they work to comprehend what they are reading. After providing some context, model through a think-aloud and how you ask and answer questions after reading a chunk, or snippet, of the text independently. So, you could read a snippet of text silently, then talk to students about what questions you have, what you will seek to find out, and any other ideas that pop up. Model how to take notes on the ideas you have. You can annotate in the margins or write thoughts out on paper. Show students both of these approaches.

Release: Help students organize their materials. You may find students are more successful if you assign just a chunk of the text for them to read independently, and then continue the remainder of the text with a shared reading. The balance between shared and independent reading will be determined by the complexity of the text students are to read and their academic language abilities in English. Provide support as necessary depending on student need.

Watch Fors and Work-Arounds

Students may take on reading more than they can comprehend at one time. Encourage students to break the text into smaller chunks, stopping more often to reflect on what they have read and think about questions they have, and questions they can answer.

Students read along and can verbally ask and answer questions, but their notebooks are empty. Model for students how to take notes about their thinking. They don't need to record the question, as this may be too much writing. They can record their thinking and notes as they answer the questions.

Read and Discuss Content: Book Study

Listening, Speaking, & Reading

WHEN TO OFFER IT

Once students are able to have social conversations and can say short sentences or phrases during academic lessons, they are ready to work on academic discussions.

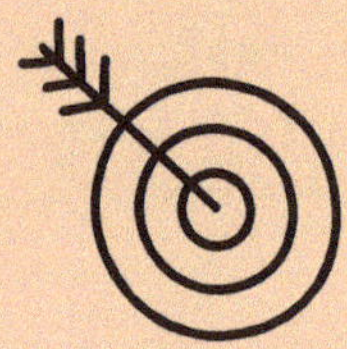

TARGET

Students can participate in academic discussions through listening, thinking, and speaking.

Students develop language acquisition not only by listening but also producing language. Students need plentiful opportunities to not only talk but also discuss topics. Discussion is different from talk as discussion involves listening to another person's ideas and thoughts, carefully considering them, and then adding new or different information. Discussion is talk plus listening and thinking. Students develop content area vocabulary and further their knowledge about things and worldly concepts when instruction is purposeful and authentic. Discussion helps to make lessons purposeful and authentic, and at first your students won't know how to have discussions—you will need to coach them.

Your Instructional Playbook

Name It: You will be working in groups to discuss the book that you have been reading. It is important that you not only talk about your thoughts but that you listen to one another.

What You Might Say Next: "A discussion is when you listen and talk, not just talk. When you listen to one another, you develop your ideas further. When you talk together, you can deepen your thinking and really focus on what the messages are in the book you are reading."

Model/Do Together: Reintroduce how you expect students to work together in their book discussion. Students likely won't need the support of sentence frames to start their conversation, but if they do, you can provide a few sentence frames to help them (see Task 20, page 60). A sequence I suggest for helping set up book discussions includes the following:

1. Conduct shared reading with students of the reading material and annotate the text.
2. Students independently read and write thoughts and wonderings about the text on a sticky note or in a journal.
3. Begin conversation by asking students to share their thinking.
4. Remind them of how to respond to one another.

Discussion Planners:

- What do you think was most important in the text? Why?
- Is your statement well reasoned or backed up by the text?
- What part of the text are you discussing?
- Did you respectfully listen to others' ideas?
- Did you state a wondering, make a prediction, or ask a question?
- Ask someone else a question to help them elaborate.

Release: Organize students into their groups and move from group to group guiding and helping them with their conversation. Your role during this time is to ensure the students are discussing on their own. Your role is not to lead, and not to answer, but to guide students to lead themselves.

If students need help with guiding their conversations, you can assign roles to students in the discussion such as facilitator (person who asks the questions), timekeeper, and recorder (person who writes down the group's thoughts and ideas and provides discussion starters). A sample of discussion starters could look like the following:

Discussion Starters:

- What was confusing?
- Is there vocabulary we need to clarify?
- Why do you think the main characters (fiction) did what they did?
- How does what the characters did matter?
- What was important in this chapter or section? Why?
- What makes the information, ideas, or events in this chapter/section interesting or important?
- Who can add to these ideas?
- Is there any other idea someone would like to share?

Watch Fors and Work-Arounds

Students are able to hold the conversation about the topic but move between their heritage language and English. Encourage students to use the language they have and the language that makes the most sense to them in sharing their message and interpreting others' messages. Moving between languages fluidly is called translanguaging. Translanguaging is the use of more than one language together and is very powerful in helping bilingual students share their thoughts, ideas, and messages.

Read, Stop, Think, Say: Independent Reading

Reading

WHEN TO OFFER IT

Once students are regularly using the read, shop, think, say strategy well during shared reading, they can try it out during independent reading.

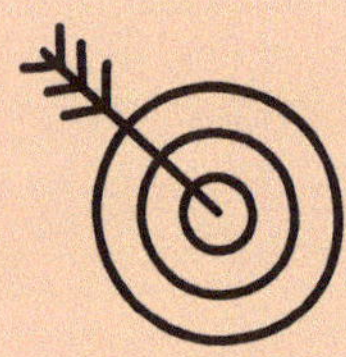

TARGET

Students will independently use the read, stop, think, say strategy to clarify meaning while reading.

Previously students have been working on this strategy while reading in groups or with a partner. Read, stop, think, say is a great strategy for students to use as they increase their independent reading time. It can serve them their whole life as a reader. It doesn't take too long to take a mental break, check in with your own understanding about what you have read, mentally focus on it, and then choose to reread if necessary or move on. As you encourage students to take on this strategy on their own, reinforce how developing a reading life can create an opportunity for them for their lives to become engaged readers that read for pleasure as well as for information. At the same time, you want to normalize self-monitoring for students. They often assume that "good" readers don't struggle or pause to check their understanding.

Your Instructional Playbook

Name It: When reading with your partner, you have been reading and then stopping to think about what you read. This is a great strategy to use as you read independently.

What You Might Say Next: "People who read a lot find reading fun and entertaining. The key is finding a book you like, and then making sure you understand what you are reading. You can check yourself and ensure that the words make sense."

Model/Do Together: Model how to take jot dots on sticky notes or in a reading notebook to keep track of what they have read. Jot dots are like bullet points. Students are not writing full sentences but instead writing short phrases that remind them of information or ideas. Remind students how to chunk the text, either after a few paragraphs in informational text, or perhaps halfway through a chapter in a novel. Model how you would take a note to remind yourself what you have read, questions you have, and thoughts you have about the text.

While modeling, pretend at some point you don't understand what you read. Model, while thinking aloud, how you would refer to your notes about what has happened previously in the text, and then rereading and referring back to the text to check for understanding. Reread a couple of times, perhaps highlighting a vocabulary word or two that you need to look up. The key idea is to model for students what to do if they don't understand what they are reading.

Strategies to Model to Fix Comprehension Break Downs:

1. Reread.
2. Stop and look up difficult or unknown vocabulary words.
3. Reread the sentences with unknown words.
4. Check previous notes and connect what you do understand in the new section to the notes.
5. Unknown words might be irregular verbs in addition to content area vocabulary. If it is a verb, check your personal word dictionary to see if the unknown word is a verb.
6. Look up information on the unknown word on the Internet to check additional information related to the word.

Read, Stop, Think, Say Sequence:

Read the designated sentences in a chunk of text (maybe sentence by sentence, a couple of sentences, or a paragraph).

1. Stop reading - reflect.
2. Think - think about what you just read, what it said, and how it relates to previous sections of text that you read.
3. Say - say what you think the text says aloud to your partner.

Release: Encourage students to use the strategy during a time of day you set aside for independent reading. After the independent reading time is over, lead a discussion with students about how the strategy worked for them and what they did if they did not understand what they had read.

Watch Fors and Work-Arounds

Students read large chunks of text before they stop to check comprehension, and then they don't know what they read. Have students stop reading in smaller chunks of text and then check their understanding. If the text is a bit more complex than they can handle in large chunks, have them read line by line.

Students don't understand many vocabulary words. Talk with them about the meaning of key words in the text. Also, show them how to look up additional information related to the word meaning to see if they can connect ideas together.

(Continued) Read, Stop, Think, Say: Independent Reading

Reading

Students can arrange and rearrange note cards until they have the sequence correct for the paper.

iStock.com/Nosyrevy

55 Write Lengthy Argument Paper

Reading & Writing

WHEN TO OFFER IT

Once students can write an opinion paper and are working with complex ideas.

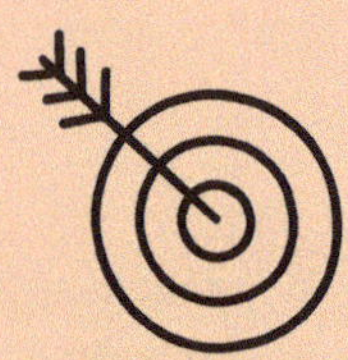

TARGET

Students will use a mnemonic to remember what goes in an argument paper.

When it comes to writing opinions, I have found that giving students a mnemonic to remember what goes in an opinion piece is important. When writing in ELA or social studies, it is common for the reason to come before the evidence. When writing in this way, the reason connects the evidence to the claim. This is the same style when writing an argument; however, in argument writing there needs to be a buildup of reasons and evidence, mostly from accepted sources, where in opinion writing the reasons and evidence can come from students' thinking. It is good for students to learn the correct form for opinion writing so that when they begin writing arguments, the transition is easy. I see many teachers have students use a mnemonic that puts the evidence before the reasons, but this is more typical of scientific writing than writing in other genres.

Your Instructional Playbook

Name It: We have been researching topics that are controversial. We are going to pick a viewpoint and write an argument paper, stating our perspective and providing reasons and evidence to inform our readers of our viewpoint.

What You Might Say Next: Show a published argument piece and point out some of the features in the argument: the claim, the reason and the evidence, the counterclaim and the warrant, that connects underlying beliefs to the claim. You could point out how the author states the claim and how the author presents the differing, or opposite, viewpoint.

Model/Do Together: As we did in Task 49, Writing Opinion Pieces: CREW, the mnemonic device to model is CREW: C for claim, R for reason, E for evidence, and W for warrant. This time we are calling it CREW^3 as an argument requires the following:

1. Referring to opinion writing (see Task 49), discuss the differences between an opinion and an argument (e.g., there are more reasons and evidence in an argument, as well as a counterclaim; writing counterclaims is most appropriate for grades seven and up).
2. Model writing a strong claim, reminding students that a claim is your clear statement that you want to persuade your audience of.
3. Once you write the claim, think aloud as you write a reason with evidence connected to the reason. (You can provide a bank of vocabulary words students can use to write the reasons and the evidence.)
4. Tell students that with argument writing, they will need at least two reasons and two to three pieces of evidence.
5. You will need to model what the paragraphs look like as they flow with reasons and evidence. You will also need to model a warrant. Note in the example below how the writing flows from the claim to the reasons and evidence, and how the warrant concludes the piece.

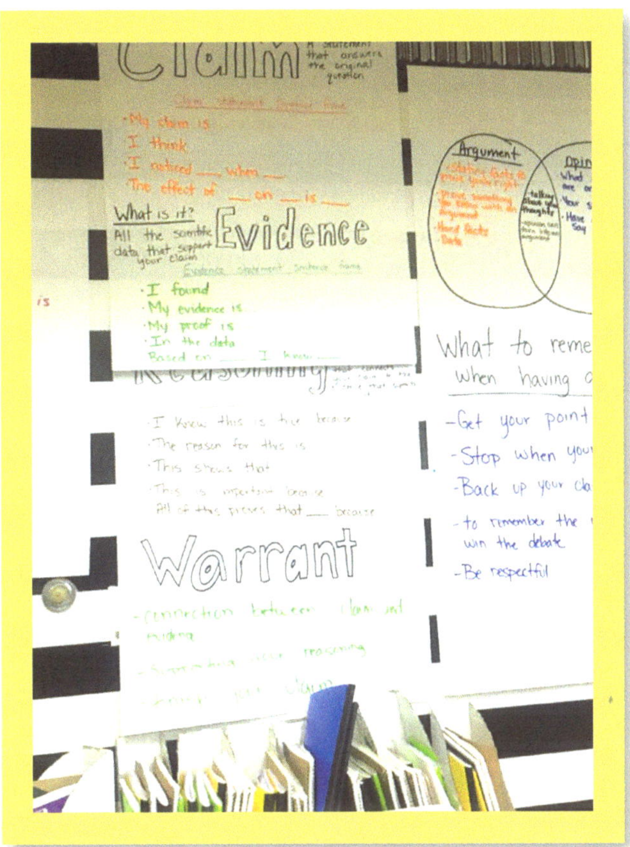

Wall charts like those shown here scaffold students as they learn the components of writing in any genre.

Release: Guide students as they write their arguments. They can refer to your modeled writing as a reference point to get their writing started. They may need the sentence frames to help them start to compose, but don't have students overrely on the scaffolds at this point in their language acquisition process.

Watch Fors and Work-Arounds

Students are stuck and cannot write. It can help to complete one piece together as a shared writing. Focusing on one or two writing techniques, compose an argument paragraph that has all parts of CREW³. Work with your students taking turns writing the sentences (or typing on a shared document if appropriate) and thinking through the next reason or piece of evidence. Model for students how to tackle what seems to be the biggest roadblocks for the students.

56 Book Reviews: Evaluate a Novel or Nonfiction Text

Reading & Writing

WHEN TO OFFER IT

As students develop the proficiency to read more complex texts, they will be ready to write about the texts to share their thinking and ideas.

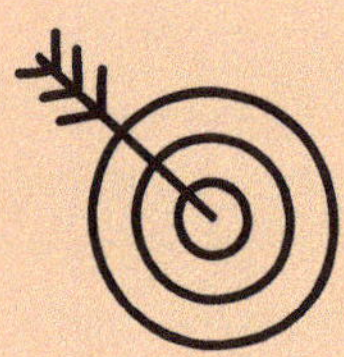

TARGET

Students will write a book review including a synopsis of the book or text and make a claim about the text.

Evaluation is what fluent readers do naturally. If we are reading a novel, we form opinions about the plot, the depth of the characters, and come to some conclusions about the skill of the writer to tell the story. We decide what we think is good or weakly developed; we rate the prose as fantastic, mediocre, or poor. When reading informative text, we evaluate all these characteristics, too, as readers. We may find some informative texts too dry, without enough text features or explanation. We may find other texts to be spot-on, even riveting. This task supports students to express their ideas and opinions about novels or informative texts. This is different than Task 51, which focuses on a book review that is more like a book report. This book review includes analysis.

Your Instructional Playbook

Name It: When we are reading, we have thoughts and ideas about the story/text. We may love a novel at the beginning but then lose interest. We may pick up a nonfiction book on a topic we are crazy about but then give up because the author's information or style or organization didn't engage us. As readers, we get to have our own ideas and opinions, but it's important for us to state for ourselves—and maybe others—precisely why we feel as we do. At the very least, this reflection helps us select engaging texts in the future. (The Book Report Writing Genre Map, which can be found in Task 51, can help; try creating a chart like this with your students, page 155.)

What You Might Say Next: "Because I want to know what you are thinking about your reading, you are going to write an evaluation of a book, story, or text. I have collected some book reviews for you to look at as models."

Model/Do Together: Present a novel or informational text that you have previously read and do a book talk about it. Talk about what the story or text was about, what you thought about it, and why. Perhaps dive into the text and share a few snippets to illustrate the points you are making. Next, model writing a book review, thinking aloud and inviting students' questions about these steps:

Book Review Writing: Fiction

1. Introduce the book with title and author.
2. State what the story is mainly about. You may describe the plot or the theme.

3. Give some information about the main characters and the problem the main character has in the book.
4. Discuss how the character solved their problem. You can decide if you want to put a spoiler in here–if you are encouraging your classmates to read the book, leave this out!
5. If the book's theme is a strong message from the author, discuss that. (Some authors foreshadow or reflect things that happen in real life.)
6. Provide a concluding sentence for this section that ties to the next section–your opinion of the book.
7. Using CREW, write your opinion about the book and be sure to include reasons and evidence from the story.
8. Provide an overall conclusion to your book review.

On another day, demonstrate how to write a review of an informational text.

Book Review Writing Template: Informational Text

1. Introduce the book or text with title and author.
2. State what the text is mainly about. You may describe the central idea. If the book is literary nonfiction, then discuss the plot.
3. Give some information about the big ideas and details in the book that support the central idea.
4. If writing about literary nonfiction, discuss how the character solved their problem. You can decide if you want to put a spoiler in here–if you are encouraging your classmates to read the book, leave this out!
5. Explain the author's purpose for writing the book or text.
6. Provide a concluding sentence for this synopsis section that ties to the next section–your opinion of the book.
7. Using CREW, write your opinion about the book or text, and be sure to include reasons and evidence from the text.
8. Provide an overall conclusion to your book review.

(Continued) Book Reviews: Evaluate a Novel or Nonfiction Text

Book-Review Writing Genre Map	
	Description
Purpose	Demonstrates ability to make a statement or claim about a situation, book, or fact(s) and provides reasons and textual evidence
Characteristics	Has clear beginning, middle, and end Makes a claim (statement), provides reasons and based on grade level multiple points of evidence Grades six and above write an argument, not an opinion, leaving out writer's thoughts and feelings If book review - identifies story's theme If book review - states judgment about the book Book reviews give enough information to entice the reader Opinion and argument essays give details to help the reader track the statement, opinion, or argument Presents justifications through references to text or research Analyzes plot, character development, and themes Analysis discusses author's purpose
Uses/types	Book review Literary analysis
Organization	Clearly developed beginning, middle, and end Beginning includes a summary of the book Has engaging beginning to hook the reader Ending brings closure, restated the opinion or argument in a new way Opinion includes writers' thoughts and feelings Presents information in logical order

Book-Review Writing Genre Map	
	Description
Techniques	*Show close reading and understanding of the book, story, theme, plot, and/or struggle of characters* *Take notes by paraphrasing and write paragraphs based on notes* *Sentence variety develops pacing* *Develop context through descriptive and analytical techniques* *Exclude extraneous detail* *Quote directly from text (as appropriate to grade level)* *Synthesize information in own words* *Track thinking in logical order* *Use notes to organize information into sections, claim, reasons, and supporting details* *Give synopsis of research at beginning of report* *Include insights connected to the book from world or personal knowledge* *Write strong claims* *Refer to evidence to back up reasons connected to the claim* *Set context through descriptive technique* *Quote directly from text* *Write a synopsis* *Analyze big ideas and write them in own words* *Analyze meaning in theme or plot and reflect on author's purpose*

Source: Adapted from Narrative Genre Map, Nancy Akhavan, Heinemann, 2009

56 (Continued) Book Reviews: Evaluate a Novel or Nonfiction Text

Release: Provide the opportunity for students to first write the synopsis of a book they read and then share their synopsis with a partner. Students can swap papers and compare the paper they are reviewing to the template. Have them give feedback to their partner about what is well done and any part that may be confusing or unclear. Students will then switch papers back and, using CREW, write their analysis of the book or text. After writing the opinion section and providing an overall conclusion to the book review, encourage students to swap papers again with a partner. Students can complete the peer evaluation by talking through their advice and ideas rather than just writing it down. Provide time for revisions.

Watch Fors and Work-Arounds

Students are retelling the story rather than writing a synopsis. When students are having trouble paraphrasing or shortening details into a synopsis, it can help them to make a list and then collapse the list into a short statement or a handful of phrases that students can put together in sentences.

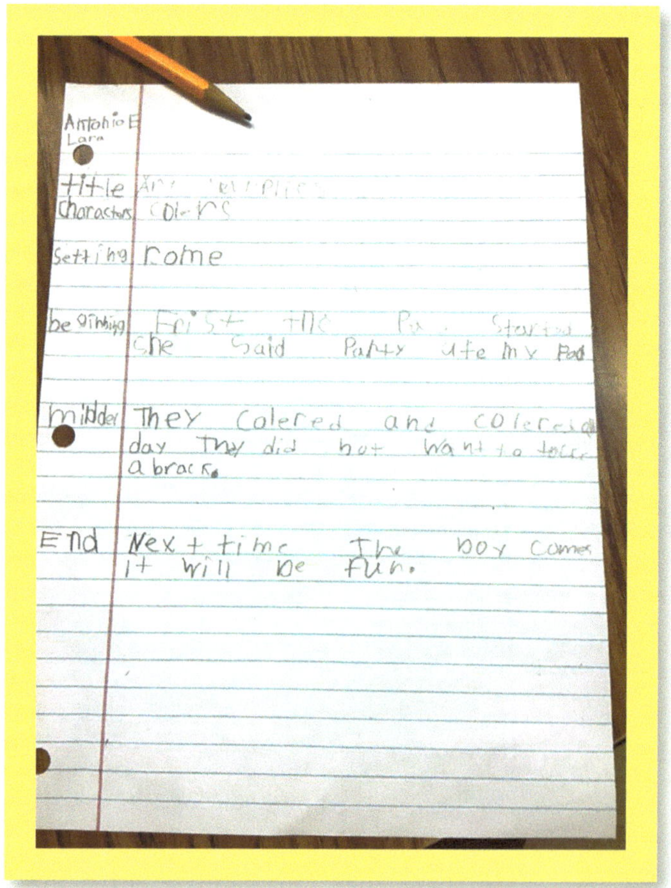

iStock.com/Nosyrevy

Paraphrasing Orally and in Writing

Speaking, Reading, & Writing

WHEN TO OFFER IT

Once students are researching to write reports, opinions, and arguments, they are ready to gather information and restate it in their own words.

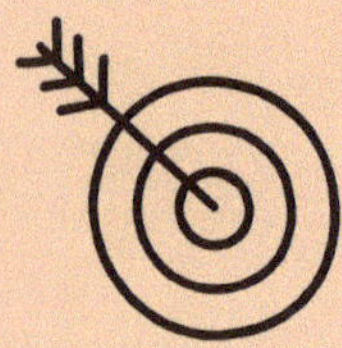

TARGET

Students can restate information they read in their own words.

When students begin to summarize, take notes on what they hear, listen, or read, students will need to paraphrase so that they are not copying information and so that they are expressing their own original thinking. Since we have all gone through school to some point, we likely have had experience with paraphrasing, and it may come easy. However, this is not an easy skill for students to learn. First, they don't always know that they can take information they are reading, viewing, or listening to and then think about it and state their own ideas in writing. Often, students want to be correct or be "right," and they are not sure if their own thinking is correct. As students build confidence and realize that as they learn, they own information for themselves, they will be able to paraphrase more easily. This task is about helping students state information in their words and realize their power.

Your Instructional Playbook

Name It: When you read texts, watch videos, or look up information on the Internet, you often write down notes exactly as you are reading it or listening to it. It is important that you begin to say what you are learning in your words. As you learn, you will own information; it will be your new knowledge and you need to be able to say your new knowledge in your own words.

What You Might Say Next: "Sometimes we restate and write down information we read or hear in our own words when the information is brand new for us. Sometimes we write down our thoughts once we learned new things and we know the information well and can say it for ourselves. Learning is a process and writing our thinking down helps us to learn and become smart about topics we are interested in."

Model/Do Together: Set up a T-chart in a notebook you project with a document camera onto a whiteboard or on a piece of chart paper. Label the left-hand side of the chart paper "paragraph #, page #/quote"and label the right-hand side "my own words."

Use an informative text that you can write on (so not a book, but a copy). First, number the paragraphs so that students can track back to where they might have taken a note from. Second, show the students a part of the text that you want to take a note about (read the text ahead, or pretend that you have already read it and zone in on a couple of parts of the text). Write, in the left-hand column, the paragraph number and, if appropriate, the sentence number on the chart, and add the most important phrase in the paragraph. In the right-hand column, model how you write the quoted phrase in your own words. Do this a couple of times, thinking aloud about how you put the quoted phrase in your own words. You may repeat a key term that cannot be restated but show over and over how much information you can say in your own way. If students are watching a video, they cannot write the paragraph or sentence number, so they will just write the fact down in the column.

Release: As students work through reading a text, working with a website, or watching a video, encourage them to take notes. Monitor that students stop often to check for the big ideas that need to be noted. If the class is watching a video together, control the flow by stopping the video in critical points and encouraging students to take a note. You can have them paraphrase the quote right then during the video, or after the video is concluded.

Watch Fors and Work-Arounds

Students have not yet acquired enough academic language to restate information in their own words. In this case, students may need to wait to do the paraphrasing after all the note-taking is completed. You can work on paraphrasing as a whole class, having students work with you as you facilitate conversation about the best way students can state information in their own words.

Arguing a Point Orally

Listening, Speaking, Reading, & Writing

WHEN TO OFFER IT

Once students have formed their arguments about a topic (Task 55) you can set them up for a debate.

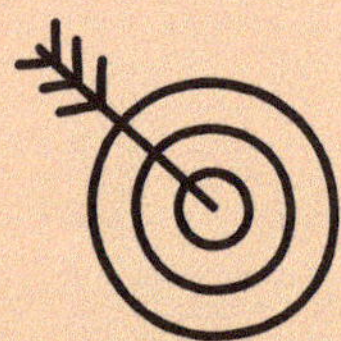

TARGET

Students will orally present their side of an issue.

This task is essentially a debate. By giving students a topic that clearly has two sides to it, you can help students create the point they want to make and help them back up their point with strong information. They will be debating with each other in class. Because students are continuing to acquire English and are not quite yet fluent, it is important to provide the opportunity for students to debate in teams or with a partner.

Your Instructional Playbook

Materials: Information on a topic of interest. The information you provide for students needs to be from credible sources and provide enough facts for both sides of an issue. Have at least two sources of information for students from books, texts, or online sources.

Name It: In the past we have learned how to write out our opinions using CREW (Task 49). As we grow in our abilities to state an opinion, we need to be able to argue a point. We are going to use CREW again, but we are going to use research to decide the points we want to argue.

What You Might Say Next: "When we argue a point, we are going beyond what we believe and using research or information from published sources to back up our ideas. When we argue a point, we form an idea based on the research we do. We are going to work on creating an argument and then presenting it in class. This is a type of debate. When people debate, there are usually people arguing a point from one viewpoint of an issue and then people arguing the opposite point."

Model/Do Together: Using a piece of writing you previously showed for argument writing (Task 55), show the students the difference between an opinion statement and an argument. In an argument, students leave out terms like *opinion,* or *I believe*. Students will now write a claim as a statement and back it up only with information they find in sources (from their research).

Explain how debate works. In a debate one team makes a point and provides information about that point as reasons and evidence for those reasons. Then the second team presents the counterpoint, also stating the reasons and the evidence.

Let students know how much fun debate can be! With a quick YouTube search, you might find an example of high school debate teams debating a point. Students of all ages can debate once they have the language proficiency developed and are able to synthesize information together, so don't let the students believe that they have to be the same age as the students in the video example you find.

Describe how they will be a bit sneaky and not tell *all* their evidence during the first round but hold a couple of pieces of evidence for round two in order to argue against the counterpoint. Team two will have the same opportunity. In round three, each team will make a closing statement. Students not involved in the debate can share their thoughts and ideas about how they are swayed by the arguments presented by the teams.

Debate Format–Two teams

Round One:

- Team 1 presents claim, reasons, and evidence.
- Team 2 presents claim, reasons, and evidence for counterpoint.

Round Two:

- Team 1 presents additional information as reasons and evidence for their point.
- Team 2 presents additional information as reasons and evidence for the counterpoint.

Round Three:

- Each team makes a closing statement.

Release: Guide students as they research their topic and write their notes. Help them to remember their point and not get confused with the counterpoint. They will need to be able to make the claim about the point they are going to debate and then have at least two reasons and a few pieces of evidence to make the debate interesting. This can take a few class sessions.

Help students prepare for the day of the debate. Show them how to organize their information for each round. Using CREW, they can write their notes for the rounds. Use CRE for round one, additional RE for round two, and W for round three, and an additional concluding statement.

(Continued) Arguing a Point Orally

Listening, Speaking, Reading, & Writing

Students can use sentence frames to get started with the sentences.

_________ is/is not _________. (Claim)

_________ is the right/wrong _________. (Claim)

_________ is how/how not things should be/are_________. (Claim)

This is true/untrue because _________. (Reason)

One reason is _________. (Reason)

Another reason is _________. (Reason)

The reason for this is _________. (Reason)

_________ discusses this point by saying _________. (Evidence)

_________ states that _________. (Evidence)

Additionally, _________. (Evidence)

Another point is _________. (Evidence)

The point is that many people _________. (Warrant–it is about beliefs)

Based on this evidence, it is apparent that _________. (Warrant - it is about beliefs)

The reasons and evidence clearly show that _________. (Warrant - it is about beliefs)

As you can see _________. (Concluding Statement)

Therefore _________. (Concluding Statement)

In closing _________. (Concluding Statement)

Watch Fors and Work-Arounds

Students cannot synthesize information from the sources. There are a few steps to helping students synthesize information from sources into big ideas they want to share as reasons. Task 57 has steps for helping students paraphrase. Students would refer specifically to the information in the text as evidence, but the big idea would be the reasons. Once students have notes to work with from more than one source, help students connect ideas together.

iStock.com/Nosyrevy

Graffiti Notes

Listening, Speaking, Reading, & Writing

WHEN TO OFFER IT

When students are involved in content studies and need to have deeper comprehension of what they are reading.

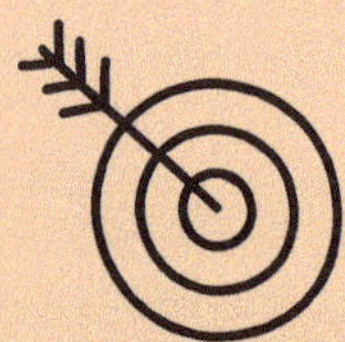

TARGET

Working in groups, students will read and annotate a text, preparing to ask questions and make statements about what they read.

As students develop proficiency in understanding the content investigations they have been doing, they can work together to read and understand a text, then write about that text to understand it at a deeper level. In the task students get to "graffiti" the walls with questions, thinking, and ideas about the text and the content that they read and are studying.

Your Instructional Playbook

Name It: You will be reading a text in groups today and then "Graffiti" the walls with what you learned about the text based on questions that I pose to you.

What You Might Say Next: "Check out the walls. I have posted chart paper around the room with a question on the top of each chart. (Use the Five Ws and One H questions.) After reading, I am going to have you work with your group and go around and write your questions on the charts (or students can write their big ideas on the chart if you prefer). After you have a chance to write on each chart, we will come together and talk."

Model/Do Together: Prepare by posting chart paper around the room (use a least five pieces) and write the questions at the top of the chart. Model writing a question based on an article you have previously read. Remind students of how questions can help them better comprehend what they are reading because the answers lead them to meaning.

Release: Organize students into groups and encourage them to read their article and annotate as they go. Once they are done, post students at the charts and give them markers. Organize students so they rotate from chart to chart writing their questions. They can also write their big ideas about the meaning of the text.

Watch Fors and Work-Arounds

Student groups are writing the same questions and there is no variety on the chart. Stop the students and bring their attention to one of the charts. Discuss how you would like them to think a bit deeper and ask questions that differ from what the other groups have asked. Discuss the questions on the chart and then model thinking up a new question and write it on the chart.

Students can work in teams to add their notes to the graffiti charts.

60 Write Family History

Listening, Speaking, Reading, & Writing

WHEN TO OFFER IT

Once students have facility with writing longer pieces and are comfortable in the nurturing and supportive classroom environment you create, they will be ready to write about their lives and their families.

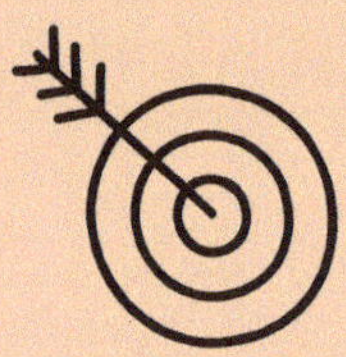

TARGET

Students can write a biographical piece about their family.

Students come to school with a rich history of family connectedness, love, and traditions. Being culturally responsive in our teaching means that we place students' lived experiences as important and honorable. Giving students the opportunity to tell their family story can be a celebration of your students' backgrounds and become almost a family biography. Honoring families is an important part of honoring students and we often don't do this enough. I once learned from a wise leader when we were discussing my students' home lives. He said, what they don't have in monetary items, they do have in love. In this task, students will have the opportunity to either write a piece telling their family story or create a multimedia presentation telling their family story. The story may be of the family's emigration to the US, or it could be a story of a tradition they honor at holidays, birthdays, or maybe, just a day-to-day routine they do as a family. It isn't about the students having a grandiose experience to share; it is about students having the opportunity to share about who they are and where they come from.

Your Instructional Playbook

Name It: We are starting a family history project. Your family history project can tell a story of your family, sharing information from many, or a few years ago, or it could be a story of now, telling your day-to-day experiences with your family. Telling a family history can help us reflect on our lives, and when we share our presentations with each other, we will learn more about who we are as a class, honoring each of us.

What You Might Say Next: "In a family history project, you may have a story you want to tell, or you may want to talk about traditions you celebrate with your family. If you cannot think of a story, or tradition, you can also tell a story about your weekly experiences with your family. Often, the smallest details make the most interesting stories to read or view. You can either write your story or show your story with a video or slide presentation."

Model/Do Together: Using the book *A House on Mango Street* by Sandra Cisneros, choose a poignant story that resonates with you. The one that resonates with me is when Sandra shares about her red sweater at school. Discuss how Sandra Cisneros shares information by showing and not telling. Brainstorm with students how they might be able to tell their family stories by sharing small details rather than a listing of facts and information. Using a ladder diagram, guide students to brainstorm what they might want to share in their family history story. They can fill in big categories. You can also encourage them to talk with their families at home about big ideas they could share if they get stuck. They can interview family members as appropriate to gather the information and details they need.

Once students brainstorm the large categories, show the excerpt from *The House on Mango Street* you previously share and talk with them about the details that Sandra Cisneros used in the excerpt. Have them look at their ladder maps and consider what details they might include in the stories and write their idea for those details on the rungs under the categories. Once students have their ladder maps fully completed, model how to lift the information from the ladder map and start drafting a piece. You will need to model how to introduce their stories (see Task 47, narrative writing); the beginning should be somewhat engaging and help set up the piece by introducing the family and perhaps naming the family members.

Release: Rather than beginning with the introduction or very first paragraph of the piece of writing, have them first draft the first category describing the story in the writing using the details from the ladder map. During the drafting process, circulate among students providing support and help. Once they get launched in the work, they can go back and create the introduction and then continue drafting their piece or their presentations. Once the writing or presentations are done, plan a day or two for students to share their work with the class. Celebrate their work!

Watch Fors and Work-Arounds

Students have a fully complete ladder map but are stuck and cannot write or create anything. Students may need you to guide the process as a we-do, rather than as a you-do (independent work). To do this work as a we-do, break the project into chunks and model each section of the project and then have students work just, and only, on that section. Then have students share their work with each other as they go, asking their peers for ideas to improve. You can go through the project step by step, piece by piece, pacing their work. You will need to model as they go so they know how to get started. Provide sentence frames as needed.

Appendix A
Research Foundation for the Tasks in This Book

	Title	Reference
1.	Total Physical Response	Bao (2014); Haynes (2007); Umansky et al. (2022).
2.	Picture Retelling	Goldenburg (2010); Haynes (2007); Newcomer et al. (2021).
3.	Building Vocabulary Using Realia	Nation (2001); Umansky et al. (2022).
4.	Building Vocabulary With Word Banks	Barr et al. (2012); Carlo et al. (2004); Umansky et al. (2022).
5.	Word Journals	Carlo et al. (2004); Newcomer et al. (2021).
6.	Choral Reading	Akhavan (2006); August et al. (2005).
7.	Zoom the Room	August and Shanahan (2006); Windsor (2010); Haigh et al. (2011); Pérez (2004); Washington-Nortey et al. (2022).
8.	Practicing Simple Phrases	Akhavan (2006); Kohnert and Pham (2010); Newcomer et al. (2021).
9.	Answering Yes or No	Bao (2014); Haynes (2007); Nation (2001).
10.	Retelling Fiction	Bear and Smith (2012); Stoutz (2011); Gamez (2009); Koskinen et al. (1988).
11.	Retelling Nonfiction	Bear and Smith (2012); T. Rasinski and Young (2014); Stoutz (2011); Gamez (2009); Koskinen et al. (1988).
12.	Read Aloud With Simple Group Discussion	Bear and Smith (2012); Cazden (2001, 2017); Clark (2020); Kara and Eveyik-Aydın (2019); Young and Hadaway (2006); Gamez (2015); Wilkinson and Son (2011).
13.	Visual Vocabulary	Barr et al. (2012); Wright (2019).
14.	Zoom the Room: Sound Walls	Blevins (2020); Bowey (2002); Ehri (2011); Goswami and Mead (1992).
15.	Shared Reading Predictable Text	Akhavan (2019); August and Shanahan (2006); Clark (2020); Ehri (2011); Kara and Eveyik-Aydın (2019); T. Rasinski and Young (2014); Young and Hadaway (2006); Lesaux et al. (2008); Ukrainetz (2000); Walpole and McKenna (2007).
16.	Read Aloud and Partner Talk	Billings and Walqui (n.d.); Kara and Eveyik-Aydın (2019); Pérez (2004); Saito (2020).
17.	Daily Activity Sequencing	August et al. (2005); Coyne et al. (2011); Haynes (2007); Donnelly and Roe (2010).
18.	Teaching Sounds and Reading Decodable Text	Akhavan (2023); Blevins (2017a, 2020, 2021); Ehri (2011); Gooch and Lambirth (2008); Ehri (2005); Templeton (2020).
19.	Word Manipulation With Onset and Rhymes	Blevins (2017b, 2020); Bowey (2002); Ehri (2011); Gooch and Lambirth (2008); Goswami and Mead (1992); Haigh et al. (2011); Templeton (2020).

	Title	Reference
20.	Writing Dialogue Journals With Sentence Frames	Linares (2019); Olson et al. (2015); Ortiz and Franquiz (2019); Palmer (1994); Walpole & McKenna (2007).
21.	Giving and Performing Two-Step Directions	Akhavan et al. (2006).
22.	Personal Dictionaries	Akhavan (2009); Ramsey (2019); Sebold (2011); Wu et al. (2021).
23.	Shared Reading: Ask-and-Answer Questions About Text	Elley (1991); Li et al. (2021); McCay (2006); Melby-Lervåg and Lervåg (2014); Mora-Flores (2018b); T. V. Rasinski, Reutzel, et al. (2011); Shanahan and Beck (2006).
24.	Language Experience Approach	Akhavan (2023); Akhavan and Walsh (2020); Beck and McKeown (2006); Cazden (2001, 2017); Celce-Murcia and Olshtain (2000); Crossley et al. (2012); Harvey and Goudvis (2013); Li et al. (2021); Mora-Flores (2018a); Uchihara et al. (2022); Wu et al. (2021).
25.	Choral Reading: Readers' Theater	Elley (1991); Li et al. (2021); McCay (2006); Melby-Lervåg and Lervåg (2014); Mora-Flores (2018b); T. V. Rasinski, Reutzel, et al. (2011) Shanahan and Beck (2006); Stahl (2004).
26.	Beginning to Write in English: Opinion Writing	Akhavan (2009); Ecchevarria and Graves (2002); Grabe and Zhang (2013); Olson et al. (2015); Peregoy and Boyle (2016).
27.	Beginning to Write in English: Informational Writing	Akhavan (2009); Grabe and Zhang (2013); Olson et al. (2015); Peregoy and Boyle (2016).
28.	Beginning to Write in English: Personal Narrative	Barr et al. (2012); Olson et al. (2015); Peregoy and Boyle (2016); Mora-Flores (2018a).
29.	Building Simple Present Tense Sentences	August (2003); Genesse and Riches (2006); Bear et al. (2009); Gottlieb (2016); Láufer (2010); Khatib & Bagherkazemi (2011).
30.	Building Sentences: Add in Adjectives/Adverbs/ Articles	Akhavan and Walsh (2020); Genesse and Riches (2006); Gottlieb (2016); Láufer (2010); Spycher (2007).
31.	Cognates Help Students Learn Vocabulary	Calderón and Soto (2017); Carlo et al. (2004); Cummins (1979, 1981); Nation (2001).
32.	Discuss Text During Read-Alouds	Bear and Smith (2012); Calderón and Slakk (2018); Cazden (2017); Celce-Murcia and Olshtain (2000); Gibbons (2009); Gutierrez et al. (2010); Harvey and Goudvis (2013).
33.	Recounting Stories Read Aloud and Together	Cummins (2011); Goldenburg (2010); Lucero (2018); Montelongo et al. (2011); Stoutz (2011); Peregoy and Boyle (2016).
34.	Match Vocabulary Words With Definitions	August et al. (2005); Beck et al. (2013); Calderón and Soto (2017); Carlo et al. (2004); Nagy (1988); Nation (2001); Ramsey (2019).
35.	Ask and Answer Questions During Shared Reading: Informational Texts	Akhavan (2014, 2023); Barr et al. (2012); Beck and McKeown (2006); Ecchevarria et al. (2017); Elley (1991); Gibbons (2009); Washington-Nortey et al. (2022).
36.	Dialogic Instruction: Main Idea and Theme	Akhavan (2023); Akhavan and Walsh (2020); Beck and McKeown (2006); Celce-Murcia and Olshtain (2000); Crossley et al. (2012); Li et al. (2021); Mora-Flores (2018a); Pressley et al. (1995); Rapp et al. (2007).

	Title	Reference
37.	Act Out Concepts of Tier 2 Words	Belhiah (2013); Johnston et al. (2000); Kieffer and Lesaux (2012).
38.	Write Short Answers to Text Questions	Cain and Oakhill (1999); Cummins (2011); Goldenburg (2010); Grabe and Zhang (2013).
39.	Building Sentences: Pronouns and Prepositions	Akhavan (2019); Fareed et al. (2016); Freeman and Freeman (2014); Hiebert (2019); Kieffer and Lesaux (2012); Lightbown and Spada (1990); WIDA (2019).
40.	Building Sentences: Conjunctions With Subordinate Clauses	Akhavan (2019); Fareed et al. (2016); Freeman and Freeman (2014); Hiebert (2019); Kieffer and Lesaux (2012); Lightbown and Spada (1990); WIDA (2019).
41.	Practicing Verb Tenses	Akhavan (2019); Freeman and Freeman (2014); Hiebert (2019); Kieffer and Lesaux (2012); Lightbown and Spada (1990); WIDA (2019).
42.	Practicing the Perfect Verb (Past, Present, and Future) Form	Akhavan (2019); Freeman and Freeman (2014); Hiebert (2019); Kieffer and Lesaux (2012); Lightbown and Spada (1990); WIDA (2019).
43.	Read, Stop, Think, Say During Shared Reading	Dejener and Burne (2016); Ecchevarria et al. (2017); Gutherie and Barber (2019); Krashen and Mason (2017); Li et al. (2021); Raphael and Au (2005); Tudor and Hafiz (1989); Pressley and Wharton-McDonald (1997).
44.	Independent Reading: Visualizing and Asking Questions About Text	Cho et al. (2019); Duke et al. (2011); Montero and Kuhn (2016); T. V. Rasinski (2010); T. V. Rasinski, Reutzel, et al. (2011); Pressley and Wharton-McDonald (1997).
45.	#HUE During Reading Strategy: Informational Texts	Dejener and Burne (2016); Ecchevarria et al. (2017); Harvey and Goudvis (2013); Kim et al. (2004); Krashen and Mason (2017); Li et al. (2021); Ness (2016); Tudor and Hafiz (1989); Pressley and Wharton-McDonald (1997).
46.	Writing Paragraphs	Akhavan (2009); Herrell and Jordan (2020); Olson et al. (2015, 2017); Spycher (2007).
47.	Writing Longer Pieces: Personal Narrative	Olson et al. (2015, 2017); Ortiz and Franquiz (2019); Wright (2019); Young and Hadaway (2006).
48.	Writing Longer Pieces: Informative	Grabe and Zhang (2013); Moss (2005); Olson et al. (2015, 2017); Tudor and Hafiz (1989); Wright (2019); Young and Hadaway (2006).
49.	Writing Longer Pieces: Opinion	Grabe and Zhang (2013); Moss (2005); Olson et al. (2015, 2017); Tudor and Hafiz (1989); Wright (2019); Young and Hadaway (2006).
50.	Writing Longer Pieces: Procedural	Olson et al. (2015, 2017); Peregoy and Boyle (2016); Wright (2019); Young and Hadaway (2006).
51.	Writing Longer Pieces: Book Reviews	Olson et al. (2015, 2017); Peregoy and Boyle (2016); Wright (2019); Young and Hadaway (2006).
52.	Ask and Answer Questions During Read-Alouds	Bear and Smith (2012); Calderón and Slakk (2018); Cazden (2017); Celce-Murcia and Olshtain (2000); Gibbons (2009); Gutierrez et al. (2010); Harvey and Goudvis (2013); Collett and Dubetz (2021).
53.	Read and Discuss Content: Book Study	Cho et al. (2019); Dejener and Burne (2016); Duke et al. (2011); James and Carter (2007); Gutherie and Barber (2019); Hoyt (2016); Li et al. (2021); Mushait and Mohsen (2019); Nagy (1988); Nowbakht and Shahnazari (2015); Swiegart (1991).

	Title	Reference
54.	Read, Stop, Think, Say: Independent Reading	Carnegie Council on Advancing Adolescent Literacy (2010); Cho et al. (2019); T. V. Rasinski (2010); T. V. Rasinski, Reutzel, et al. (2011); Wright (2019).
55.	Write Lengthy Argument Paper	Fareed et al. (2016); Olson et al. (2015, 2017); Shi (2004); Spycher (2007).
56.	Book Review: Evaluate a Novel or Nonfiction Text	Cervetii and Hiebert (2015); James and Carter (2007); Keck (2006); Kittley-Koshenina (2009); Moss (2005); Mushait and Mohsen (2019); Nagy (1988); Swiegart (1991).
57.	Paraphrasing Orally and in Writing	Himmele and Himmele (2009); Moss (2005); Nowbakht and Shahnazari (2015); T. V. Rasinski (2010); Scarcella (2003); Schumaker et al. (1984); Sebold (2011).
58.	Arguing a Point Orally	Dejener and Burne (2016); Himmele and Himmele (2009); Kong and Fitch (2002); Mora-Flores (2018a); T. V. Rasinski (2010); Scarcella (2003); Sebold (2011); Shanahan and Beck (2006).
59.	Graffiti Noes	Dejener and Burne (2016); Kong and Fitch (2002); Mora-Flores (2018a); T. V. Rasinski (2010); Scarcella (2003); Sebold (2011); Shanahan and Beck (2006); Swiegart (1991).
60.	Write Family History	Fareed et al. (2016); Olson et al. (2015, 2017); Shi (2004); Spycher (2007).

Resources from Appendix A and Appendix B can be downloaded for your convenience. Go to **resources.corwin.com/bigbookELD**.

Appendix B
Reproducible for Instructional and Student Use

- Conjunctions
- CREW Graphic Organizer (pages 1 & 2)
- Phoneme/Grapheme Assessment
- Preposition Chart
- Common Tier 2 Words
- Spanish Cognate List
- Readers' Theater Script Example
- Tiny Sentence Expand
- Word Journal
- Three-Column Note-Taking Sheet

Conjunctions

Coordinating conjunctions join phrases or clauses that are equal to each other, in other words, two independent clauses.

A subordinating conjunction joins unequal clauses. In other words, an independent and a dependent clause

Examples of coordinating conjunctions are:

- *and*
- *but*
- *or*
- *nor*
- *for*

Coordinating conjunction in a sentence:

- *She wasn't my friend,* ***but*** *I loaned her my skateboard.*

Notice how the phrases either side of "but" each contain complete thoughts—they are independent clauses.

The subordinate clause adds valuable information to the independent clause it is connected to, but the independent clause doesn't need the subordinate to be a sentence.

Examples

1. *I will not start the lesson* ***unless*** *you are all quiet.*
2. ***Although*** *it is lunch time, there isn't too much traffic.*
3. *You can have a drink in the car* ***as long as*** *you're careful not to spill it!*
4. ***If*** *it's an emergency, go ask for help from the yard attendant.*
5. ***Whenever*** *I see a dog, I have to stop to pet it.*
6. *Wash your hands* ***before*** *you leave for lunch.*
7. ***Though*** *I'd love to say yes, the answer is no.*
8. *You may not begin reading* ***until*** *everyone has found their place in the book.*

CREW Graphic Organizer (Pages 1 & 2)

CREW OPINION WRITING

Name________________________

CLAIM

REASON

EVIDENCE

- ____
- ____
- ____
- ____

WRAP UP

____

____

____

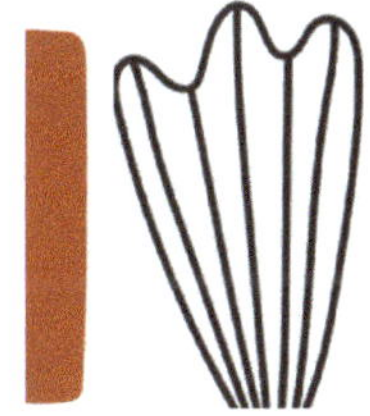

____

Credit line: iStock.com/Jennifer Kosig

C(RE)^{3}W OPINION WRITING

Name________________________

CLAIM

REASON & EVIDENCE

- ____

REASON & EVIDENCE

- ____

REASON & EVIDENCE

- ____

WRAP UP

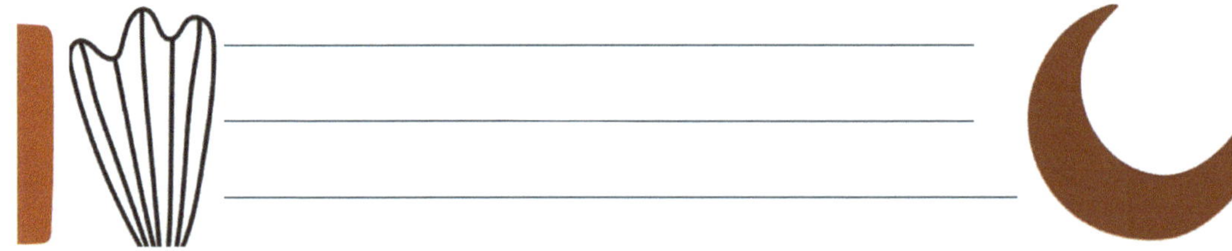

Credit line: iStock.com/Jennifer Kosig

Phoneme/Grapheme Assessment

NAME: ______________________ DATE: ______________

Phoneme/Grapheme Assessment

Letters		Score			Score
Names	m t a s i r d o f g l h u c n b j k y e w p v qu x z	__/ 26	Sounds	/m/ /t/ / a/ / s/ / i / /r/ /d/ /o/ /f/ /g/ /l/ /h/ /u/ /k/ /n/ /b/ /j/ /k/ /y/ /e/ /w/ /p/ /v/ /kw/ /ks/ /z/	Consonants ___/21 Vowels ____/5
VC & CVC					
	ab seb tid nop nug og cak lem pip huv				__/10
Consonant Digraphs					
	mosh cack chun shup mith hing whak thit soch nath				__/10
Silent e					
	pice hine gile pade pote fane tate kole tose zile				__/10
r-Controlled Vowels					
	tirk merl mort tarn forn pern lirk lurn merm cark				__/10
Vowel Teams					
oa, ea, oo, ai, oi, ay, ou, oi,oy, au, aw, oe, ew al igh	toast neam moom laist poit may mouth moist noy raul graw loe mew gray pald light				--/16

Preposition Chart

Preposition	How It's Used	Example
at	at exact times parts of the day age mealtime	**at** ten a.m. **at** noon **at** age fifteen **at** breakfast
by	a limit in time in the sense of "at the latest"	**by** nightfall **by** the due date
in	seasons months years durations after a certain period of time	**in** the spring **in** June **in** 2023 **in** the same month **in** 30 minutes
on	days of the week parts of the day where the day is named dates	**on** Friday **on** Saturday morning **on** December 25th
ago	a certain time in the past	ten years **ago**
after	a certain point in time that follows another point in time	**after** school
before	before a point in time that precedes another point in time	**before** school **before** bedtime **before** 2023
during	something that happened or will happen in a specific period of time	**during** school **during** winter
for	over a certain period in the past	**for** three summers **for** a long time
past	telling the time	Fifteen **past** five
since	From a certain period of time	**since** 1992 **since** I went to middle school
throughout	something that happened or will happen continuously during a specific period of time	**throughout** the school year **throughout** my childhood
to	telling time from an earlier time to a later time	ten minutes **to** seven 9 a.m. **to** 11 a.m.
until up (to)	up to a certain point in time how long something is going to last	**until** the end of the summer **until** midnight

Preposition	How It's Used	Example
at	showing an object's position or position after it has moved meeting place or location point of direction a target	**at** school turn **at** the corner throw the ball **at** the batter **at** the swings
by	close to alongside of	**by** the school **by** the desk
in	in an enclosed space in a geographic area in a print medium	**in** the classroom **in** the refrigerator **in** a book
on	a certain location	**on** the right **on** the Internet **on** the bus
about	around or outside of but not exactly related to	**about** town **about** the book **about** three feet long
above	suspended higher than something else superior to	**above** the door **above** me in school
after	a point farther from an earlier point	chasing **after** my kid brother the house **after** the green house
against	leaning on opposite to or facing	**against** the table **against** the wall
along	tracing the length of something without emphasis on the ends	**along** the whiteboard **along** the road
among	in the company of (three or more) in a crowd the end of a long list	**among** friends **among** the crowd **among** many other things
around	location of something explaining a period of time	**around** 11 o'clock **around** the school
before	in the front in terms of space	**before** the students **before** the front of the class
behind	on the back side of a point in space	**behind** the bus **behind** her eyes
below	something lower than or underneath something else	**below** the stairs **below** standard

Preposition	How It's Used	Example
from	in a sense of where	**from** the playground
into	Enter a room or building	go **into** the classroom
onto	movement to the top of something	jump **onto** the table
over	covered by something else more than getting to the other side overcoming an obstacle	put your coat **over** your clothes **over** ten years old walk **over** the bridge get **over** the problem
through	something with limits on top, bottom and sides	drive **through** the tunnel
toward	movement in the direction of something (but not directly to it)	walk **toward** the cafeteria
about	for topics—meaning what a topic is about	we were talking **about** you
at	for age	she learned to ride a bike **at** six
by	who made it rise or fall of something traveling (other than walking or horseback riding)	the book is **by** a doctor prices have been lowered **by** 10 percent **by** car
from	from who gave something	a present **from** Nancy
in	entering a car	get **in** the car
of	who or what	did the word come from a page **of** the book
off	leaving a public transport vehicle	get **off** the bus
on	walking or riding on horseback entering public transport vehicle	**on** foot get **on** the bus
out of	leaving a car	get **out of** the car

Source: Adapted from St. Mary's College CWAC (2015)

For more information on using prepositions, see the following resources:

Azar, Betty S., and Stacy A. Hagen. *Understanding and Using English Grammar*, 4th ed.

Beason, Larry, and Mark Lester. *A Commonsense Guide to Grammar and Usage*, 6th ed.

Johnston, Ted, and Joe Old. *English Beyond the Basics*, 2nd ed.

Common Tier 2 Words

A Words	collaborate	engage	**H Words**
accomplish	conduct	era	habit
achieve	connect	examine	harassment
adequate	construct	example	harsh
advance	contrast	execute	hesitate
advocate	contribute	exempt	hierarchy
analogy	convenient	experience	hinderance
argument	culminate	expectation	historic
arrange		explore	horizontal
articulate	**D Words**		hostility
assess	decision	**F Words**	hypothesis
assist	deduce	facilitate	
associate	deepen	factor	**I Words**
attract	defense	familiar	illustrate
attribute	delineate	fasten	image
authority	detect	feasible	implication
	determine	figure	improve
B Words	develop	form	incorporate
beam	diagram	frequent	infer
belligerent	differentiate	frequencies	infer
benefit	disappoint		inform
bewilder	discern	**G Words**	interact
bias	discriminate	gall	interpret
boast	discriminate	gather	investigate
border	distinguish	gauged	
briskly	diverse	generate	**J Words**
broaden	draft	gigantic	jaded
build		gist	jabbed
	E Words	glare	jaunt
C Words	elaborate	government	jeer
cite	employ	graph	jell
classify	enhance	grueling	jest

judge
juggle
justify
juxtapose

K Words

karat
keen
kingdom
knack

L Words

label
lanky
lastly
lark
latent
launch
lawful
lethal
link

M Words

majority
malice
manipulation
marvel
measure
member
mesh
modify
monitor
multiply

N Words

narrate
native
navigation
nearby
neatly
neither
normal
novice
nudge
nurse

O Words

obedient
obligation
oblige
observe
occurrence
openly
opposed
opposite
orient
origin

P Words

patient
passage
perspective
persuade
phenomenon
pivotal
plausible
proficient
pronounce

Q Words

qualification
qualify
quality
qualm
queasy
quest
question
quieted
quirky
quote

R Words

recall
recede
recognize
refer
report
represent
research
resolve
reverence
revisit

S Words

seek
selection
significant
similar
simplify
specification
strength
subsequent
substitute
symbol

T Words

tension
tentative
test
tolerate
transfer
transformational
translate
trivial
turbulent
typical

U Words

undone
unexpected

unfamiliar	verify	widen
unite	vertical	widen
unique	vice versa	width
unnatural	violate	withdrawn
unusual	visual	
update	voracious	**Z Words**
usage		zany
usual	**W Words**	zapped
	wafted	zeal
V Words	waiver	zenith
validity	wane	zesty
valuable	wasted	zigzag
variable	weird	zipped
vast	whisk	zone

Spanish Cognate List

A		C	
English Cognate	**Spanish Word**	**English Cognate**	**Spanish Word**
accident	accidente	cabin	cabina (de teléfono, avión, etc.)
accidental	accidental	cable	cable
active	activo (a)	cafeteria	cafetería
activities	actividades	camera	cámara
admire (to)	admirar	camouflage	camuflaje
admit (to)	admitir	canyon	cañón
adult	adulto	captain	capitán (a)
adventure	aventura	capture (to)	captura
adopt (to)	adoptar	catastrophe	catástrofe
adoption	adopción	cause	causa
African	Africano (a)	celebrate (to)	celebrar
agent	agente	cement	cemento
air	aire	center	centro
alarm	alarma	ceramic	cerámica
allergic	alérgico (a)	cereal	cereal

A		C	
English Cognate	**Spanish Word**	**English Cognate**	**Spanish Word**
anaconda	anaconda	ceremony	ceremonia
animal	animal	chimney	Chimenea
announce (to)	anunciar	chimpanzee	chimpancé
appear (to)	aparecer	cholera	cólera
appetite	apetito	circle	círculo
area	área	circular	circular
arithmetic	Aritmética (o)	class	clase
artist	artista	coast	costa
association	asociación	colony	colonia
astronomer	Astrónomo (a)	color	color
atmosphere	atmósfera	committee	comité
attention	atención	common	común
August	agosto	complete	completo(a)
autograph	autógrafo	completely	completamente
automobile	automóvil	company	compañía
B		concert	concierto
banana	banana	confetti	confeti
banjo	banjo	constellation	constelación
bicycle	bicicleta	construction	construcción
biography	biografía	contagious	contagioso(a)
blouse	blusa	continent	continente
brilliant	brillante	continue (to)	continuar
		contract	contrato
		contribution	contribución

English Cognate	Spanish Word	English Cognate	Spanish Word
coyote	coyote	especially	especialmente
crocodile	cocodrilo	examine (to)	examinar
curious	curioso(a)	exclaim	exclamar
D		explosion	explosión
December	diciembre	exotic	exótico(a)
		extra	extra

English Cognate	Spanish Word	English Cognate	Spanish Word
decide (to)	decidir	extraordinary	extraordinario(a)
decoration	decoración, adorno		
delicate	delicado(a)	F	
depend (to)	depender	family	familia
deport (to)	deportar	famous	famoso(a)
describe (to)	describir	fascinate (to)	fascinar
desert	desierto (a)	favorite	favorito(a)
destroy (to)	destruir	ferocious	feroz
detain (to)	detener	finally	finalmente
determine (to)	determinar	firm	firme
dictator	dictador (a)	flexible	flexible
different	diferente	flower	flor
determine (to)	determinar	fortunately	afortunadamente
dinosaur	dinosaurio	fruit	fruta
direction	dirección	funeral	funeral
directions	direcciones	furious	furioso(a)
directly	directamente	G	
director	director (a)	galaxy	galaxia
disappear (to)	desaparecer	gallon	galón
disaster	desastre	garden	jardín
disgrace	desgracia	gas	gas
discrimination	discriminación	giraffe	jirafa
Debate	discutir	golf	golf
distance	distancia	glorious	glorioso(a)
distribute (to)	distribuir	gorilla	gorila
dollar	dólar	group	grupo
double	doble	guide	guía
dragon	dragón	H	
dynamite	dinamita	helicopter	helicóptero
E		hippopotamus	hipopótamo
electric	eléctrico(a)	history	historia

English Cognate	Spanish Word	English Cognate	Spanish Word
elephant	elefante	honor	honor
enormous	enorme	hospital	hospital
energy	energía	hotel	hotel
enter (to)	entrar	hour	hora
elephant	elefante	human	humano(a)
escape (to)	escapar	I	
especially	especialmente	idea	idea
examine (to)	examinar	medal	medalla
exclaim	exclamar	memory	memoria
identification	identificación	metal	metal
imagine (to)	imaginar	microscope	microscopio
immediately	inmediatamente	million	millón
immigrants	inmigrantes	miniature	miniatura
importance	importancia	minute	minuto
important	importante	minutes	minutos
impressed	impresionando(a)	moment	momento
impression	impresión	monument	monumento
incredible	increíble	much	mucho (a)
incurable	incurable	music	música
independence	independencia	N	
information	información	natural	natural
insects	insectos	necessity	necesidad
inseparable	inseparable	nectar	néctar
insist (to)	insistir	nervous	nervioso(a)
inspection	inspección	notice	noticia
intelligence	inteligencia	O	
interesting	interesante	obedience	obediencia
interrupt (to)	interrumpir	object	objeto
introduce (to)	introducir	observatory	observatorio
introduction	introducción	occasion	ocasión
invent (to)	inventar	ocean	océano
investigate (to)	investigar	October	octubre

English Cognate	Spanish Word	English Cognate	Spanish Word
invitation	invitación	office	oficina
invite (to)	invitar	operation	operación
island	isla	ordinary	ordinario (a)
L			
leader	líder	P	
lemon	limón	palace	palacio
lens	lente	panic	pánico
leopard	leopardo	paper	papel
lesson	lección	park	parque
lessons	lecciones	part	parte
line	línea	patience	paciencia
lion	león	penguin	pingüino (a)
list	lista	perfect	perfecto (a)
locate (to)	localizar	perfume	perfume
M		permanent	permanente
machine	máquina	photo	foto
magic	magia	photograph	fotografía
magician	mago(a)	piano	piano
magnificent	magnífico(a)	pioneer	pionero
map	mapa	pirate	pirata
March	Marzo	planet	planeta
march (to)	marchar, caminar	T	teléfono
marionettes	marionetas, títeres	telephone	telescopio
planetarium	planetario	telescope	televisión
plans	planes	television	terrible
plants	plantas	terrible	tomate
plates	platos	tomato	totalmente
police	policía	totally	turista
practice	práctica	tourist	tráfico
practice (to)	practicar	traffic	atrapar
prepare (to)	preparar	trap (to)	triple

English Cognate	Spanish Word	English Cognate	Spanish Word
present (to)	presentar	triple	trompeta
problem	problema	trumpet	tubo
professional	profesional	tube	
R		U	
radio	radio	uniform	uniforme
ranch	rancho	V	
really	realmente	vegetables	vegetales
restaurant	restaurante	version	versión
retire (to)	retirarse	visit (to)	visitar
reunion	reunión	volleyball	vóleibol
rich	rico(a)	vote (to)	votar
rock	roca		
route	ruta		
S			
secret	secreto (a)		
September	Septiembre		
series	serie		
sofa	sofá		
special	especial		
splendid	espléndido(a)		
statistics	estadísticas		
stomach	estómago		
study (to)	estudiar		
surprise	sorpresa		

Source: Calderon, August, Duran, Madden, Slavin & Gil (2003)

Readers' Theater Script Example

"Furry Friends Unleashed"

Characters:

1. Narrator
2. Sarah - a young girl
3. Max - a mischievous dog
4. Whiskers - a curious cat
5. Mr. Johnson - a neighbor

Scene 1: Sarah's Living Room

Narrator: Once upon a time, in a cozy living room, young Sarah was busy playing with her toys.

Sarah: (excitedly) Oh, I wish I had a pet to play with!

Scene 2: Pet Adoption Day

Narrator: One sunny day, Sarah and her parents visited the local pet adoption center.

Sarah: (looking around) So many pets! I want them all!

Scene 3: Meeting Max and Whiskers

Narrator: Among the furry friends, Sarah's eyes sparkled as she met Max, a mischievous dog, and Whiskers, a curious cat.

Max: (barking) Woof! Woof! Play with me!

Whiskers: (meowing) What's going on here? Anything interesting?

Scene 4: Bringing Them Home

Narrator: With hearts full of joy, Sarah, Max, and Whiskers headed home together.

Scene 5: Mischief at Home

Narrator: In their new home, Max and Whiskers couldn't resist exploring and causing a bit of mischief.

Sarah: (giggling) Oh, you two are a handful, but I love you!

Scene 6: Neighborly Encounter

Narrator: One day, Mr. Johnson, the neighbor, witnessed Max and Whiskers' playful antics.

Mr. Johnson: (smiling) Looks like you've got some lively pets there!

Scene 7: Pet Playdate

Narrator: Soon, Max and Whiskers became friends with Mr. Johnson's pet, creating a furry friendship that brought joy to the neighborhood.

Scene 8: Life with Furry Friends

Narrator: And so, Sarah, Max, and Whiskers lived happily ever after, creating delightful memories filled with love, laughter, and the joy that only pets can bring.

The end.

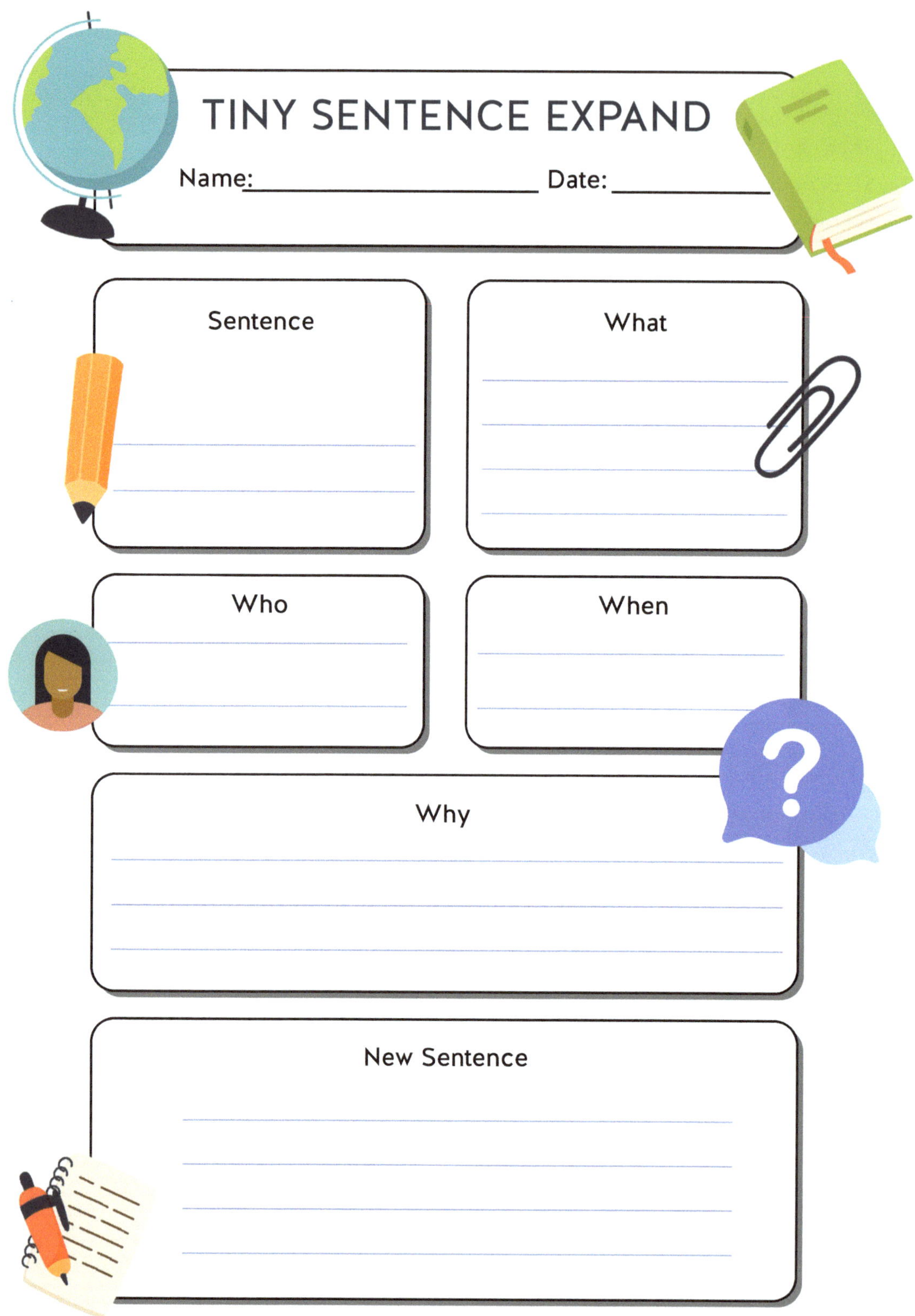

iStock.com/Tatiana Smirnova; iStock.com/RLT_Images; iStock.com/calvindexter

Name ______________

PERSONAL SPELLING DICTIONARY

A	B

C	D

Name ________________

PERSONAL SPELLING DICTIONARY

E	F

G	H

Name ________________

PERSONAL SPELLING DICTIONARY

I	J

K	L

Name ____________________

PERSONAL SPELLING DICTIONARY

M	N

O	P

Name ________________

PERSONAL SPELLING DICTIONARY

Q	R

S	T

Name ______________

PERSONAL SPELLING DICTIONARY

U	V

W	X

Name ________________

PERSONAL SPELLING DICTIONARY

Y	Z

Name: ____________________ Date: ____________________

Three Column Notes

Point One	Point Two	Point Three

What is the big idea overall?

Credit line: iStock.com/vladwel

References

Akhavan, N. (2006). *Help! my kids don't all speak English: How to set up a language workshop in your linguistically diverse classroom.* Heinemann.

Akhavan, N. (2007). *Accelerated vocabulary instruction: Strategies for closing the achievement gap for all students.* Scholastic.

Akhavan, N. (2009). *Teaching writing in a title one school.* Heinemann.

Akhavan, N. (2014). *The nonfiction now lesson bank, grades 4-8: Strategies and routines for higher-level comprehension in the content areas.* Corwin.

Akhavan, N. (2019). *At the reading table with striving readers: Achieving equity by scaffolding skills and strategies.* Benchmark Education.

Akhavan, N. (2023). *Small group reading with multilingual learners.* Corwin.

Akhavan, N., & Walsh, N. (2020). Cognitive apprenticeship learning approach in K-8 writing instruction: A case study. *Journal of Education and Learning, 9*(3), 123–142. https://doi .org/10.5539/jel.v9n3p123

August, D. (2003). *Supporting the development of English literacy in English language learners: Key isuesissues and promising practices* (Reports-DescritiveDescriptive No. 61). Center for Research on the Education of Students Placed at Risk.

August, D., Carlo, M., Dressler, C., & Snow, C. (2005). The critical role of vocabulary development for English language learners. *Learning Disabilities Research & Practice, 20*(1), 50–57.

August, D., & Shanahan, T. (2006). *Developing literacy in second-language learners: Report of the National Literacy Panel on language-minority children and youth.* Lawrence Erlbaum.

Bao, D. (2014). *Understanding silence and reticence: Ways of participating in second language acquisition.* Bloomsbury.

Barr, S., Islami, Z. R., & Joshi, R. M. (2012). Core strategies to support English learners. *The Educational Forum, 76*(1), 105–117.

Bear, D. R., Helman, L., & Woessner, L. (2009). Word study assessment and instruction with English learners in a second grade classroom: Bending with students' growth. In J. Coppola & E. Primas (Eds.), *Teaching and learning in linguistically and culturally diverse classrooms: Bringing theory and research to practice* (pp. 11–40). International Reading Association.

Bear, D. R., & Smith, R. E. (2012). The literacy development of English learners: What do we know about each student's literacy development. In L. Helman (Ed.), *Literacy development with English learners: Research based instruction grades K-6* (pp. 87–116). Routledge.

Beck, I. L., & McKeown, M. G. (2006). *Improving comprehension with questioning the author: A fresh and expanded view of a powerful approach.* Scholastic.

Beck, I. L., McKeown, M. G., & Kucan, L. (2013). *Bringing words to life: Robust vocabulary instruction* (2nd ed.). Guilford Press.

Belhiah, H. (2013). Using the hand to choreograph instruction: On the functional role of gesture in definition talk. *The Modern Language Journal, 97*(2), 417–434. https://doi.org/10.1111/ j.1540-4781.2013.12012.x

Bialik, K., Scheller, A., & Walker, K. (2018). *6 facts about English language learners in U.S. public schools.* Pew Research Center. https://www.pewresearch.org/fact-tank/2018/10/25/6-facts-about-english-language-learners-in-u-s-public-schools/

Billings, E., & Walqui, A. (n.d.). *Dispelling the myth of "English only": Understanding the importance of the first language in second language learning.* NYSED Office of bilingual and world languages. http://www.nysed.gov/common/nysed/files/dispelling_myth_rev-2.pdf

Blevins, W. (2017a). *Teaching phonics and word study in the intermediate grades, second edition.* Scholastic.

Blevins, W. (2017b). *A fresh look at phonics.* Corwin.

Blevins, W. (2020). *From phonics to reading, grades K-3.* Sadlier. file:///C:/Users/Nancy/AppData/Local/Temp/publisher-background_K-2-1.pdf

Blevins, W. (2021). *Choosing and using decodable text: Practical tips and strategies for enhancing phonics instruction.* Scholastic.

Bowey, J. A. (2002). Reflections on onset-rime and phoneme sensitivity as predictors of beginning word reading. *Journal of Experimental Child Psychology, 82,* 29–40.

Britton, J. N. (1972). Writing to learn and learning to write. In National Council of Teacher of English, *The humanity of English.* NCTE distinguished lectures (pp. 31–53). NCTE.

Busholtz, M. & Lee, J. S. (2017). Language and culture as sustenance. In *Culturally sustaining pedagogies: Teaching and learning for justice in a changing world.* Django Paris & H. Samy Alim (eds.), 43-60. Teachers College Press.

Cain, K., & Oakhill, J. V. (1999). Inference making ability and its relation to comprehension failure in young children. *Reading and Writing: An Interdisciplinary Journal, 11*(5-6), 489-503.

Calderón, M., & Slakk, S. (2018). *Teaching reading to English learners, grades 6-12: A framework for improving achievement in the content areas.* Corwin. https://doi. org/10.4135/978154435742

Calderón, M., & Soto, I. (2017). *Academic language mastery: Vocabulary in context.* Corwin. https://doi. org/10.4135/9781506338293

Carlo, M. S., August, D., McLaughlin, B, Snow, C. E., Dressler, C., Lippman, D. N., Lively, T. J., & White, C. E. (2004). Closing the gap: Addressing the vocabulary needs of English language learners in bilingual and mainstream classrooms. *Reading Research Quarterly, 39*(2), 188–215.

Carnegie Council on Advancing Adolescent Literacy. (2010). *Time to act: An agenda for advancing adolescent literacy for college and career success.* Carnegie Corporation of New York.

Cazden, C. B. (2001). *Classroom discourse: The language of teaching and learning* (2nd ed.). Heinemann.

Cazden, C. B. (2017). *Communicative competence, classroom interaction, and educational equity the selected works of Courtney B. Cazden.* Routledge.

Celce-Murcia, M., & Olshtain, E. (2000). *Discourse and context in language teaching: A guide for language teachers*. Cambridge University Press.

Cervetii, G. N., & Hiebert, E. H. (2015). The sixth pillar of reading instruction: Knowledge development. *Reading Teacher, 68*(7), 548–551.

Chapin, S., O'Connor, C., & Anderson, N. (2009). *Classroom discussions: Using math talk to help students learn, Grades K–6* (2nd ed.). Math Solutions Publications.

Chacón-Beltrán, R., Abello-Contesse, C., & del Mar Torreblanca, M. (2010). *Insights into non- native vocabulary teaching and learning*. Channel View Publications.

Cho, E., Capin, P., Roberts, G., Roberts, G. J., & Vaughn, S. (2019). Examining sources and mechanisms of reading comprehension difficulties: Comparing English learners and non-English learners within the simple view of reading. *Journal of Educational Psychology, 111*(6), 982–1000.

Clark, A. (2020). Cultural relevance and linguistic flexibility in literature discussions with emergent bilingual children. *Bilingual Research Journal, 43*(1), 50–70. https://doi.org/10.1080/15235882.2020.1722974

Cloud, N., Genesee, F., & Hamayan, E. (2009). *Literacy instruction for English language learners: A teacher's guide to researchbased practices*. Heinemann.

Collett, J., & Dubetz, N. (2021). Instruction to engage multilingual learners with grade-level content. *The Reading Teacher, 75*(5), 593–602.

Coyne, M. D., Kame'enui, E. J., & Carnine, D. W. (2011). *Effective teaching strategies that accommodate diverse learners* (4th ed.). Pearson.

Crossley, S. A., Allen, D., & McNamara, D. S. (2012). Text simplification and comprehensible input: A case for an intuitive approach. *Language Teaching Research* , *16*(1), 89–108. https://doi.org/10.1177/1362168811423456

Cummins, J. (1979). Linguistic interdependence and the educational development of bilingual children. *Review of Educational Research, 49*(2), 222–251.

Cummins, J. (1981). Four misconceptions about language proficiency in bilingual education. *NABE: The Journal for the National Association for Bilingual Education, 5*(3), 17–31.

Cummins, J. (2008). BICS and CALP: Empirical and theoretical status of the distinction. *Encyclopedia of Language and Education*, 487-499.

Cummins, J. (2011). Literacy engagement: Fueling academic growth for English learners. *The Reading Teacher, 65*(2), 142–146.

Donnelly, W. B., & Roe, C. J. (2010). Using sentence frames to develop academic vocabulary for English learners. *The Reading Teacher, 64*(2), 131–136. https://doi.org/10.1598/RT.64.2.5

Duke, N., Pearson, D., Strachan, S., & Billman, A. (2011). Essential elements of fostering and teaching reading comprehension. In S. J. Samuels & A. E. Farstrup (Eds.), *What research has to say about reading instruction* (pp. 51–93). IRA. https://doi.org/10.1598/0829.03

Ecchevarria, J., & Graves, A. (2002). *Sheltered content instruction: Teaching English-language learners with diverse abilities* (2nd ed.). Allyn & Bacon.

Ecchevarria, J., Vogt, M., & Short, D. J. (2017). *Making content comprehensive for English learners, the SIOP model* (5th ed.). Pearson/Allyn & Bacon.

Edelman, E. R., Amirazizi, S. A., Feinberg, D. K., Quirk, M., Scheller, J., Pagán, C. R., & Persoon, J. (2022). A comparison of integrated and designated ELD models on second and third graders' oral English language proficiency. *TESOL Journal, 13*, e659. https://doi.org/10.1002/tesj.659

Ehri, L. C. (2005). Learning to read words: Theory, findings, and issues. *Scientific Studies of Reading, 9*, 167–188.

Ehri, L. C. (2011). Teaching phonemic awareness and phonics in the language arts classroom. In D. Lapp & D. Fisher (Eds.), *Handbook of research on teaching the English language arts* (3rd ed., pp. 231–237). Routledge.

Elley, W. B. (1991). Acquiring literacy in a second language: The effect of book-based programs. *Language learning, 41*(3), 375–411.

Ellis, R., & Shintani, N. (2013). *Exploring language pedagogy through second language acquisition research*. Routledge.

Fareed, M., Ashraf, A., & Bilal, M. (2016). ESL learners' writing skills: Problems, factors and suggestions. *Journal of Education and Social Sciences, 4*, 81–92.

Fillmore, L. W. (2009). *English language development: Acquiring the language needed for literacy and learning.* Pearson Research into Practice.

Fisher, D., Frey, N., & Akhavan, N. (2019). *This is balanced literacy*. Corwin.

Freeman, D., & Freeman, Y. (2014). *Essential linguistics: What teachers need to know to teach ESL, reading, spelling and grammar* (2nd ed.). Heinemann.

Gamez, P. B. (2009). *Academic oral language development in Spanish-speaking English language learners: The effect of teacher talk*. The University of Chicago. ProQuest Dissertations Publishing.

Gamez, P. B. (2015). Classroom-based English exposure and English language learners' expressive language skills. *Early Childhood Research Quarterly, 31*, 135–146.

García, O. & Lin, A. (2016). Translanguaging and bilingual education. In O. García, A. Lin, & S. May (Eds.), Bilingual and multilingual education (pp. 117–130). *Encyclopedia of Language and Education 5*. Springer.

Genesee, F., Lindholm-Leary, K., Saunders, W., & Christian, D. (2005). English language learners in U.S. schools: An overview of research findings. *Journal of Education for Students Placed at Risk, 10*(4), 363–385.

Genesse, F., & Riches, C. (2006). Literacy: Instructional issues. In F. Genesse, K. Lindholm-Leary, W. Saunder, & D. Christian (Eds.), *Educating English language learners* (pp. 363–384). Cambridge University Press.

Gibbons, P. (2009). *English learners, academic literacy and thinking.* Heinemann.

Gibbons, P. (2015). *Scaffolding language, scaffolding learning: Teaching English language learners in the mainstream classroom.* Heineman.

Goldenburg, C. (2010). Improving achievement for English learners: Conclusions from recent reviews and emerging research. In G. Li & P. A. Edwards (Eds.), *Best practices in ELL instruction* (pp. 15–43). Guilford Publications.

Gooch, K., & Lambirth, A. (2008). *Understanding phonics and the teaching of reading.* McGraw-Hill Education.

Goswami, U., & Mead, F. (1992). Onset and rime awareness and analogies in reading. *Reading Research Quarterly, 27*, 152–162.

Gottlieb, M. (2016). *Assessing English language learners: Bridges to educational equity: Connecting academic language proficiency to student achievement* (2nd ed.). Corwin.

Grabe, W., & Zhang, C. (2013). Reading and writing together: A critical component of English for academic purposes teaching and learning. *TESOL Journal, 41*(1), 9–24.

Gutherie, J. T., & Barber, A. T. (2019). Best practices for motivating students to read. In L. M. Morrow & L. B. Gambrell (Eds.), *Best practice in literacy instruction* (pp. 52–72). Guilford Press.

Gutierrez, K. D., Zepeda, M., & Castro, D. C. (2010). Advancing early literacy learning for all children: Implications of the NELP report for dual-language learners. *Educational Researcher, 39*(4), 334–339.

Haigh, C. A., Savage, R., Erdos, C., & Genesse, F. (2011). The role of phoneme and onset-rime awareness in second language reading acquisition. *Journal of Research in Reading, 34*(1), 94–113.

Hammond, Z. (2015). *Culturally responsive teaching and the brain: Promoting authentic engagement and rigor among culturally and linguistically diverse students*. Corwin / Sage.

Harvey, S., & Goudvis, A. (2013). Comprehension at the core. *The Reading Teacher, 66*(6), 432–439.

Haynes, J. (2007). *Getting started with English language learners: How educators can meet the challenge*. ASCD.

Herrell, A. L., & Jordan, M. (2020). *50 strategies for teaching English language learners* (6th ed.). Pearson.

Hiebert, E. (2019). *Teaching words and how they work: Small changes for big vocabulary results*. Teachers College Press.

Himmele, P., & Himmele, W. (2009). *The language-rich classroom*. ASCD.

Honigsfeld, A., & Dove, M. G. (2013). *Collaborating for English Learners: A foundational guide to integrated practices* (2nd ed.). Corwin.

Howard, T. C. (2020). *Why race and culture matter in schools: Closing the achievement gap in America's classrooms*. Routledge.

Hoyt, L. (2016). *Interactive read-alouds, grades 2-3: Linking standards, fluency, and comprehension*. Heinemann.

Hymes, D. (1971). *On communicative competence*. University of Pennsylvania Press.

James, I., & Carter, T. S. (2007). *Questioning and informational texts: Scaffolding students' comprehension of content areas*. Forum on Public Policy.

Johnston, S. S., Tulbert, B. L., Sebastian, J. P., Devries, K., & Gompert, A. (2000). Vocabulary development: A collaborative effort for teaching content vocabulary. *Intervention in School and Clinic, 35*(5), 311–313.

Kara, K., & Eveyik-Aydın, E. (2019). Effects of TPRS on very young learners' vocabulary acquisition. *Advances in Language and Literary Studies, 10*(1), 135–146. https://doi.org/10.7575/aiac.alls.v.10n.1p.135

Keck, C. (2006). The use of paraphrase in summary writing: A comparison of L1 and L2 writers. *Journal of Second Language Writing, 15*(4), 261–278.

Khatib, M., & Bagherkazemi, M. (2011). The potential of learner output for enhancing EFL learners? Short-term and long-term learning of the English simple present tense. *Theory and Practice in Language Studies, 1*(4), 400–407. https://doi.org/10.4304/tpls.1.4.400-407

Kieffer, M. J., & Lesaux, N. K. (2012). Knowledge of words, knowledge about words: Dimensions of vocabulary in first and second language learners in sixth grade *Reading and Writing: An Interdisciplinary Journal, 25*, 347–373.

Kim, A., Vaughn S., Wanzek J., & Wei, S. (2004). Graphic organizers and their effects on the reading comprehension of students with LD: A synthesis of research. *Journal of Learning Disabilities, 37*, 105–118. https://doi.org/10.1177/00222194040370020201

Kittley-Koshenina, C. W. (2009). *The effects of video instruction on science vocabulary development of the English language learners in elementary education*. ProQuest Dissertations Publishing.

Kohnert, K., & Pham, G. (2010). The process of acquiring first and second languages. In M. Shatz & L. Wilkinson (Eds.), *Preparing to educate English language learners* (pp. 48–66). Guilford.

Kong, A., & Fitch, E. (2002) . Using book club to engage culturally and linguistically diverse learners in reading, writing, and talking about books. *The Reading Teacher, 56*(4), 352–362.

Koskinen, P. S., Gambrell, L. B., Kapinus, B. A., & Heathington, B. S. (1988). Retelling: A strategy for enhancing students' reading comprehension. *The Reading Teacher, 41*(9), 892–896. http://www.jstor.org/stable/20199962

Krashen, S. (1982). *Principles and practices in second language acquisition*. Pergamon Press.

Krashen, S. (1988). *Second language acquisition and second language learning*. Prentice Hall.

Krashen, S. D. (2003). *Explorations in language acquisition and use*. Heinemann.

Krashen, S., & Mason, B. (2017). Sustained silent reading in foreign language education: An update. *Turkish Online Journal of English Language Teaching, 2*(2), 70–73.

Láufer, B. (2010). Form-focused instruction in second language vocabulary learning. In R. Chacón-Beltrán, C. Abello-Contesse, & M. del Mar Torreblanca-López (Eds.), *Insights into non-native vocabulary teaching and learning* (pp. 15–27). Channel View Publications.

Lesaux, N. K., Geva, E., Koda, K., Siegel, L. S., & Shanahan, T. (2008). Development of literacy in second-language learners. In D. August & T. Shanahan (Eds.), *Developing reading and writing in second-language learners* (pp. 27–60). International Reading Association & Center for Applied Linguistics.

Li, J.-T., Tong, F., Irby, B. J., Lara-Alecio, R., & Rivera, H. (2021). The effects of four instructional strategies on English learners' English reading comprehension: A meta-analysis. *Language Teaching Research*. Advance online publication. https://doi.org/10.1177/1362168821994133

Lightbown, P. M., & Spada, N. (1990). Focus-on-form and corrective feedback in communicative language teaching: Effects on second language learning. *Studies in Second Language Acquisition, 12*, 429–448.

Linares, R. E. (2019). Meaningful writing opportunities: Write-alouds and dialogue journaling with newcomer and English learner high schoolers. *Journal of Adolescent & Adult Literacy, 62*(5), 521–530. https://doi.org/10.1002/jaal.932

Lucero, A. (2018). The development of bilingual narrative retelling among Spanish-English dual language learners over two years. *Language, Speech and Hearing Services in Schools, 49*(3), 607–621.

Mastrothanasis, K., Kladaki, M. & Andreou, A. (2023). A systematic review and meta-analysis of the Readers' Theatre impact on the development of reading skills. *International Journal of Educational Research Open, 4*.

McCay, S. L. (2006). *Researching second language classrooms*. Routledge.

Melby-Lervåg, M., & Lervåg, A. (2014). Reading comprehension and its underlying components in second-language learners: A meta-analysis of studies comparing first- and second-language learners. *Psychology Bulletin, 140*, 409–433.

Min-Young K., Wilkinson. I. A. G. (2019). What is dialogic teaching? Constructing, deconstructing, and reconstructing a pedagogy of classroom talk. *Learning, Culture and Social Interaction, 21*, 70-86.

Montelongo, J. A., Hernández, A. C., Herter, R. J., & Cuello, J. (2011). Using cognates to scaffold context clue strategies for Latino Els. *The Reading Teacher, 64*(6), 429–434.

Montero, M. K., & Kuhn, M. R. (2016). English learners and fluency development. In L. Helman (Ed.), *Literacy development with English learners: Research based instruction in grades K-6* (2nd ed., pp. 182–205). Guilford Press.

Mora-Flores, E. (2018a). *Integrated English language development: Supporting English learners across the curriculum* (Epub). Shell Education.

Mora-Flores, E. (2018b). Part II: Comprehensible input and output strategies. In *Integrated English language development: Supporting English learners across the curriculum* (Epub, p. 83). Shell Educational Publishing.

Moss, B. (2005). Making a case and a place for effective content area literacy instruction in the elementary grades. *The Reading Teacher, 59*(1), 46–55.

Mushait, S., & Mohsen, M. A. (2019). Is listening comprehension a comprehensible input for L2 vocabulary acquisition? *International Journal of English Linguistics, 9*(6), 77–84. https://doi.org/10.5539/ijel.v9n6p77

Nagy, W. E. (1988). *Teaching vocabulary to improve reading comprehension*. National Council of Teachers of English.

Nation, I. S. P. (2001). *Learning vocabulary in another language*. Cambridge University Press.

National Center for Education Statistics (NCES). (2002). 2022 NAEP Reading Assessment: Highlighted Results at Grades 4 and 8 for the Nation, States, and Districts. NCES 2022126.

Ness, M. K. (2016). Reading comprehension strategies in secondary content area classrooms: Teacher use of and attitudes towards reading comprehension instruction. *Reading Horizons: A Journal of Literacy and Language Arts, 49*(2). https://scholarworks.wmich.edu/reading_horizons/vol49/iss2/5

Newcomer, S. N., Ardasheva, Y., Morrison, J. A., Ernst-Slavit, G., Morrison, S. J., Carbonneau, K. J., & Lightner, L. K. (2021). "Whoa... Welcome to America!": Supporting refugee background students' socioemotional well-being, English language development, and content area learning. *Journal of Research in Childhood Education, 35*(3), 417–437.

Nowbakht, M., & Shahnazari, M. (2015). The comparative effects of comprehensible input, output and corrective feedback on the receptive acquisition of L2 vocabulary items. *Advances in Language and Literary Studies, 6*(4), 103–114. https://doi.org/10.7575/aiac.alls.v.6n.4p.103

Olson, C. B., Matuchniak, T., Chung, H. Q., Stumpf, R., & Farkas, G. (2017). Reducing achievement gaps in academic writing for Latinos and English learners in grades 7–12. *Journal of Educational Psychology, 109*(1), 1–21.

Olson, C. B., Scarcella, R., & Matuchniak, T. (2015). English learners, writing, and the common core. *Elementary School Journal, 115*(4), 570–592. https://doi-org.hmlproxy.lib.csufresno.edu/10.1086/681235

Ortiz, A. A., & Franquiz, M. E. (2019). Co-editors introduction: Challenges to the success of English learners in the context of language instruction educational programs. *Bilingual Research Journal, 42*(1), 1–5.

Palmer, C. (1994). *Developing cultural literacy through the writing process: Empowering all learners*. Allyn & Bacon.

Peregoy, S. F., & Boyle, O. F. (2016). *Reading, writing and learning in ESL: A resource book for K-12 teachers* (7th ed.). Pearson.

Pérez, B. (2004). *Sociocultural contexts of language and literacy* (2nd ed.). Lawrence Erlbaum Associates.

Pressley, M., Brown, R., El-Dinary, P. B., & Allferbach, P. (1995). The comprehension instruction that students need: Instruction fostering constructively responsive reading. *Learning Disabilities Research & Practice, 10*(4), 215–224.

Pressley, M., & Wharton-McDonald, R. (1997). Skilled comprehension and its development through instruction. *School Psychology Review, 26*(3), 448–466.

Ramsey, J. (2019). *Teaching academic vocabulary to increase comprehension in content areas for ELLs from grades 3-5*. ProQuest Dissertations & Theses Global. The Humanities and Social Sciences Collection.

Raphael, T. E., & Au, K. H. (2005). QAR: Enhancing comprehension and test taking across grades and content areas. *The Reading Teacher, 59*(3), 206–221.

Rapp, D. N., van den Broek, P., McMaster, K. L. Kendeou, P., & Espin, C. A. (2007). Higher-order comprehension processes in struggling readers: A perspective for research and intervention. *Scientific Studies of Reading, 11*(4), 289–312.

Rasinski, T. V. (2010). *The fluent reader: Oral and silent reading strategies for building word recognition, fluency, and comprehension* (2nd ed.). Scholastic.

Rasinski, T. V., Reutzel, D. R., Chard, D., & Linan-Thompson, S. (2011). Reading fluency. In M. L. Kamil, P. D. Pearson, E. B. Moje, & P. P. Afflerbach (Eds.), *Handbook of reading research* (Vol. IV, pp. 286–319). Routledge.

Rasinski, T., & Young, C. (2014). Assisted reading-A bridge from fluency to comprehension. *New England Reading Association Journal, 50*(1), 1–4.

Saito, K. (2020). Multi- or single-word units? The role of collocation use in comprehensible and contextually appropriate second language speech. *Language Learning, 70*(2), 548–588. https://doi.org/10.1111/lang.12387

Scarborough, H. S. (2001). Connecting early language and literacy to later reading (dis)abilities: Evidence, theory, and practice. In S. B. Neuman & D. K. Dickinson (Eds.), *Handbook of early literacy research* (Vol. 1, pp. 97–110). Guilford.

Scarcella, R. (2003). *Academic English: A conceptual framework* (Technical Report 2003-1). University of California Linguistic Minority Research Institute.

Schumaker, J. B., Denton, P. H., & Deshler, D. D. (1984). *The paraphrasing strategy*. University of Kansas Press.

Sebold, C. (2011). Building English language learners' academic vocabulary: Strategies & tips. Linguistically Diverse Students & Their Families. *Multicultural Education, 18*(2), 24–28.

Shanahan, T., & Beck, I. L. (2006). Effective literacy teaching for English-language learners. In D. August & T. Shanahan (Eds.), *Developing literacy in second-language learners: Report of the national literacy panel on language-minority children and youth* (pp. 415–488). Erlbaum.

Shi, L. (2004). Textual borrowing in second-language writing. *Written Communication, 21*(2), 171–200. https://doi.org/10.1177/0741088303262846

Souers, K.V.M. & Hall, P. (2018). *Relationship, responsibility and regulation: Trauma-invested practices for fostering resilient learners*. ASCD.

Spear-Swerling, L. (2011). Patterns of reading disabilities across development. In A. McGill-Franzen & R. Allington (Eds.), *Handbook of reading disability research* (pp. 149-161). Routledge.

Spycher, P. (2007). Academic writing of adolescent English learners: Learning to use "although". *Journal of second Language Writing, 16*(4), 238–254.

Stahl, S. A. (2004). What do we know about fluency? Findings of the national reading panel. In P. McCardle & V. Chhabra (Eds.), *The voice of evidence in reading research* (pp. 187–211). Paul H. Brookes Publishing Co.

Steele, C.M. & Aaronson, J. M. (1995). Stereotype threat and the intellectual test-performance of African-Americans. *Journal of personality and social psychology, 69*(5), 797-811.

Stembridge, A. (2020). *Culturally responsive education in the classroom: An equity framework for pedagogy*. (1st ed.). Routledge.

Stoutz, S. (2011). *Retelling using different methods* [Dissertation, Education Masters. Paper 199]. https://fisherpub.sjfc.edu/education_ETD_masters/199

Swiegart, W. (1991). Classroom talk, knowledge development, and writing. *Research in the Teaching of English, 25*(4), 469–496.

Templeton, S. (2020). Stages, phases, repertoires, and waves: Learning to spell and read words. *The Reading Teacher, 74*(3), 315–323. https://doi.org/10.1002/trtr.1951

Tudor, I., & Hafiz, F. (1989). Extensive reading as a means of input to L2 learning. *Journal of Research in Reading, 12*(2), 164–178. https://doi.org/10.1111/j.1467-9817.1989.tb00164.x

Uchihara, T., Webb, S., Saito, K., & Trofimovich, P. (2022). Does mode of input affect how second language learners create form–Meaning connections and pronounce second language words? *The Modern Language Journal, 106*(2), 351–370. https://doi.org/10.1111/modl.12775

Ukrainetz, T. A., Cooney, M. H., Dyer, S. K., Kysar, A. J., & Harris, T. J. (2000). An investigation into teaching phonemic awareness through shared reading and writing. *Early Childhood Research Quarterly, 15*(3), 331–355.

Umansky, I. M., Thompson, K. D., Soland, J., & Kibler, A. K. (2022). Understanding newcomer English learner students' English language development: Comparisons and predictors. *Bilingual Research Journal, 45*(2), 180–204.

U.S. Department of Education (2022). Our nation's English learners: What are their characteristics? Retrieved from https://www2.ed.gov/datastory/el-characteristics/index.html.

Valdés, G., Poza, L. E., & Brooks, M.D. (2015). Language acquisition in bilingual education.

van der Veen, C., de Mey, L., van Kruistum, C., & van Oers, B. (2017). The effect of productive classroom talk and metacommunication on young children's oral communicative competence and subject matter knowledge: An intervention study in early childhood education. *Learning and Instruction*, 48, 14-22.

Vygotsky, L. S. (1978). *Mind in society: Development of higher psychological processes*. Harvard University Press.

Walpole, S., & McKenna, M. C. (2007). *Differentiated reading instruction: Strategies for the primary grades*. Guilford Publications.

Washington-Nortey, P.-M., Zhang, F., Xu, Y., Ruiz, A. B., Chen, C.-C., & Spence, C. (2022). The impact of peer interactions on language development among preschool English language learners: A systematic review. *Early Childhood Education Journal, 50*(1), 49–59.

WIDA Consortium. (2012). *Amplification of the English Language Development Standards, Kindergarten-Grade 12*. Board of Regents of the University of Wisconsin System.

WIDA. (2020). *WIDA English language development standards framework, 2020 edition: Kindergarten–grade 12*. Board of Regents of the University of Wisconsin System.

Wilkinson, I. A. G., & Son, E. H. (2011). A dialogic turn research on learning and teaching to comprehend. In M. L. Kamil, P. D. Pearson, E. B. Moje, & P. P. Afflerbac (Eds.), *Handbook of reading research* (Vol. IV, pp. 359–387). Routledge.

Windsor, J., Kohnert, K., Lobitz, K., Pham, G. (2010). Cross-language nonword repetition by bilingual and monolingual children. *American Journal of Speech-Language Pathology*, 19, 298–310.

Wright, W. E. (2019). *Foundations for teaching English language learners: Research, theory, policy and practice*. Caslon, Inc.

Wu, S., Dixon, Q., Sun, H., & Zhang, P. (2021). Breadth or depth: The role of vocabulary in Chinese English-language beginning writers' development. *International Journal of Bilingual Education and Bilingualism, 24*(9), 1356–1372.

Young, T. A., & Hadaway, N. L. (2006). *Supporting the literacy development of English learners*. International Reading Association.

Zweirs, J. (2014). *Building academic language: Meeting common core standards across disciplines, grades 5-12, second edition*. Jossey-Bass.

Index

Zeitfracht Medien GmbH
Ferdinand-Jühlke-Straße 7
99095 Erfurt, Deutschland
produktsicherheit@kolibri360.de